T0234017

Pro Google Kubernetes Engine

Network, Security, Monitoring, and Automation Configuration

Navin Sabharwal
Piyush Pandey

Apress®

Pro Google Kubernetes Engine: Network, Security, Monitoring, and Automation Configuration

Navin Sabharwal
New Delhi, Delhi, India

Piyush Pandey
New Delhi, India

ISBN-13 (pbk): 978-1-4842-6242-9
https://doi.org/10.1007/978-1-4842-6243-6

ISBN-13 (electronic): 978-1-4842-6243-6

Managing Director, Apress Media LLC: Welmoed Spahr
Acquisitions Editor: Celestin Suresh John
Development Editor: Laura Berendson
Coordinating Editor: Aditee Mirashi

Cover designed by eStudioCalamar

Cover image designed by Pixabay

Distributed to the book trade worldwide by Springer Science+Business Media New York, 233 Spring Street, 6th Floor, New York, NY 10013. Phone 1-800-SPRINGER, fax (201) 348-4505, e-mail orders-ny@springer-sbm.com, or visit www.springeronline.com. Apress Media, LLC is a California LLC and the sole member (owner) is Springer Science+Business Media Finance Inc (SSBM Finance Inc). SSBM Finance Inc is a **Delaware** corporation.

For information on translations, please e-mail booktranslations@springernature.com; for reprint, paperback, or audio rights, please e-mail bookpermissions@springernature.com.

Apress titles may be purchased in bulk for academic, corporate, or promotional use. eBook versions and licenses are also available for most titles. For more information, reference our Print and eBook Bulk Sales web page at www.apress.com/bulk-sales.

Any source code or other supplementary material referenced by the authors in this book is available to readers on GitHub via the book's product page, located at www.apress.com/978-1-4842-6242-9. For more detailed information, please visit www.apress.com/source-code.

Printed on acid-free paper

Table of Contents

About the Authors

 **Navin Sabharwal** has more than 20 years of industry experience and is an innovator, thought leader, patent holder, and author in the fields of cloud computing, artificial intelligence and machine learning, public cloud, AIOps, DevOps, infrastructure services, monitoring and management platforms, big data analytics, and software product development. Navin is responsible for DevOps, artificial intelligence, cloud lifecycle management, service management, monitoring and management, IT Ops analytics, AIOps and machine learning, automation, operational efficiency of scaled delivery through Lean Ops, and strategy and delivery for HCL Technologies. He can be reached at Navinsabharwal@gmail.com and www.linkedin.com/in/navinsabharwal.

ABOUT THE AUTHORS

 **Piyush Pandey** has more than ten years of industry experience. Currently, he works at HCL Technologies as an automation architect, delivering solutions related to hybrid cloud, using cloud-native and third-party solutions. Automation solutions include such use cases as enterprise observability, infrastructure as code, server automation, runbook automation, cloud management platforms, cloud native automation, and dashboard/visibility. Piyush is responsible for designing end-to-end solutions and architecture for enterprise automation adoption. He can be contacted at piyushnsitcoep@gmail.com and www.linkedin.com/in/ piyush-pandey-704495b.

About the Technical Reviewers

Ankur Verma is a DevOps consultant at OpsTree Solutions with more than nine years of experience in the IT industry

He has in-depth experience in building highly complex, scalable, secure, and distributed systems.

Jaspreet Singh is a skilled DevOps engineer currently associated with OpsTree Solutions. Technically proficient, he has more than six years of professional experience in the areas of IT infrastructure technologies, web application technologies, Cloud (AWS, GCP, Alibaba), virtualization technologies, and containerization and automation.

Acknowledgments

To my family, Shweta and Soumil, for always being by my side and allowing me to sacrifice their time to my intellectual and spiritual pursuits and for taking care of everything while I have been immersed in writing this book. This and my other accomplishments would not have been possible without your love and support. To my mom and my sister, for their constant love and support. Without your blessings nothing is possible.

To my coauthors Piyush Pandey, Siddharth Choudhary & Saurabh Tripathi, thank you for the hard work and quick turnarounds.

To my team at HCL, who have been a source of inspiration, with their hard work, ever-engaging technical conversations, and their technical knowledge. Your ever-flowing ideas are a source of happiness and excitement every single day. To Piyush Pandey, Sarvesh Pandey, Amit Agrawal, Vasand Kumar, Punith Krishnamurthy, Sandeep Sharma, Amit Dwivedi, Gauarv Bhardwaj, Nitin Narotra, and Vivek, thank you for being there and making technology fun. Special thanks to Siddharth Choudhary & Saurabh Tripathi who contributed to research input for this book.

To Celestin, Aditee, and the entire team at Apress, thank you for turning our ideas into reality. It has been an amazing experience collaborating with you and over the years. The speed of decision making and the editorial support have been excellent.

To all with whom I have had the opportunity to work—coauthors, colleagues, managers, mentors, and guides—in this world of 7 billion, it was coincidence that brought us together, but it was and is an enriching experience to be associated with you and learn from you. All the ideas I've had and paths I've followed are an assimilation of the conversations that I have had and experiences I have shared with you. Thank you.

ACKNOWLEDGMENTS

Thank you Goddess Saraswati, for guiding me to the path of knowledge and spirituality.

असतो मा साद गमय

तमसो मा ज्योतिर् गमय

मृत्योर मा अमृतम् गमय

asato mā sadgamaya
tamaso mā jyotirgamaya
mrtyor mā'mrtam gamaya
Lead us from ignorance to truth,
Lead us from darkness to light,
Lead us from death to immortality.

CHAPTER 1

Introduction to GKE

This first chapter of this book will introduce you to the world of containers, microservice applications, and associated monitoring and management tools ecosystems. It also looks at how containers and the ecosystem around them are assembled. The following topics are covered:

- Introduction to Docker

- Introduction to Kubernetes

- Managing Kubernetes

- GCP Container Solutions for Container Ecosystems

- Google Kubernetes Engine

- Container Registry

- Network

- Cloud Run

- Anthos

Introduction to Docker

With the rise of containerization technologies for modern application development, Docker is now widely used as a containerization framework. Containers are a way to bundle an application into its own isolated package, along with dependencies. Everything the application requires

© Navin Sabharwal, Piyush Pandey 2020
N. Sabharwal and P. Pandey, *Pro Google Kubernetes Engine*,
https://doi.org/10.1007/978-1-4842-6243-6_1

to run successfully as a process is now captured and executed within the container. This enables standardization and consistency across environments, as now the container will always come preloaded with all the prerequisites/dependencies required to run the application service. Now you can develop application code on your personal workstation and then safely deploy it to run on production-level infrastructure. Thus, the issues that one faced in terms of dependencies on operating system (OS) or virtualization software are no longer applicable on the container infrastructure (Figure 1-1).

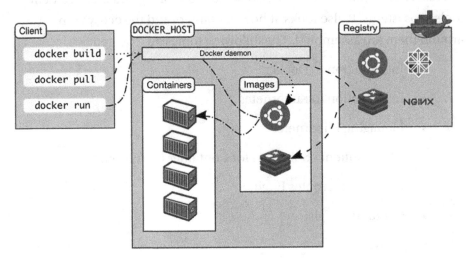

Figure 1-1. *Docker architecture*

Docker eliminates the divergence between development systems and software that is released in production. A Docker container works in the same OS configuration as is used to develop the software.

Following are some components of the Docker ecosystem (Figure 1-2):

Docker client: Docker users can interact with Docker through a client.

Docker host: The Docker host provides a base environment to run containerized applications. It provides all the necessary infrastructure base components from the Docker daemon, images, containers, and networks to storage.

Docker images: Docker images are equivalent to OS template or Virtual Machine images, the primary difference being that instead of packaging the OS, it contains the application binaries and all the dependencies required to run the application. By using these images, we can achieve application portability across infrastructure, without worrying about the infrastructure technologies used.

Registries: Registries are used to manage Docker images. There are two main types of registries: public and private. This is where Docker images are stored and can be pulled for instantiation on containers.

Docker Engine: Docker Engine enables developing, packaging, deploying, and running applications.

Docker daemon: Docker daemon is the core process that manages Docker images, containers, networks, and storage volumes.

Docker Engine REST API: This is the API used by containerized applications to interact with the Docker daemon.

Docker CLI: Docker CLI provides a command-line interface for interacting with the Docker daemon.

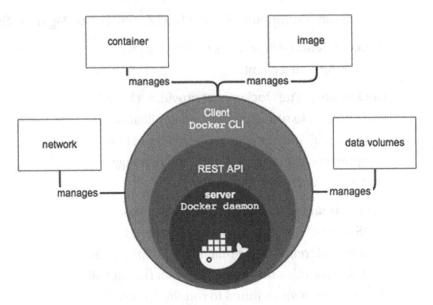

Figure 1-2. *Docker management interfaces (CLI and API)*

Introduction to Kubernetes

Kubernetes is an open source container management (orchestration) tool that provides an abstraction layer over containers, to manage container fleets leveraging REST APIs. Kubernetes is portable in nature and is supported to run on various public and private cloud platforms, such as physical servers, GCP, AWS, Azure, OpenStack, or Apache Mesos.

Similar to Docker, Kubernetes also follows a client-server architecture. It has a master server which is used to manage target nodes in which containerized applications are deployed. It also has a feature for service discovery.

The master server consists of various components, including a kube-apiserver, an etcd key-value store, a kube-controller-manager, a cloud-controller-manager, a kube-scheduler, and a DNS server for Kubernetes services. Node components include kubelet and kube-proxy (Figure 1-3).

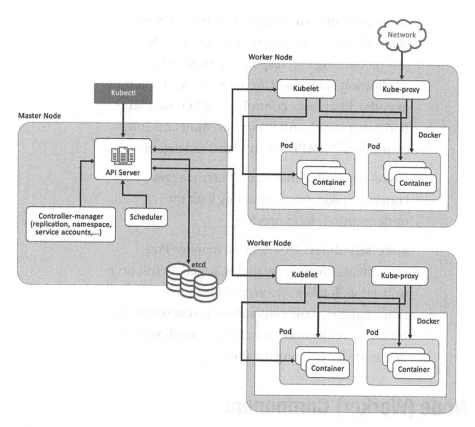

Figure 1-3. Kubernetes architecture

Master Node

Following are the main components found on the master node:

etcd cluster: An etcd cluster is a distributed key value store used for storing Kubernetes cluster data (such as the number of Pods, their state, namespace, etc.), API objects, and service discovery details.

kube-apiserver: This Kubernetes API server provides a programmatic interface for container management activities, such as Pods management, services, and replication sets/controllers, using REST APIs.

kube-controller-manager: This is used to manage controller processes, such as Node controller (for monitoring and responding to node health), Replication controller (for maintaining the number of Pods), Endpoints controller (for Service and Pod integration), and Service account and Token controllers (for API/Token access management).

cloud-controller-manager: This manages controller processes interacting with the underpinning cloud provider.

kube-scheduler: This helps to manage Pod placement across target nodes, based on resource utilization. It takes into account resource requirements, hardware/software/security policy, affinity specifications, etc., before deciding on the best node for running the Pod.

Node (Worker) Component

Following are the main components found on a node (worker) component:

Kubelet: The agent component running on a worker node. Its main purpose is to ensure that containers are running in a Pod. Any containers that are outside the management of Kubernetes are not managed by Kubelet. This ensures that worker nodes, Pods, and their containers are in a healthy state, as well as reporting these metrics back to Kubernetes master nodes.

kube-proxy: A proxy service that runs on worker node, to manage inter-Pod networking and communication.

Managing Kubernetes

kubectl is a command-line tool used for Kubernetes cluster management, using APIs exposed by kube-apiserver.

Kubernetes Workload

The Kubernetes workload includes the following main components:

Pod: A logical collection of one or more containers that formulate a single application and are represented as running processes on worker nodes. A Pod packages application containers, storage, network, and other configuration required for running containers. Pods can horizontally scale out and enable application deployment strategies, such as rolling updates and blue-green deployment, which aims at reducing application downtime and risks during upgrades.

Service: This provides an interface for the collection of one or more Pods bounded by policy. Since the life cycle of Pods is ephemeral in nature, Service helps to ensure application access without worrying, even if a back-end Pod dies abruptly.

Namespace: Namespace is a logical construct used to divide cluster resources across multiple users. You can use a resource quota with a namespace, to manage resource consumption by multiple application teams.

Deployment: Deployment represents the collection of one or more running Pods' It works closely with a deployment controller to ensure that the Pod is available, per the user specification mentioned in the Pod specification.

Introduction to GCP

Google Cloud Platform (GCP) is the public cloud offering of Google which provides a collection of IaaS/PaaS services to end customers. The Google Cloud Platform (GCP) is a suite of cloud computing services offered by Google. They run on the same infrastructure that Google uses internally for its own end-user products, such as Google search, Google Photos, YouTube, Gmail, etc. GCP services are well positioned for the modern application development user and have some unique offerings in the areas of data storage, Big Data analytics, artificial intelligence, and containerization. Google continues to innovate and strengthen its offerings.

GCP offers a wide range of services, which can be divided into the following areas: computing and hosting, storage, networking, big data, and machine learning. To build cloud applications, GCP provides various products. Some of the popular services are shown in Table 1-1.

Table 1-1. *GCP Services*

Services	Description
Google Compute Engine	Helps in creating a VM to run an operating system and allow creation of different computers in the cloud
Google Kubernetes Engine	Helps in managing Container Orchestrator and to deploy, scale, and release, using Kubernetes as a managed service
Google Cloud Function	Helps in implementing event-driven serverless cloud platforms and to create infrastructure as code, i.e., infrastructure designed and implemented by the code
Google Container Registry (GCR)	Google Container Registry provides secure, private Docker image storage on Google Cloud Platform. It provides a single place for teams to manage Docker images, perform vulnerability analysis, and decide who can access what, with fine-grained access control.
Google Stackdriver (now known as Google Operations)	Helps to get performance and diagnostics data to public cloud users. Stackdriver (Google Operations) provides support for both Google Cloud and AWS cloud environments, making it a hybrid cloud solution.

GCP Container Solutions for Container Ecosystems

GCP provides various services to run the containers ecosystem. It ranges from *Google Cloud Run,* which provides a fully managed environment, to *Kubernetes Engine*, which provides cluster management. *Google Compute Engine* provides roll-it-yourself compute infrastructure. Collectively, GCP provides an ideal solution for running containers. GCP also provides the tools you require to use containers, from development to production.

Cloud Build and *Container Registry* provide Docker image storage and management, backed with high security standards and highly efficient networks. Google's Container-Optimized OS provides a lightweight, highly secure operating system that comes with the Docker and Kubernetes runtimes preinstalled (Figure 1-4).

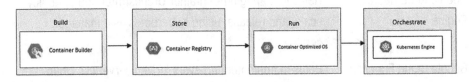

Figure 1-4. *GCP container ecosystem services*

Table 1-2 provides details of GCP services for the container ecosystem.

Table 1-2. *Details of GCP Services for the Container Ecosystem*

GCP Solution Name	Features	User Needs
Kubernetes Engine	• Fully automated container orchestration, including health monitoring, node auto-scaling, upgrading, repairing, and roll back • Focuses only on application components rather than VMs • Provides highly available heterogeneous and multi-zone clusters	• User will get highly managed, secure and scalable containers in the production environment. • Efficient for running microservice-based applications on containers on VM pools • Eliminates the need to focus on managing the cluster software or infrastructure

(*continued*)

Table 1-2. (*continued*)

GCP Solution Name	Features	User Needs
Compute Engine	• Facilitates auto-scaling, auto-healing, rolling updates, multi-zone deployments, and load balancing at the VM level • No container orchestration. Consider using Kubernetes Engine for automated container orchestration with managed Kubernetes. • Direct access to specialized hardware, including local SSDs, GPUs, and TPUs	• Allows easy integration of containerized applications with existing IaaS infrastructure • Easily deploys a single container per VM • Adopts containers, even if you are not yet familiar with orchestration tools. Migrates to Kubernetes Engine, for full orchestration, when ready.
Cloud Run	• Fast auto-scaling • Supports custom domains, to map your service with your domain • Pay when your code is running.	• No language barrier; uses any language with any libraries, in a fully managed serverless environment • Builds and runs public or private microservices

(*continued*)

Table 1-2. (*continued*)

GCP Solution Name	Features	User Needs
App Engine Flexible Environment	• Fully managed PaaS service to run an application in one container • Provides automatic high availability with built-in auto-scaling and load balancing • App versioning with zero-downtime upgrades • Native support for microservices, authorization, SQL and NoSQL databases, logging, security scanning, and content delivery networks	• Deploys custom runtimes for App Engine application in a container • Builds highly reliable and scalable serving apps or components without having to deal with servers, clusters, or infrastructure • Focuses on writing code and developer velocity over infrastructure control

Google Kubernetes Engine

Today, Kubernetes is the leading container orchestration tool in the industry. All major cloud providers offer managed Kubernetes services.

Google offers the managed Kubernetes service to its client known as *Google Kubernetes Services,* or *Google Kubernetes Engine (GKE).* GKE helps to manage containerized environments that facilitate development of microservices-based applications, and management and scaling of a client's containerized applications, using the Google infrastructure. It uses Kubernetes APIs, commands and resources to deploy and manage the applications, perform administration tasks, set policies, and monitor the health of the deployed applications.

When a GKE cluster runs, it provides the benefit of advanced cluster management features that GCP provides. These include

- GCP's load-balancing for Compute Engine instances
- Node pools to designate subsets of nodes within a cluster, for additional flexibility
- Automatic scaling of your cluster's node instance count
- Automatic upgrades for your cluster's node software
- Node auto-repair to maintain node health and availability
- Logging and monitoring with Stackdriver (Google operations), for visibility into your cluster

Figure 1-5 illustrates the GKE components.

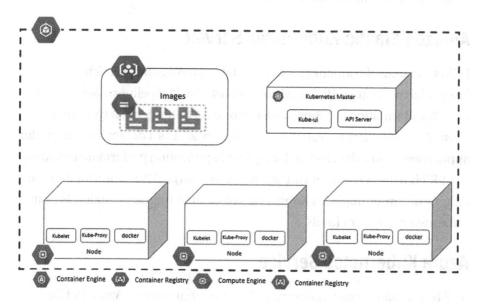

Figure 1-5. *GKE components*

GKE organizes its platform through Kubernetes Master. Every container cluster has a single master end point, which is managed by Kubernetes Engine. The master provides a unified view into the cluster and, through its publicly accessible end point, is the doorway for interacting with the cluster.

The managed master also runs the Kubernetes API server, which services REST requests, schedules Pod creation and deletion on worker nodes, and synchronizes Pod information (such as open ports and location) with service information.

Comparing EKS, AKS, and GKE

Let us now compare the features of the Kubernetes offerings from three cloud providers: Amazon Elastic Kubernetes Service (EKS) from Amazon Web Services (AWS), Azure Kubernetes Service (AKS) from Microsoft Azure, and GKE from Google Cloud.

Amazon Elastic Kubernetes Service

EKS is a managed container service available on AWS. It has a rich integration with other AWS services, such as CI/CD pipelines, Cloudwatch and Cloudformation etc. Since EKS is based on Kubernetes, it works with most of the use cases prevalent in the industry and as a deployment target for applications and a data source for logs and application performance metrics.

EKS is a good choice if you already have a large AWS footprint and are either experimenting with Kubernetes or want to migrate workloads from Kubernetes to other clouds.

Azure Kubernetes Service

AKS is a managed container service by Azure that runs on Azure Public Cloud, Government Cloud and, on premises, on Azure Stack. It has seamless integration with the other Azure services and has managed worker nodes. It also provides integration with Microsoft's other cross-platform development tools, including VS Code and DevOps (formerly Visual Studio Team Services).

AKS is a good choice if you are a Microsoft Shop and no strong desire for another cloud.

Google Kubernetes Engine

GKE is a managed service for Kubernetes that is available on the Google Cloud Platform. GKE has the services for the marketplace to deploy applications and the highest service-level agreement (SLA) guarantee for uptime. It secures the running containers using its Istio service mesh and gVisor. It also has an on-premises offering in development, as part of Google's Anthos offering for hybrid/multi cloud environments on dedicated hardware.

Table 1-3 compares the features of AKS, EKS, and GKE.

Table 1-3. *Feature Comparison of GKE, AKS & EKS*

	GKE	AKS	EKS
Kubernetes Version	1.14.10-gke.27	1.15	1.15
Multi AZ	Yes	Partial	Yes
Upgrades	Auto/On-demand	On-demand	Not clear
Auto-scale	Yes	Self-deployed	Self-deployed
Network Policy	Yes	Self-deployed	Self-deployed
Persistent Volume	Yes	Yes	Yes
Load Balancer	Yes	Yes	Yes
CLI Support	Partial	Yes	Yes
Service Mesh	Istio	In development	Yes (App Mesh)
RBAC	Yes	Yes	Yes

(continued)

15

Table 1-3. (*continued*)

	GKE	AKS	EKS
Compliance	HIPAA, SOC, ISO, PCI DSS	HIPAA, SOC, ISO, PCI DSS	HIPAA, SOC, ISO, PCI DSS
App Secret Encryption	Yes	No	No
SLA	99.5% (zone) 99.95% (regional)	99.5%	99.9%
Marketplace	Yes	No	No
Pricing	Standard costs of GCE machines and other resources	Standard costs of node VMs and other resources	$0.10/hour (USD) per cluster plus standard costs of EC2 instances and other resources

GKE Architecture

Google Kubernetes Engine consists of a cluster that has at least one master and multiple worker machines known as nodes. The orchestration of the Kubernetes system runs with the help of master and node machines. The basic unit of any GKE ecosystem is the cluster. The object that represents the application run on top of clusters is represented in the following diagram (Figure 1-6).

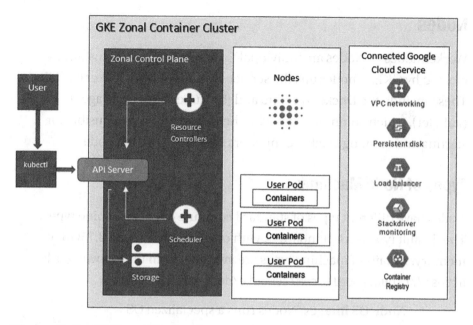

Figure 1-6. *GKE architecture*

Cluster Master

The Kubernetes control plane processes and Kubernetes API server, scheduler, and core resource controllers are run in the cluster master. GKE manages the life cycle of the master when a cluster is created or deleted. Upgrading the Kubernetes version running on the master is achieved by GKE, either automatically or manually, at the user's request.

Cluster Master and the Kubernetes API

Interactions with the cluster master are performed through Kubernetes API calls. The master handles the requests by the Kubernetes API Server process. Kubernetes API calls can be made through gRPC/HTTP, kubectl, or by interacting with the UI in the cloud console.

Nodes

Worker nodes or Nodes are individual Compute Engine VM instances created by GKE. A node runs the services to support the Docker container. These include the Docker runtime and the Kubernetes node agent (kubelet), which communicates with the master and is responsible for starting and running Docker containers scheduled on that node.

Types of Node Machines

Nodes have different types of standard compute engine machine types. The default type is n1-standard-1, with one virtual CPU and 3.75GB of memory. Details of machine types are available from the following url: https://cloud.google.com/compute/docs/machine-types/.

Node OS images: Nodes runs a specialized OS image, e.g., Linux RHEL, Ubuntu, for running containers. While creating clusters, we can choose which type of OS image to use in node pools.

Types of clusters: GKE provides various types of clusters that can be used while creating the cluster. After creating a cluster type, it cannot be changed.

Single-zone cluster: A single-zone cluster has a single master, also known as a control plane, running in single zone and manages workloads on nodes running in the same zone.

Multi-zonal clusters: This is a single replica of a control plane running in a single zone and having nodes running in multiple zones.

Regional clusters: Within a given region, these multiple replicas of control planes run in multiple zones, and nodes also run on each zone where a replica of a control plane runs.

Node pools: A group of nodes having the same types of configurations are known as Node pools. Each node in the pool has a Kubernetes node label, cloud.google.com/gke-nodepool, which has the node pool's name as its value. A node pool can contain a single node or many nodes. While creating a cluster, the number and types of nodes provided become the default node pool. Additional custom node pools of different sizes and types can be added to the cluster. All nodes in any given node pool are identical to one another.

Container Registry

Google Cloud Container Registry is a private registry for managed Docker images. Container Registry can be accessed through HTTPS end points, and you can manage, push, and pull the Docker images for VM instances provided by Google Cloud from any other system or cloud or your own systems.

Cloud Container Registry is a highly secure private registry available only to users who have valid access to it. It detects vulnerabilities in images and ensures safe container image deployment. It uses up-to-date vulnerabilities-based databases that ensure images will be scanned against new malware.

It automatically builds and pushes images to a private registry when you commit code to Cloud Source Repositories, GitHub, or Bitbucket. Users can easily set up CI/CD pipelines with integration to Cloud Build or deploy directly to Google Kubernetes Engine, App Engine, Cloud Functions, or Firebase. Container Registry supports Docker Image Manifest V2 and OCI image formats.

Network

This section provides an overview of the core concepts of Google Kubernetes Engine networking. Kubernetes uses declarative language to define how applications are deployed, how applications communicate with one another as well as the Kubernetes plane, and how clients can access the deployed applications.

While using Kubernetes orchestration for applications, the network design of the applications and their hosts are designed with regard to Pods, Services, and external client communications, rather than thinking about how hosts or VMs are connected.

Kubernetes's advanced software-defined networking (SDN) enables packet routing and forwarding for Pods, Services, and nodes across different zones in the same regional cluster. Kubernetes and Google Cloud also dynamically configure IP filtering rules, routing tables, and firewall rules on each node, depending on the declarative model of your Kubernetes deployments and cluster configuration on Google Cloud.

Services, Pods, containers, and nodes communicate using IP addresses and ports. Kubernetes provides different types of load balancing to direct traffic to the correct Pods.

- **ClusterIP**: The IP address assigned to a service. In other documents, it may be called the "Cluster IP." This address is stable for the lifetime of the service, as discussed under the "Introduction to GCP" section of this chapter.

- **Pod IP**: The IP address assigned to a given Pod. This is ephemeral, as discussed under "Introduction to GCP."

- **Node IP**: The IP address assigned to a given node.

Cloud Run

To deploy and run container-based applications in cloud requires a service that can manage the complexity of the servers, networking security, and storage.

Google Cloud provides such a service, called Cloud Run. It is serverless and enables you to run stateless containers that you invoke via web requests and PUB/SUB events. Cloud Run is built on an open cloud native standard, enabling the portability of applications.

Key Features

The key features of Cloud Run are as follows:

- **Uses any language, binary, or library:** It allows use of any programming language or system libraries.

- **Uses container workflows and standards:** Cloud Run leverages container workflows and standards, such as Docker, Container Registry, and Cloud Build.

- **Pricing:** GCP offers pay-per-use for its Cloud Run service.

Anthos

Anthos is the Google multi-cloud application platform that modernizes existing applications based on the concept of building once and running anywhere.

Anthos is not a single product but a bunch of multiple services that perform application modernization, cloud migration, and multi-cloud and hybrid cloud management. Anthos enables consistency between on-premises and cloud environments and helps accelerate application development (Figure 1-7).

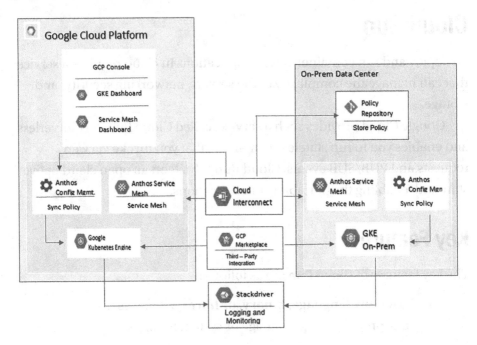

Figure 1-7. Anthos components

Components of Anthos

Anthos GKE

Anthos GKE components provide overall container management, with quick installation and upgrades with Google validation.

Google Cloud Console offers a single-pane-of-glass view for managing clusters across on-premises and cloud environments.

Anthos Config Management

This enables rapid and secure application deployment and allows you to create a common configuration for administrative policies that apply on Kubernetes clusters, whether it be on-premises or in the cloud.

Anthos Service Mesh

A fully managed service mesh that manages complex microservices architectures. It simplifies operating services across the board, from traffic management and mesh telemetry to securing communications between services.

Although a detailed discussion of Anthos is not within the scope of this book, we have provided an extensive discussion of GKE and its components.

Summary

In this chapter, we have covered the container ecosystem evolution, Docker and Kubernetes architecture, and the benefits and challenges of container technology. The next chapter begins with practical exercises to set up an environment on GCP.

CHAPTER 2

Setting Up an Environment on GCP

This second chapter of this book introduces you to setting up an environment on GCP. You also will learn how to sign up for a Google account and set up an environment for the GCP container ecosystem. The chapter covers the following topics:

- Signing Up for Google Cloud

- Setting Up an Environment for Google GKE

- Supporting Services for Containers

Signing Up for Google Cloud

Let's get started with GCP. The first step is to sign up to access GCP. The following covers the steps required for signing up and is directed more toward first-time users.

The primary prerequisite for signing up for the platform is a Google account. GCP uses Google accounts for access management and authentication. As shown in Figure 2-1, enter the URL `https://cloud.google.com/free#` in your browser window.

© Navin Sabharwal, Piyush Pandey 2020
N. Sabharwal and P. Pandey, *Pro Google Kubernetes Engine*,
https://doi.org/10.1007/978-1-4842-6243-6_2

Figure 2-1. Google Cloud Platform

Click the Get started for free button, which will bring up the following Sign-in screen (Figure 2-2).

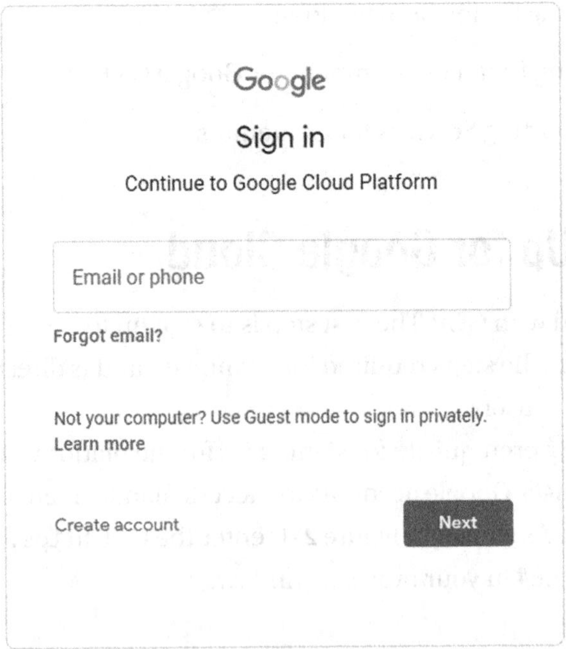

Figure 2-2. GCP Sign in screen

You will be prompted for a Google account. If you don't have a Google account, follow the Create account process to create one.

Note   If the account is already signed in, you will be redirected to the GCP console (Figures 2-3 and 2-4).

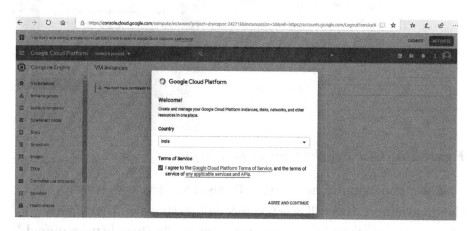

Figure 2-3. *GCP console*

Figure 2-4. *GCP project activation*

If you are eligible for a free tier, you will be prompted for the account details, as shown in Figure 2-5.

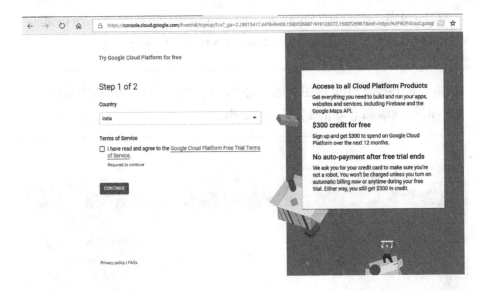

Figure 2-5. *GCP free tier registration, Step 1*

Select your country, agree to the Terms of Service, and click the Continue button. This will take you to Step 2, as shown in Figure 2-6, wherein you create and select your payment profile. Provide the required billing details; however, be aware that auto-debit will not occur unless you manually upgrade for it.

Try Google Cloud Platform for free

Dhaulagiri Apartments, Kaushambi
Ghaziabad, Uttar Pradesh 201010
India

Step 2 of 2

Payments profile ⓘ

Choose the payments profile that will be associated with
this account or transaction. A payments profile is shared
and used across all Google products.

How you pay

📅   Monthly automatic payments

You pay for this service on a regular
monthly basis, via an automatic charge
when your payment is due.

θ   Individual profile for Play and YouTube ∨
Payments profile ID: 1   43

Customer info

θ   Account type ⓘ
Individual

Payment method ⓘ

💳   Mastercard ···   5   ∨

🪪   Tax information

Tax status

The personal information that you provide here will be
added to your payments profile. It will be stored securely
and treated in accordance with the Google Privacy
Policy.

🏢   Name and address ⓘ   🖊

START MY FREE TRIAL

Figure 2-6. *GCP free tier registration, Step 2*

While you create your payment profile and sign yourself in, the right-
hand panel displays details, as shown in Figure 2-7.

Access to all Cloud Platform products

Get everything that you need to build and run your apps, websites and services, including Firebase and the Google Maps API.

$300 credit for free

Sign up and get $300 to spend on Google Cloud Platform over the next 12 months.

No autocharge after free trial ends

We ask you for your credit card to make sure that you are not a robot. You won't be charged unless you manually upgrade to a paid account.

Figure 2-7. *GCP free tier information*

As you can see, Google offers a free trial credit of $300 for a period of 12 months, which is sufficient not only to explore all the exercises in the book but also to evaluate GCP further. Once you have specified all the details, click the Start My Free Trial button.

It will take a while for the registration to be completed. Once the necessary validations are done, you will be redirected to the Google console, and you are ready to get started.

Click the Create button on the VM creation console, to activate GCP Compute Engine services which will be used for creating VM (Figure 2-8).

Figure 2-8. *GCP Compute engine activation for VM creation via console*

Click the Activate button at the top-right corner of the page. It will prompt you to upgrade. Click Upgrade (Figure 2-9).

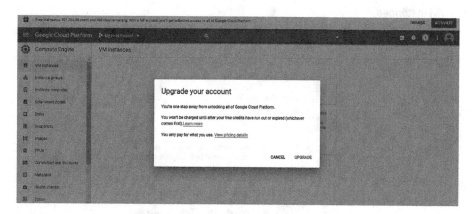

Figure 2-9. *VM creation console upgrade*

31

Refresh the page, as prompted (Figure 2-10).

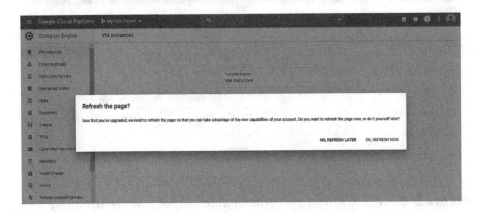

Figure 2-10. *VM creation console refresh prompt*

Once the activation process is complete, the following screen (Figure 2-11) will be displayed.

VM instances

Compute Engine
VM instances

Compute Engine lets you use virtual machines that run on Google's infrastructure. Create micro-VMs or larger instances running Debian, Windows or other standard images. Create your first VM instance, import it using a migration service or try the quickstart to build a sample app.

Create   or   Import   or   Take the quickstart

Figure 2-11. *Post-activation screen*

Setting Up an Environment for Google GKE

Setting Up the GCP CLI

The gcloud command-line interface (CLI) is the primary CLI tool for managing the GCP.

Google Cloud SDK (software development kit) offers a variety of command-line tools to interact with GCP, namely

- **gcloud**: GCP's primary CLI

- **gsutil**: The CLI to interact with Google Cloud Storage

- **bq**: The CLI to interact with Google BigQuery

- **kubectl**: Kubernetes Engine's CLI

You can use the gcloud CLI to perform many common platform tasks, either from the command line or in scripts and via other automation tools like Jenkins/Ansible etc.

For example, you can use it gcloud CLI to create and manage

- Google Compute Engine VM instances and other resources

- Google Cloud SQL instances

- Google Kubernetes Engine clusters

- Google Cloud Dataproc clusters and jobs

- Google Cloud DNS managed zones and record sets

- Google Cloud Deployment Manager deployments

You can also use the gcloud CLI to deploy App Engine applications and perform other associated tasks. The gcloud CLI is a part of the Google Cloud SDK.

By default, the SDK installs the gcloud CLI commands that are at the General Availability level only. Additional functionality is available in

SDK components named alpha and beta. These components allow you to use the gcloud CLI to work with Google Cloud Bigtable, Google Cloud Dataflow, and other parts of the Cloud Platform at earlier release levels than General Availability.

Table 2-1 depicts the gcloud CLI command release levels.

Table 2-1. *gcloud CLI Command Release Levels*

Release level	Label	Description
General Availability	None	Commands are considered fully stable and available for production use. Advance warnings are given for commands that break current functionality, and they are documented in the release notes.
Beta	beta	Commands are functionally complete but may still have some outstanding issues. Breaking changes to these commands may be made without notice.
Alpha	alpha	Commands are in early release and may change without notice.

The alpha and beta components are not installed by default when you install the SDK. You must install these separately, using the gcloud components' install command. If you try to run an alpha or beta command and the corresponding component is not installed, the gcloud command-line tool will prompt you to install it.

The gcloud CLI releases have the same version number as the SDK. The current SDK version is 278.0.0.

Note   The gcloud command-line tool is available automatically in Google Cloud Shell. If you are using Cloud Shell, you do not have to install the gcloud CLI manually in order to use it.

GCP Cloud Shell

Google Cloud Shell provides you with command-line access to computing resources hosted on GCP and is available from the GCP console. Cloud Shell makes it easy for you to manage your Cloud Platform console projects and resources without having to install the Google Cloud SDK and other tools. With Cloud Shell, the Cloud SDK gcloud command and other utilities you need are always available when you need them.

Creating a Project

A project is essentially a container for regrouping all IT and non-IT resources connected with a specific cloud project. Every project is identified by some specific parameter, as follows (Table 2-2).

Table 2-2. *Project Parameters*

Parameter	Description
Name	This is used to identify and describe a project. The name is only for user reference and can be changed at any stage. Free tier access allows creation of 24 projects.
Project ID	This is a unique string for identifying a project globally. It is created by starting with the project name. The project ID can be edited and changed. To create a project ID, you can use any lowercase letter, number, and hyphens. The only requirement is that the name be unique. After a unique ID is entered, it can no longer be changed.
Project Number	This is a parameter that is auto-generated by GCP. You can't manage or change this number.

To create a new project, click the Create a new project button. This leads to the following steps:

1. Go to the Manage resources page in the Cloud console.

2. On the Select organization drop-down list at the top of the page, select the organization with which you want to create a project. If you are a free-trial user, skip this step.

3. Click Create Project.

4. In the New Project window that appears, enter a project name and select a billing account, as applicable (Figure 2-12).

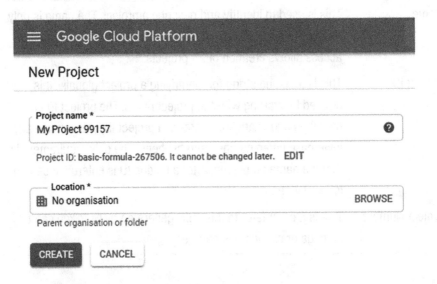

Figure 2-12. *New Project detail screen*

Remember that the project ID must have a unique name that will be used across all Google Cloud projects. (The project name in the preceding figure has already been taken and will not work for you.) The project name will be PROJECT_ID.

5. When you've finished entering the new project details, click Create. New Project will be selected and will appear as follows (Figure 2-13).

Figure 2-13. *New Project view*

Launching Cloud Shell

Activate Google Cloud Shell from the GCP console Cloud Shell icon on the top-left toolbar (Figure 2-14).

Figure 2-14. *Cloud Shell button*

The following screen will be displayed. Click Continue (Figure 2-15).

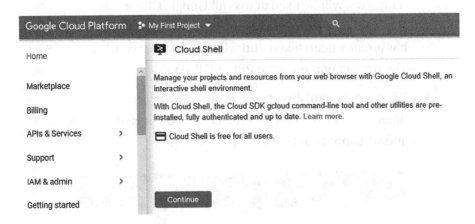

Figure 2-15. *Cloud Shell screen*

After clicking the Continue button, Click the Start Cloud Shell button to start the Cloud Shell session (Figure 2-16).

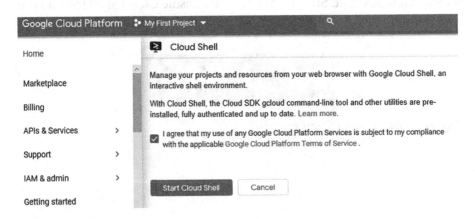

Figure 2-16. *Cloud Shell start screen*

It should take a few minutes to provision and connect to the environment. The preceding is a one-time activity. The next time, clicking the Shell button will lead to the following screen (Figure 2-17).

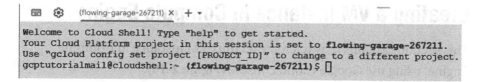

Figure 2-17. Cloud Shell screen

This VM is loaded with all the development tools you'll require. It offers a persistent 5GB home directory and runs on the Google Cloud, greatly enhancing network performance and authentication. Much, if not all, of your work in this lab can be done with simply a browser or your Google Chromebook.

Once connected to Cloud Shell, you should first check that you are already authenticated and that the project is already set to your PROJECT_ID.

Run the following command in Cloud Shell to confirm that you are authenticated.

Command: gcloud config list project

Output: The output should display as follows (Figure 2-18).

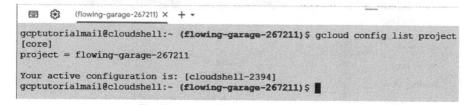

Figure 2-18. List project command output

Creating a VM Instance in Compute Engine

This section explains how to create a Linux VM instance in Compute Engine, using the Google Cloud console (Figure 2-19).

1. On Cloud console option, click on the VM instances link, as in Figure 2-19.

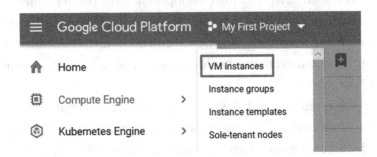

Figure 2-19. *Cloud console page—VM instances option*

2. From the Cloud console option, click on the Create button, to create a new instance (Figure 2-20).

Figure 2-20. *Cloud console page—Create VM option*

3. On the Create Instance page's Boot disk section, click Change, to begin configuring your boot disk (Figure 2-21).

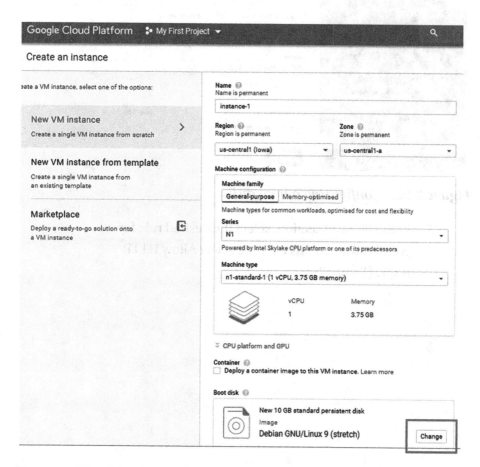

Figure 2-21. *Cloud console page—Create an instance page*

4. On the Public images tab, choose your preferred Operating system and Version. In this case, we are selecting Debian version 9 (Figure 2-22).

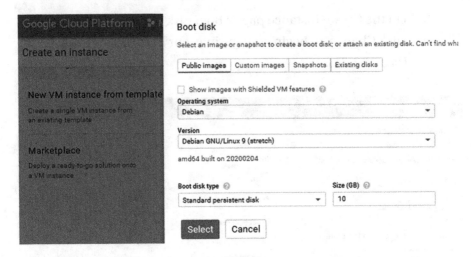

Figure 2-22. *Configuring a boot disk*

5. In the Firewall section, select the desired rule for your firewall. In this case, we select Allow HTTP traffic (Figure 2-23).

New 10 GB standard persistent disk

Image

Debian GNU/Linux 9 (stretch)   [Change]

Identity and API access ⊘

Service account ⊘

Compute Engine default service account   ▼

Access scopes ⊘
● Allow default access
○ Allow full access to all Cloud APIs
○ Set access for each API

Firewall ⊘
Add tags and firewall rules to allow specific network traffic from the Internet.
☑ Allow HTTP traffic
☐ Allow HTTPS traffic

⌄ Management, security, disks, networking, sole tenancy

You will be billed for this instance. Compute Engine pricing ↗

[Create] [Cancel]

Figure 2-23. *Selecting the firewall rule*

6. Click Create to create the instance.

   Allow some time for the instance to start. After the
   instance is ready, it is listed with a green status icon
   on the VM instances page(Figure 2-24).

Figure 2-24. *VM instances page status icon*

7. In the list of VM instances, click SSH in the row of
    the instance that you want to connect (Figure 2-25).

Figure 2-25. *VM instances dashboard*

8. Now you have a terminal window for interacting
    with your Linux instance, as in Figure 2-26.

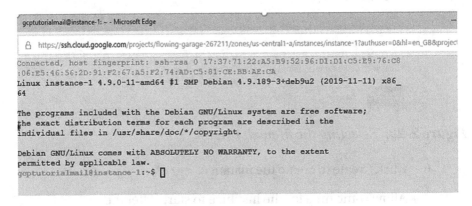

Figure 2-26. *VM instance terminal*

Setting Up CLI on the Created VM

In this section, we will set up CLI on the new VM created in the preceding
section.

Step 1: Log on to the preceding created VM. Select
the appropriate download from the SDK package at
https://cloud.google.com/sdk/docs/downloads-

versioned-archives and scroll down to find the
required package to install (Figure 2-27).

2. Download the appropriate archive compatible with your version:

Platform	Package	Size	SHA256 Checksum
Linux 64-bit (x86_64)	google-cloud-sdk-283.0.0-linux-x86_64.tar.gz	56.6 MB	13b4bbe79238e35a975e21514caca9c e77a8359800d85c5afb9ca188cef834 1c

Figure 2-27. *Package download page*

Right-click the highlighted package and select Copy
link address (Figure 2-28).

2. Download the appropriate archive compatible with your version:

Platform	Package	Size	SHA256 Checksum
Linux 64-bit (x86_64)	google-cloud-sdk-283.0.0-linux-x86_64.tar.	56.6	13b4bbe79238e35a975e21514caca9c 0d85c5afb9ca188cef834
Linux 32-bit (x86)	google-cloud-sdk linux-x86.tar.gz		a1b25d0ffd30283a07c26 132070e5057206512218

Open link in new tab
Open link in new window
Open link in incognito window
Save link as...
Copy link address
Inspect   Ctrl+Shift+I

Figure 2-28. *Package download page*

Step 2: Check for the current working directory and
run the package download command to download
the SDK package, using the link copied in the
preceding step.

Command: pwd—check for current working
directory

Output: The result of pwd will be displayed as
follows (Figure 2-29).

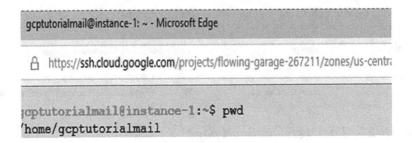

Figure 2-29. *Output of pwd command*

Command: wget https://dl.google.com/dl/
cloudsdk/channels/rapid/downloads/google-
cloud-sdk-279.0.0-linux-x86_64.tar.gz

Output: The result of wget will be displayed as
follows (Figure 2-30).

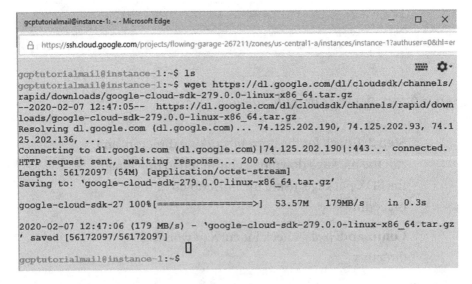

Figure 2-30. *Output of wget command*

Once downloaded, the SDK package can be listed as follows.

Command: ls

Output: The result of the ls command will be displayed as follows (Figure 2-31).

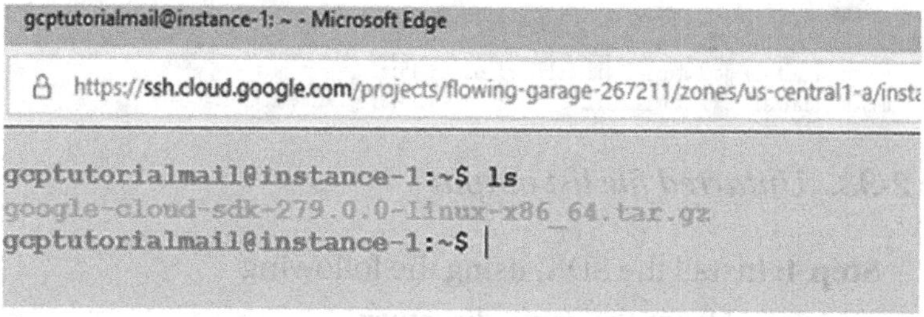

Figure 2-31. *List downloaded package using ls command with output as above*

Step 3: Untar the SDK package using the following command.

Command: tar -xvf google-cloud-sdk-279.0.0-linux-x86_64.tar.gz

Output: The result of the preceding command will be displayed as follows (Figure 2-32).

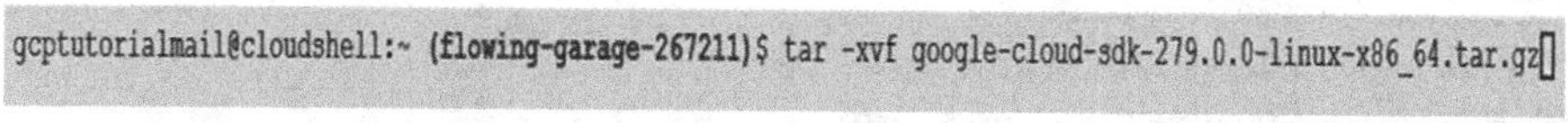

Figure 2-32. *Untar package command output*

The untarred file can be listed as follows, using

Command: `ls -lrt`

Output: The result of the preceding command will be displayed as in Figure 2-33.

```
gcptutorialmail@instance-1:~$ ls -lrt
total 54860
-rw-r--r-- 1 gcptutorialmail gcptutorialmail 56172097 Feb  4 15:50 google-cloud-sdk-279.0.0-linux-x86_64.tar.gz
drwxr-xr-x 9 gcptutorialmail gcptutorialmail     4096 Feb  7 13:01 google-cloud-sdk
```

Figure 2-33. *Untarred file list output*

Step 4: Install the SDK, using the following command from the same directory.

Command: `./google-cloud-sdk/install.sh`

Output: The result of the preceding command will be displayed as follows (Figures 2-34, 2-35, and 2-36).

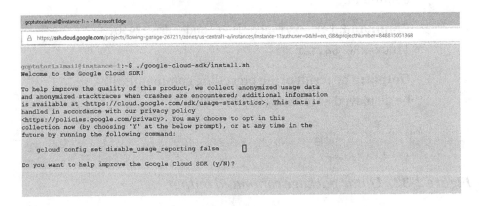

Figure 2-34. *Install SDK output screen—continued*

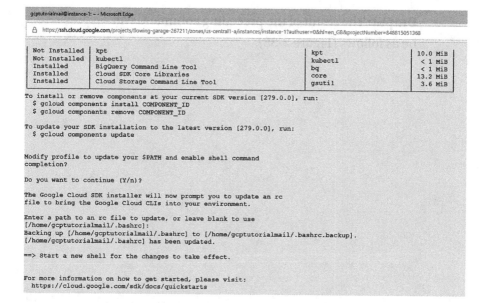

```
gcptutorialmail@instance-1: - - Microsoft Edge

  https://ssh.cloud.google.com/projects/flowing-garage-267211/zones/us-central1-a/instances/instance-1?authuser=0&hl=en_GB&projectNumber=848815051368

 Not Installed │ Cloud Datalab Command Line Tool                           │ datalab                    │  < 1 MiB
 Not Installed │ Cloud Datastore Emulator                                  │ cloud-datastore-emulator   │ 18.4 MiB
 Not Installed │ Cloud Firestore Emulator                                  │ cloud-firestore-emulator   │ 40.4 MiB
 Not Installed │ Cloud Pub/Sub Emulator                                    │ pubsub-emulator            │ 34.9 MiB
 Not Installed │ Cloud SQL Proxy                                           │ cloud_sql_proxy            │  3.8 MiB
 Not Installed │ Emulator Reverse Proxy                                    │ emulator-reverse-proxy     │ 14.5 MiB
 Not Installed │ Google Cloud Build Local Builder                         │ cloud-build-local          │  6.0 MiB
 Not Installed │ Google Container Registry's Docker credential helper      │ docker-credential-gcr      │  1.8 MiB
 Not Installed │ Kind                                                      │ kind                       │  4.5 MiB
 Not Installed │ Minikube                                                  │ minikube                   │ 18.1 MiB
 Not Installed │ Skaffold                                                  │ skaffold                   │ 12.1 MiB
 Not Installed │ gcloud Alpha Commands                                     │ alpha                      │  < 1 MiB
 Not Installed │ gcloud Beta Commands                                      │ beta                       │  < 1 MiB
 Not Installed │ gcloud app Java Extensions                                │ app-engine-java            │ 62.2 MiB
 Not Installed │ gcloud app PHP Extensions                                 │ app-engine-php             │
 Not Installed │ gcloud app Python Extensions                             │ app-engine-python          │  6.1 MiB
 Not Installed │ gcloud app Python Extensions (Extra Libraries)           │ app-engine-python-extras   │ 27.1 MiB
 Not Installed │ kpt                                                       │ kpt                        │ 10.0 MiB
 Not Installed │ kubectl                                                   │ kubectl                    │  < 1 MiB
 Installed     │ BigQuery Command Line Tool                                │ bq                         │  < 1 MiB
 Installed     │ Cloud SDK Core Libraries                                  │ core                       │ 13.2 MiB
 Installed     │ Cloud Storage Command Line Tool                          │ gsutil                     │  3.6 MiB

To install or remove components at your current SDK version [279.0.0], run:
  $ gcloud components install COMPONENT_ID
  $ gcloud components remove COMPONENT_ID

To update your SDK installation to the latest version [279.0.0], run:
  $ gcloud components update


Modify profile to update your $PATH and enable shell command
completion?
```

Figure 2-35. *Install SDK output screen—continued*

```
gcptutorialmail@instance-1: - - Microsoft Edge

  https://ssh.cloud.google.com/projects/flowing-garage-267211/zones/us-central1-a/instances/instance-1?authuser=0&hl=en_GB&projectNumber=848815051368

 Not Installed │ kpt                                       │ kpt       │ 10.0 MiB
 Not Installed │ kubectl                                   │ kubectl   │  < 1 MiB
 Installed     │ BigQuery Command Line Tool                │ bq        │  < 1 MiB
 Installed     │ Cloud SDK Core Libraries                  │ core      │ 13.2 MiB
 Installed     │ Cloud Storage Command Line Tool           │ gsutil    │  3.6 MiB

To install or remove components at your current SDK version [279.0.0], run:
  $ gcloud components install COMPONENT_ID
  $ gcloud components remove COMPONENT_ID

To update your SDK installation to the latest version [279.0.0], run:
  $ gcloud components update


Modify profile to update your $PATH and enable shell command
completion?

Do you want to continue (Y/n)?

The Google Cloud SDK installer will now prompt you to update an rc
file to bring the Google Cloud CLIs into your environment.

Enter a path to an rc file to update, or leave blank to use
[/home/gcptutorialmail/.bashrc]:
Backing up [/home/gcptutorialmail/.bashrc] to [/home/gcptutorialmail/.bashrc.backup].
[/home/gcptutorialmail/.bashrc] has been updated.

==> Start a new shell for the changes to take effect.


For more information on how to get started, please visit:
  https://cloud.google.com/sdk/docs/quickstarts
```

Figure 2-36. *Install SDK output screen—continued*

Press Y.

Step 5: After the installation, you must initialize gcloud to execute commands.

Configuring Google Cloud CLI on Local Machine

Take the following steps, to configure the Google Cloud SDK.

1. Initialize the SDK using the following command.

    Command: gcloud init (Figure 2-37)

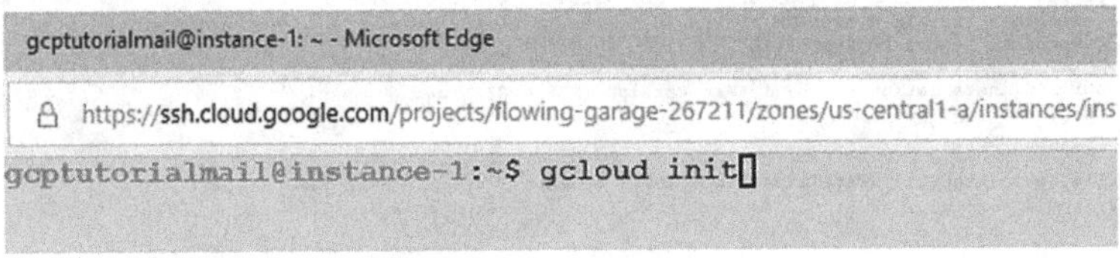

Figure 2-37. *SDK initialization*

Output: The result of the preceding command will be as follows (Figure 2-38).

```
gcptutorialmail@instance-1: ~ - Microsoft Edge          —    □    ×

🔒  https://ssh.cloud.google.com/projects/flowing-garage-267211/zones/us-central1-a/instances/instance-1?authuser=0&hl=er

gcptutorialmail@instance-1:~$ gcloud init
Welcome! This command will take you through the configuration of gcloud.

Your current configuration has been set to: [default]

You can skip diagnostics next time by using the following flag:
  gcloud init --skip-diagnostics

Network diagnostic detects and fixes local network connection issues.
Checking network connection...done.
Reachability Check passed.
Network diagnostic passed (1/1 checks passed).

Choose the account you would like to use to perform operations for
this configuration:
 [1] 848815051368-compute@developer.gserviceaccount.com
 [2] Log in with a new account
Please enter your numeric choice:  1
```

Figure 2-38. *SDK initialization output*

How to Get Project ID

To get the project ID, return to the project list and copy the appropriate project ID as shown in Figure 2-39. Enter the project ID when asked as shown in Figure 2-40 and continue by pressing Enter (Figure 2-39).

Select a project		⚙ NEW PROJECT
🔍 Search projects and folders		
RECENT ALL		
Name	ID	
✓ ‰ My First Project ❓	flowing-garage-267211	
‰ My First Project ❓	copper-array-267209	

Figure 2-39. *Select a project screen*

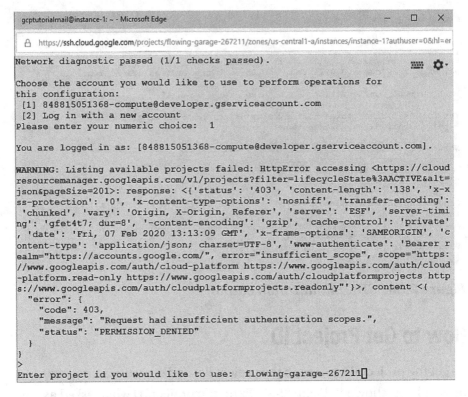

Figure 2-40. SDK initialize output

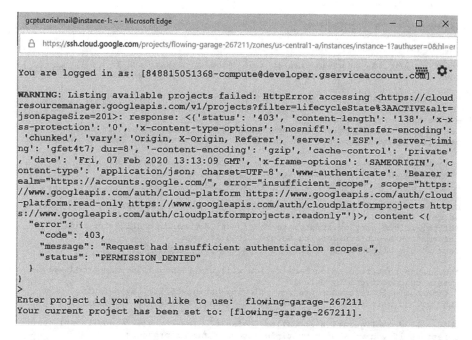

gcptutorialmail@instance-1: ~ - Microsoft Edge   —   ☐   ✕

🔒 https://**ssh.cloud.google.com**/projects/flowing-garage-267211/zones/us-central1-a/instances/instance-1?authuser=0&hl=er

You are logged in as: [848815051368-compute@developer.gserviceaccount.com]. ⚙▾

WARNING: Listing available projects failed: HttpError accessing <https://cloud
resourcemanager.googleapis.com/v1/projects?filter=lifecycleState%3AACTIVE&alt=
json&pageSize=201>: response: <{'status': '403', 'content-length': '138', 'x-x
ss-protection': '0', 'x-content-type-options': 'nosniff', 'transfer-encoding':
'chunked', 'vary': 'Origin, X-Origin, Referer', 'server': 'ESF', 'server-timi
ng': 'gfet4t7; dur=8', '-content-encoding': 'gzip', 'cache-control': 'private'
, 'date': 'Fri, 07 Feb 2020 13:13:09 GMT', 'x-frame-options': 'SAMEORIGIN', 'c
ontent-type': 'application/json; charset=UTF-8', 'www-authenticate': 'Bearer r
ealm="https://accounts.google.com/", error="insufficient_scope", scope="https:
//www.googleapis.com/auth/cloud-platform https://www.googleapis.com/auth/cloud
-platform.read-only https://www.googleapis.com/auth/cloudplatformprojects http
s://www.googleapis.com/auth/cloudplatformprojects.readonly"'}>, content <{
    "error": {
      "code": 403,
      "message": "Request had insufficient authentication scopes.",
      "status": "PERMISSION_DENIED"
    }
}
>
Enter project id you would like to use: flowing-garage-267211
Your current project has been set to: [flowing-garage-267211].

Figure 2-41. *SDK initialize output—continued*

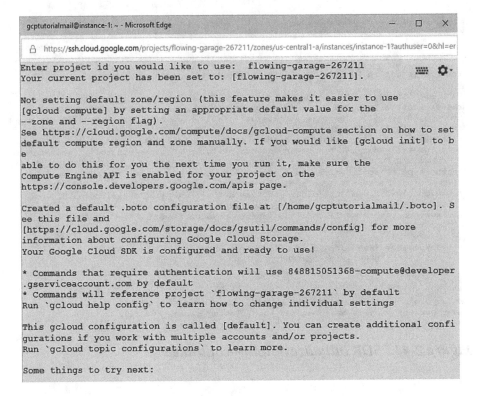

Figure 2-42. SDK initialize output—continued

The Cloud Shell is connected to the Google project.

Run the following command in Cloud Shell to confirm that you are authenticated.

Command: gcloud config list project (Figure 2-43)

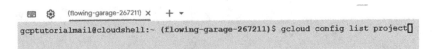

Figure 2-43. List project screen

Output: The result of the preceding command will be as follows (Figure 2-44).

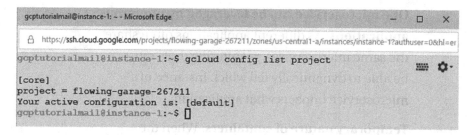

Figure 2-44. *List project output screen*

Supporting Services for Containers

With the rise of container technology came the requirement to support ecosystems with which enterprises could run mission-critical workloads on containers. The introduction of container technology and adoption of microservices architecture for application requires monitoring solution. Monitoring solutions now requires management of data for non-ephemeral and ephemeral services for vast amount of objects. Collecting data from applications composed of so many services has become vastly complex. Following are nuances to be considered when it comes to container services:

> **Short life span of containers**: If used to host microservices, containers are constantly provisioned and decommissioned, based on demand at a specific point in time. This can lead to cycles, where, in the morning, a container host cluster is filled up with microservices belonging to Workload A, while in the afternoon, this same host is serving Application B. This means that the business impact of a security breach, slow performance, or downtime on a certain host will have a very different business impact, depending on when it occurs.

One microservice can be leveraged by numerous applications: As different applications often share the same microservices, monitoring tools must be able to dynamically tell which instance of a microservice impacts what application.

Temporary nature of containers: When the assembly of a new container is triggered based on a container image, networking connections, storage resources, and integration with other required corporate services have to be provided instantly. This dynamic provisioning can impact the performance of related and unrelated infrastructure components.

More levels to watch: In the case of Kubernetes, enterprise IT must monitor at the levels of Nodes (host servers), PODs (host clusters), and individual containers. In addition, monitoring has to occur at the VM and storage level, as well as at the microservices level.

Different container management frameworks: Amazon EC2 Container Services run on Amazon's homegrown management platform, while Google naturally supports Kubernetes (as does VMware), and Docker supports Swarm. Container monitoring solutions must be aware of the differences between these container-management platforms.

Microservices change fast and often: Anomaly detection for microservices-based applications is much more difficult than for standard apps, as apps consisting of microservices are in constant change.

New microservices are added to the app, and
existing ones are updated in a very quick sequence,
leading to different infrastructure usage patterns.
The monitoring tool needs to be able to differentiate
between "normal" usage patterns caused by
intentional changes and actual "anomalies" that
have to be addressed.

Table 2-3 explains various metrics collected at multiple layers of a
container ecosystem.

***Table 2-3.** Metrics Explosion View with Container Technology
Evolution*

Per Host Metrics Explosion			
Component	# of Metrics for a Traditional Stack	for 10 Container Cluster with 1 Underlying Host	for 10 Container Cluster with 1 Underlying Host
Operating System	100	100	200
Orchestrator	n/a	50	50
Container	n/a	500 (50 per container)	5,000 (50 per container)
Application	50	500 (50 per container)	5,000 (50 per container)
Total # of Metrics	150	1,150	10,250

In order to have complete visibility of containerized applications, you
now must have data from various components, which formulates the base
infrastructure for running containers. This means you must monitor the
following:

- Application services

- Pods and containers

- Clusters running the containers

- Network for service/Pod/cluster communication

- Host OS/machine running the cluster

Choosing the right monitoring tool set is certainly important, based on pros and cons of the solution. Following are the options available on the market for container ecosystems (Table 2-4).

Table 2-4. *Tools for the Container Ecosystem*

Functionality	Services	Description
Monitoring	Prometheus	Prometheus is one of the oldest and most popular open source container monitoring solutions available. It's a graduated cloud-native computing foundation (CNCF) project that offers powerful querying capabilities, visualization, and alerting.
Reporting and Dashboarding	Grafana	Grafana is a popular reporting dashboarding tool for container environments. It has the capability to leverage data feeds from Prometheus and other sources, for visualizing information in a Kubernetes environment.
Monitoring	cAdvisor	cAdvisor is another container resource-monitoring tool that works at the worker node level instead of Pod level. It has the capability to discover all the containers running on worker nodes and provide metrics about CPU, memory, filesystems, etc. This solution does not provide long-term storage of metric data or analytics services on top, for driving insights for operations teams.
Monitoring	Heapster	Heapster aggregates monitoring data across multiple nodes, using kubelet and cAdvisor at the back end. Unlike cAdvisor, Heapster works at the Pod level, instead of the worker node level.

(continued)

Table 2-4. (*continued*)

Functionality	Services	Description
Monitoring and Security	Sysdig Monitor and Secure	Sysdig Monitor helps in monitoring container applications, by providing end-to-end visibility from application service to Pod to container to node-level availability, performance, and faults, across multiple container technologies and clouds. Additionally, Sysdig Secure container image and cluster level security vulnerability views.
Monitoring	Dynatrace	With its Ruxit acquisition, Dynatrace now has a new suite of tools available for container monitoring and alerting. Leveraging an agent-based approach, it can discover and fetch data related to containerized application services, Pods, containers, worker nodes, etc.
Monitoring	AppDynamics	This application and business performance software collects data from agents installed on hosts and collects data using Docker APIs.
Log Management	Fluentd	This is an open source collector for unified logging layers.
Monitoring	Collectd	This is a small daemon that periodically collects system information and provides mechanisms to store and monitor container metrics.
Monitoring	Cloud native	Leading cloud providers, such as AWS (Cloudwatch), Azure (Azure Monitor), and Google Cloud (Stackdriver or Google Operations) have their own native mechanisms to monitor container ecosystems on AWS EKS, Azure AKS, and Google GKE.

(*continued*)

Table 2-4. (*continued*)

Functionality	Services	Description
Security	Aqua Security	The Aqua Container Security Platform provides granular, context-aware security, while automating the entire image-to-production process, allowing enterprises to focus on deploying and running applications.
Security	Sysdig Security	Sysdig is a unified platform that provides such services as monitoring, troubleshooting, and alerting, offering in-depth visibility into dynamic distributed environments. It captures, co-relates, and visualizes full-stack data and provides a dashboard for reporting.
Security	Twistlock	The Twistlock Cloud Native Cybersecurity Platform provides full life cycle security for containerized environments. Twistlock helps to scale securely and deploy containers with confidence.
Security and Networking	Istio	Istio is an open source service mesh that layers transparently onto existing distributed applications. It includes APIs that allow it to integrate into any logging platform or telemetry or policy system. It run a distributed microservice architecture successfully and efficiently and provides a uniform way to secure, connect, and monitor microservices.

(*continued*)

Table 2-4. (*continued*)

Functionality	Services	Description
Registry	Harbor	Harbor is an open source container image registry that secures images with role-based access control, scans images for vulnerabilities, and signs images as trusted. Harbor delivers compliance, performance, and interoperability that helps consistently and securely manage images across cloud-native compute platforms such as Kubernetes and Docker.
CI/CD	Spinnaker	Spinnaker is an open source, multi-cloud, continuous delivery platform that helps in releasing software changes quickly and securely with no issues. It combines a powerful and flexible pipeline management system, with integrations with the major cloud providers.
CI/CD	Jenkins	Jenkins is a popular open source automation server that provides a number of plug-ins to support building, deploying, and automating project build and release.
Infra As Code	Ansible	Ansible is a popular Infra as Code automation tool which is used by Infrastructure and Application teams for automating tasks such as provisioning,application deployment,Security management etc. This enables Application and IT teams with productivity, quality & security improvement for delivering services to Business.

(*continued*)

Table 2-4. (*continued*)

Functionality	Services	Description
Infra As Code	Terraform	Terraform is a tool for building, changing, and versioning infrastructure safely and efficiently. Terraform can manage existing and popular service providers as well as custom in-house solutions. Terraform is cloud-agnostic. Configuration files describe to Terraform the components required to run a single application or your entire data center. Terraform generates an execution plan describing what it will do to reach the desired state and then executes it to build the described infrastructure. As the configuration changes, Terraform is able to determine what changed and create incremental execution plans that can be applied. The infrastructure Terraform can manage includes low-level components, such as compute instances, storage, and networking, as well as high-level components, such as DNS entries, SaaS features, etc.
Infra As Code	Google Deployment Manager	Deployment Manager is a Google Cloud infrastructure-deployment service that automates the creation and management of Google Cloud resources.
Networking	coreDNS	CoreDNS is an elastic and flaccid DNS server that can work as the Kubernetes cluster DNS. The CoreDNS project is hosted by the CNCF.

(continued)

Table 2-4. (*continued*)

Functionality	Services	Description
API Management	Envoy	Envoy works as an API gateway in Kubernetes with Ambassador. Ambassador operates as a specialized control plane to expose Envoy's functionality as Kubernetes annotations.
Infra As Code	Helm	Kubernetes applications can be managed using Helm. For this, Helm uses Charts, which defines the application deployment details. It helps in installing and upgrading complex applications. Charts can be easily managed in terms of versioning, sharing creation, and publishing.
Security	Falco	This is an open source cloud-native runtime security tool that is commonly used as a Kubernetes threat-detection engine. Falco catches unexpected application behavior and alerts on threats at runtime.
Monitoring, Analytic and Reporting	Splunk	Splunk products help search, analyze, and visualize the data gathered from different components of IT infrastructure or businesses. It can gather data from applications, websites, etc., and once the data source is configured, it indexes the data stream. The indexed data stream is parsed into a series of individual events that can be further searched and visualized.

Summary

In this chapter, you have seen how to set up an environment in GCP. We also covered the complexity involved in monitoring and managing the container ecosystem. We covered important open source and enterprise tools used for monitoring and managing the container based applications. In the next chapter, we begin with practical exercises to set up GKE and continue by deploying our first containerized application.

CHAPTER 3

Container Image Management Using Google Container Registry

In this chapter, readers will be introduced to Google Container Registry (GCR) service and they will learn the following:

- Introduction to Google Container Registry
- Setting Up Google Container Registry
- Pushing a Docker Image into the GCP Container Registry
- Managing and Securing the GCP Container Registry

Introduction to Google Container Registry

Container Registry is a single place to manage Docker images, perform vulnerability analysis, and control which users can access what images. GCR provides extensive integration features for CI/CD and security thereby making it easy for developers and administrators to manage

© Navin Sabharwal, Piyush Pandey 2020
N. Sabharwal and P. Pandey, *Pro Google Kubernetes Engine*,
https://doi.org/10.1007/978-1-4842-6243-6_3

images in a secure policy-driven fashion. It provides features to automatically build and push images to private registry whenever you commit code to Cloud Source Repositories, GitHub, or Bitbucket.

Google Container Registry provides features to detect vulnerabilities at the early stages of software deployment cycle. It can assess whether container images are safe for deployment. Google Container Registry uses native integration with binary authorization to define policies and prevent deployment of images conflicting with the set policies. It can trigger automatic lockdown of container images thereby prohibiting risky images from being deployed to Google Kubernetes Engine. With regional private repositories, you can store images close to your compute instances in Europe, Asia, or the United States and access Google's global network, for fast deployment. Following are key features of GCR:

- **Vulnerability scanning:** This feature enables scanning of Docker image containers, to identify vulnerabilities. It identifies package vulnerabilities for Ubuntu, Debian, and Alpine.

- **Tagging:** Tagging of the image ensures better manageability. The adding and removing of tags can be performed easily from the GCP console.

- **Building trigger on code or tag changes:** GCR allows automatic build trigger of container images on code or tag changes to a code repository. This feature also provides consolidated views of build details, e.g., source steps, logs, and steps.

Setting Up Google Container Registry

Setting up GCR is pretty simple and straightforward. The following steps explain how to quickly setup GCR service.

In Chapter 2, you learned how to create Google Compute Engine. We will use the same Compute Engine instance to demonstrate image pull from and push to GCP Container Registry. For this demonstration, and execution of the Pull and Push commands, we must first install Docker version 18.03 on the Compute Engine instance. Follow these steps to install Docker.

Step 1: Log in to the VM created earlier.

Step 2: Run the following command to update the existing list of packages.

Command: sudo apt update (Figure 3-1)

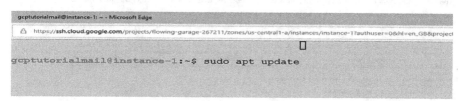

Figure 3-1. *Updating list package command*

Output: The result of the preceding command will be as follows (Figure 3-2).

```
gcptutorialmail@instance-1: ~ - Microsoft Edge
   https://ssh.cloud.google.com/projects/flowing-garage-267211/zones/us-central1-a/instances/instance-1?authuser=0&hl=en_GB&projectNumber=848815051368

Hit:1 http://security.debian.org/debian-security stretch/updates InRelease
Ign:2 http://deb.debian.org/debian stretch InRelease
Hit:3 http://packages.cloud.google.com/apt cloud-sdk-stretch InRelease
Get:4 http://deb.debian.org/debian stretch-updates InRelease [91.0 kB]
Hit:5 http://packages.cloud.google.com/apt google-compute-engine-stretch-stable InRelease
Get:6 http://deb.debian.org/debian stretch-backports InRelease [91.8 kB]
Hit:7 http://packages.cloud.google.com/apt google-cloud-packages-archive-keyring-stretch InRelease
Hit:8 http://deb.debian.org/debian stretch Release
Fetched 183 kB in 0s (279 kB/s)

Reading package lists... Done
```

Figure 3-2. *Updating list package output*

Step 3: Install a few prerequisite packages that allow apt to use packages over HTTPS.

Command: `sudo apt install apt-transport-https ca-certificates curl gnupg2 software-properties-common` (Figure 3-3)

```
gcptutorialmail@instance-1:~$ sudo apt install apt-transport-https ca-certificates curl gnupg2 software-properties-common
```

Figure 3-3. *Package install command*

Output: Result of preceding command will be as follows (Figures 3-4 and 3-5).

Figure 3-4. *Package install output*

Enter Y.

```
Setting up libdbus-python-dumind47.43.00228-0+deb9u1) ...

Setting up apgstransport-httpamd544(9)10.4-1) ...
Setcap worked! gst-ptp-helper is not suid!
Setting up libdbus-glib-1-2:amd64 (0.108-2) ...
Setting up libpolkit-agent-1-0:amd64 (0.105-18+deb9u1) ...
Setting up python3-gi (3.22.0-2) ...
Setting up libpolkit-backend-1-0:amd64 (0.105-18+deb9u1) ...
Setting up python3-software-properties (0.96.20.2-1) ...

Setting up dbus (1.10.28-0+deb9u1) ...
Setting up libpam3systemd1amd641B32-25+deb9u12) ...

Removing /pup/system/system/polkitdebdevice..
polkit.service is a disabled or a static unit not running, not starting it.
Setting up packagekit (1.1.5-2+deb9u1) ...
Setting up software-properties-common (0.96.20.2-1) ...

Setting up packagekitotoedml(base5{2+deb9u1) ...
Processing triggers for libc-bin (2.24-11+deb9u4) ...
Processing triggers for systemd (232-25+deb9u12) ...
Processing triggers for dbus (1.10.28-0+deb9u1) ...

gcptutorialmail@instance-1:~$ |
```

Figure 3-5. *Package install output*

Step 4: Add the GPG key for the official Docker repository to your system.

Command: `curl -fsSL https://download.docker.com/linux/debian/gpg |` `sudo apt-key add -` (Figure 3-6)

```
gcptutorialmail@instance-1: ~ - Microsoft Edge
🔒 https://ssh.cloud.google.com/projects/flowing-garage-267211/zones/us-central1-a/instances/instance-1?authuser=0&hl=en_GB&projectNumber=848815051368
gcptutorialmail@instance-1:~$ curl -fsSL https://download.docker.com/linux/debian/gpg | sudo apt-key add -
```

Figure 3-6. *Adding GPG key command*

Output: The result of the preceding command will be as follows (Figure 3-7).

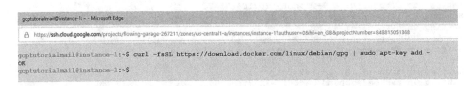

Figure 3-7. *Adding GPG key output*

Step 5: Add the Docker repository to the APT sources.

Command: `sudo add-apt-repository "deb [arch=amd64] https://download.docker.com/ linux/debian $(lsb_release -cs) stable"` (Figure 3-8)

```
gcptutorialmail@instance-1:~$ sudo add-apt-repository "deb [arch=amd64] https://download.docker.com/linux/debian
$(lsb_release -cs) stable"
```

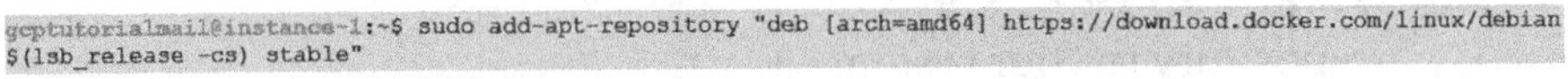

Figure 3-8. *Adding Docker repository to ATP command and output*

Step 6: Update the package database with the Docker packages from the newly added repo.

Command: `sudo apt update` (Figure 3-9)

```
gcptutorialmail@instance-1:~$ sudo apt update
```

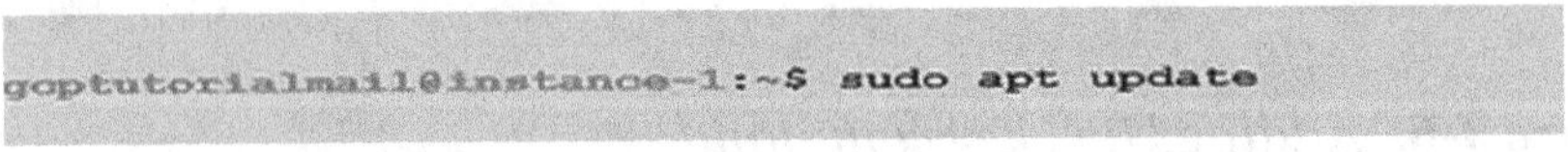

Figure 3-9. *Updating package command*

Output: The result of the preceding command will be as follows (Figure 3-10).

```
🔒 https://ssh.cloud.google.com/projects/flowing-garage-267211/zones/us-central1-a/instances/instance-1?authuser=0&hl=en_GB&projectNumber=848815051368

goptutorialmail@instance-1:~$ sudo apt update
Hit:1 http://security.debian.org stretch/updates InRelease
Ign:2 http://deb.debian.org/debian stretch InRelease
Hit:3 http://packages.cloud.google.com/apt cloud-sdk-stretch InRelease
Hit:4 http://deb.debian.org/debian stretch-updates InRelease
Hit:5 http://deb.debian.org/debian stretch-backports InRelease
Hit:6 http://packages.cloud.google.com/apt google-compute-engine-stretch-stable InRelease
Hit:7 http://deb.debian.org/debian stretch Release
Hit:8 http://packages.cloud.google.com/apt google-cloud-packages-archive-keyring-stretch InRelease
Get:9 https://download.docker.com/linux/debian stretch InRelease [44.8 kB]
Get:11 https://download.docker.com/linux/debian stretch/stable amd64 Packages [11.9 kB]
Fetched 56.7 kB in 0s (69.1 kB/s)
Reading package lists... Done

Building dependency tree... Done
5 packages can be upgraded. Run 'apt list --upgradable' to see them.
goptutorialmail@instance-1:~$
```

Figure 3-10. *Updating package output*

Step 7: Install Docker repo by executing the following command.

Command: `apt-cache policy docker-ce`

Output: The result will be as follows (Figure 3-11).

```
goptutorialmail@instance-1:~$ apt-cache policy docker-ce
docker-ce:
  Installed: (none)
  Candidate: 5:19.03.5~3-0~debian-stretch
  Version table:
     5:19.03.5~3-0~debian-stretch 500
        500 https://download.docker.com/linux/debian stretch/stable amd64 Packages
```

Figure 3-11. *Installing Docker policy*

Step 8: Finally, install Docker by executing the following command.

Command: `sudo apt install docker-ce`
(Figure 3-12)

```
goptutorialmail@instance-1:~$ sudo apt install docker-ce
```

Figure 3-12. *Installing Docker command*

Output: The result will be as shown in Figure 3-13.

```
gcptutorialmail@instance-1:~$ sudo apt install docker-ce

Reading package lists... Done
Building dependency tree
Reading state information... Done
The following additional packages will be installed:
  aufs-dkms aufs-tools binutils cgroupfs-mount containerd.io cpp cpp-6 dkms docker-ce-cli fakeroot gcc gcc-6 git git-man less libasan3
  libatomic1 libc-dev-bin libc6-dev libcc1-0 libcilkrts5 liberror-perl libfakeroot libgcc-6-dev libgomp1 libisl15 libitm1 liblsan0 libltdl7
  libmpc3 libmpfr4 libmpx2 libperl5.24 libquadmath0 libtsan0 libubsan0 linux-compiler-gcc-6-x86 linux-headers-4.9.0-12-amd64
  linux-headers-4.9.0-12-common linux-headers-amd64 linux-kbuild-4.9 linux-libc-dev make manpages manpages-dev patch perl perl-base
  perl-modules-5.24 pigz rename rsync
Suggested packages:
  aufs-dev binutils-doc cpp-doc gcc-6-locales python3-apport menu gcc-multilib autoconf automake libtool flex bison gdb gcc-doc
  gcc-6-multilib gcc-6-doc libgcc1-dbg libgomp1-dbg libitm1-dbg libatomic1-dbg libasan3-dbg liblsan0-dbg libtsan0-dbg libubsan0-dbg
  libcilkrts5-dbg libmpx2-dbg libquadmath0-dbg git-daemon-run | git-daemon-sysvinit git-doc git-el git-email git-gui gitk gitweb git-arch
  git-cvs git-mediawiki git-svn glibc-doc make-doc ed diffutils-doc perl-doc libterm-readline-gnu-perl | libterm-readline-perl-perl
The following NEW packages will be installed:
  aufs-dkms aufs-tools binutils cgroupfs-mount containerd.io cpp cpp-6 dkms docker-ce docker-ce-cli fakeroot gcc gcc-6 git git-man less
  libasan3 libatomic1 libc-dev-bin libc6-dev libcc1-0 libcilkrts5 liberror-perl libfakeroot libgcc-6-dev libgomp1 libisl15 libitm1 liblsan0
  libltdl7 libmpc3 libmpfr4 libmpx2 libperl5.24 libquadmath0 libtsan0 libubsan0 linux-compiler-gcc-6-x86 linux-headers-4.9.0-12-amd64
  linux-headers-4.9.0-12-common linux-headers-amd64 linux-kbuild-4.9 linux-libc-dev make manpages manpages-dev patch perl perl-modules-5.24
  pigz rename rsync
The following packages will be upgraded:
  perl-base
1 upgraded, 52 newly installed, 0 to remove and 4 not upgraded.
Need to get 138 MB/140 MB of archives.
After this operation, 631 MB of additional disk space will be used.
Do you want to continue? [Y/n]
```

Figure 3-13. *Installing Docker output*

Enter Y (Figure 3-14).

```
Setting up git (1:2.11.0-3+deb9u5) ...
Setting up gcc (4:6.3.0-4) ...
Setting up linux-compiler-gcc-6-x86 (4.9.210-1) ...
Setting up linux-headers-4.9.0-12-amd64 (4.9.210-1) ...
Setting up dkms (2.3-2) ...
Setting up linux-headers-amd64 (4.9+80+deb9u10) ...
Setting up aufs-dkms (4.9+20161219-1) ...
Loading new aufs-4.9+20161219 DKMS files...
Building for 4.9.0-11-amd64
Module build for kernel 4.9.0-11-amd64 was skipped since the
kernel headers for this kernel does not seem to be installed.
Processing triggers for libc-bin (2.24-11+deb9u4) ...
Processing triggers for systemd (232-25+deb9u12) ...
gcptutorialmail@instance-1:~$
```

Figure 3-14. *Installing Docker output—continued*

Step 9: Verify that Docker has been installed successfully, by executing the following query.

Command/Output: `sudo systemctl status docker` (Figure 3-15)

```
gcptutorialmail@instance-1:~$ sudo systemctl status docker

● docker.service - (Docker Application Container Engine enabled; vendor preset: enabled)
   Active: active (running) since Mon 2020-02-10 09:50:26 UTC; 1min 41s ago
     Docs: https://docs.docker.com
 Main PID: 13947 (dockerd)
   CGroup: /system.slice/docker.service
           └─13947 /usr/bin/dockerd -H fd:// --containerd=/run/containerd/containerd.sock
```

Figure 3-15. *Verifying install Docker command/output*

> To execute the Docker command without sudo, do
> the following:
>
> **Step 1**: Execute the following query.
>
> **Command:** sudo usermod -aG docker ${USER}
> (Figure 3-16)

```
gcptutorialmail@instance-1:~$ sudo usermod -aG docker ${USER}
```

Figure 3-16. *sudo privilege command*

> **Step 2**: Log out and log in again, to see the applied
> effect. Confirm that your user is now added to the
> Docker group, by typing the following:
>
> **Command/Output:** id -nG (Figure 3-17)

```
gcptutorialmail@instance-1:~$ id -nG
gcptutorialmail adm dip video plugdev docker google-sudoers
```

Figure 3-17. *Verifying Docker group privilege*

Pushing a Docker Image into the GCP Container Registry

Step 1: Log in with your account ID created earlier. In our case, we are using gcptutorialmail@gmail. com to push the image into the GCP registry. Reinitialize using the following command, and enter 1 when indicated, to pick the configuration.

Command/Output: gcloud init (Figure 3-18)

```
gcptutorialmail@instance-1:~$ gcloud init
Welcome! This command will take you through the configuration of gcloud.
Settings from your current configuration [default] are:
core:
  account: 848815051368-compute@developer.gserviceaccount.com
  disable_usage_reporting: 'False'
  project: flowing-garage-267211

Pick configuration to use:
 [1] Re-initialize this configuration [default] with new settings
 [2] Create a new configuration
Please enter your numeric choice:  1
```

Figure 3-18. *Initializing Google account*

Step 2: Select option 2 to configure the account to perform the image upload operation (Figure 3-19).

```
Your current configuration has been set to: [default]
You can skip diagnostics next time by using the following flag:
  gcloud init --skip-diagnostics

Network diagnostic detects and fixes local network connection issues.
Checking network connection...done.

Reachability diagnostic passed.(1/1 checks passed).

Choose the account you would like to use to perform operations for
this configuration:
 [1] 848815051368-compute@developer.gserviceaccount.com
 [2] Log in with a new account
Please enter your numeric choice:  2
```

Figure 3-19. *Initializing Google account*

Step 3: After entering "2," you will be asked to continue, enter "Y." Open the link displayed onscreen onto a browser, copy the verification code, and paste it onto the screen in "Enter Verification Code:" and you will be successfully logged in (Figures 3-20 and 3-21).

```
You are running on a Google Compute Engine virtual machine.
It is recommended that you use service accounts for authentication.

You can run:

  $ gcloud config set account `ACCOUNT`

to switch accounts if necessary.

Your credentials may be visible to others with access to this
virtual machine. Are you sure you want to authenticate with
your personal account?

Do you want to continue (Y/n)?  y

Go to the following link in your browser:

    https://accounts.google.com/o/oauth2/auth?code_challenge=9Qlpr6wCi5gsKpctiTX63m9
method=S256&access_type=offline&redirect_uri=urn%3Aietf%3Awg%3Aoauth%3A2.0%3Aoob&res
nt.com&scope=https%3A%2F%2Fwww.googleapis.com%2Fauth%2Fuserinfo.email+https%3A%2F%2F
ww.googleapis.com%2Fauth%2Fappengine.admin+https%3A%2F%2Fwww.googleapis.com%2Fauth%2
s.reauth


Enter verification code: 4/wQEgKpUV3jMqGP0Ln6dvXXaa4yLjiF_lLcV-LsnhZ8gPSs2FIbdfBzA
You are logged in as: [gcptutorialmail@gmail.com].
```

Figure 3-20. *Initializing Google account—continued*

Google

Sign in

Please copy this code, switch to your application and paste it there:

4/wQEgKpUV3jMqGP0Ln6dvXXaa4yLjiF_lLcV-
LsnhZ8gPSs2FIbdfBzA

Figure 3-21. *Sign-in code*

Step 4: After step 3, the system will ask you to select
the Compute Engine zone from the list displayed.
Enter the respective number. In our case, the
number will be 8 for us-central1 (Figure 3-22).

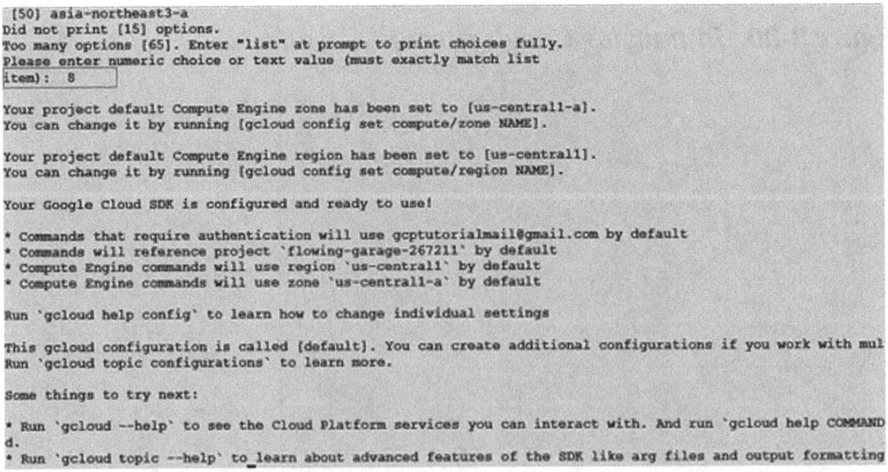

```
[50] asia-northeast3-a
Did not print [15] options.
Too many options [65]. Enter "list" at prompt to print choices fully.
Please enter numeric choice or text value (must exactly match list
item):  8

Your project default Compute Engine zone has been set to [us-central1-a].
You can change it by running [gcloud config set compute/zone NAME].

Your project default Compute Engine region has been set to [us-central1].
You can change it by running [gcloud config set compute/region NAME].

Your Google Cloud SDK is configured and ready to use!

* Commands that require authentication will use gcptutorialmail@gmail.com by default
* Commands will reference project `flowing-garage-267211` by default
* Compute Engine commands will use region `us-central1` by default
* Compute Engine commands will use zone `us-central1-a` by default

Run `gcloud help config` to learn how to change individual settings

This gcloud configuration is called [default]. You can create additional configurations if you work with mul
Run `gcloud topic configurations` to learn more.

Some things to try next:

* Run `gcloud --help` to see the Cloud Platform services you can interact with. And run `gcloud help COMMAND
d.
* Run `gcloud topic --help` to learn about advanced features of the SDK like arg files and output formatting
```

Figure 3-22. *Compute Engine zone*

Now the CLI setup for pushing the image into GCP
Container Registry is ready to use.

Step 5: After step 4, to test pushing the image into
the GCP Container Registry, we will first download
a sample `nginx` image from the Docker Hub. Check
the download using the following command.

Command: 1) `docker pull nginx` This will pull the
image `nginx` from the public Docker Hub; 2) `docker`
`images` This will list the images existing on the local
machine.

Output: The result of the preceding command will
be as follows (Figure 3-23).

```
goptutorialmail@instance-1:~$ docker pull nginx
Using default tag: latest
latest: Pulling from library/nginx
bc51dd8edc1b: Pull complete
66ba67045f57: Pull complete
bf317aa10aa5: Pull complete
Digest: sha256:ad5552c786f128e389a0263104ae39f3d3c7895579d45ae716f528185b36bc6f
Status: Downloaded newer image for nginx:latest
docker.io/library/nginx:latest
goptutorialmail@instance-1:~$ docker images
REPOSITORY          TAG                 IMAGE ID            CREATED             SIZE
nginx               latest      _       2073e0bcb60e        9 days ago          127MB
```

Figure 3-23. *Compute Engine zone—continued*

Step 6: After step 5, we must tag the image, to
upload it to the Container Registry. Once tagged,
it can be listed using the second of the following
commands.

Command: 1) `docker tag nginx gcr.io/flowing-`
`garage-267211/nginx:v1` This will tag the image
that is required to be the version and image before it
can be pushed into the GCP container.

2) docker images This will list all the images existing in the local machine.

Output: The result of the preceding command will be as follows (Figure 3-24).

```
gcptutorialmail@instance-1:~$ docker images
REPOSITORY                              TAG       IMAGE ID        CREATED
nginx                                   latest    2073e0bcb60e    10 days ago
gcr.io/flowing-garage-267211/nginx      v1        2073e0bcb60e    10 days ago
```

Figure 3-24. Image list

Step 7: After step 6, we will now push the image into the Container Registry, using the following command to tag the image that is required to be versioned, so that it can be pushed into the GCP container.

Command: docker push gcr.io/flowing-garage-267211/nginx:v1

Output: The result of the preceding command will be as follows (Figure 3-25).

```
gcptutorialmail@instance-1:~$ docker push gcr.io/flowing-garage-267211/nginx:v1
The push refers to repository [gcr.io/flowing-garage-267211/nginx]
22439467ad99: Layer already exists
b4a29beac87c: Layer already exists
488dfecc21b1: Layer already exists
v1: digest: sha256:62f787b9465faddb79f96c84ac0877aaf28fb325bfc3601b9c0934d4c107ba94 size: 948
```

Figure 3-25. Docker push image

The image can be viewed in the Container Registry via the GCP console. Navigate to Tools ➤ Container Registry ➤ Images, as shown in Figure 3-26.

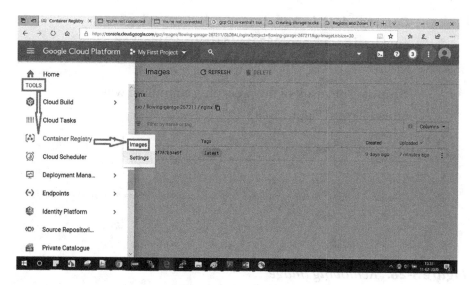

Figure 3-26. *Image navigation*

On clicking the Image link, the following page will
display the list of Images (Figure 3-27).

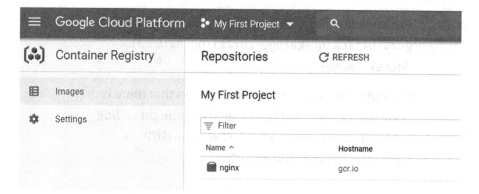

Figure 3-27. *Pushed image view*

Step 8: After step 7, we will pull the image from the
GCP Container Registry.

Before that, we will delete the image available on the
local VM.

Command: 1) `docker images` 2)`docker rmi gcr. io/flowing-garage-267211/nginx:v1` 3)`docker images`

Output: The result of the preceding command will be as follows (Figure 3-28).

```
gcptutorialmail@instance-1:~$ docker images
REPOSITORY                                    TAG           IMAGE ID          CREATED         SIZE
nginx                                         latest        2073e0bcb60e      10 days ago     127MB
gcr.io/flowing-garage-267211/nginx            v1            2073e0bcb60e      10 days ago     127MB
gcptutorialmail@instance-1:~$ docker rmi gcr.io/flowing-garage-267211/nginx:v1
Untagged: gcr.io/flowing-garage-267211/nginx:v1
Untagged: gcr.io/flowing-garage-267211/nginx@sha256:62f787b94e5faddb79f96c84ac0877aaf28fb325bfc3601b9c09:
a94
gcptutorialmail@instance-1:~$ docker images
REPOSITORY            TAG           IMAGE ID          CREATED         SIZE
nginx                 latest        2073e0bcb60e      10 days ago     127MB
gcptutorialmail@instance-1:~$ ▮
```

Figure 3-28. *Removing image*

Step 9: After step 8, we will pull the image from the GCP Container Registry, with the following commands.

Commands: 1) `docker images` 2) `docker pull gcr.io/flowing-garage-267211/nginx:v1` 3) `docker images`

Output: The following snapshot shows that there is no image on the local machine. Using the preceding commands, we pull the image from the GCP Container Registry (Figure 3-29).

```
gcptutorialmail@instance-1:~$ docker images
REPOSITORY            TAG                IMAGE ID          CREATED           SIZE
nginx                 latest             2073e0bcb60e      10 days ago       127MB
gcptutorialmail@instance-1:~$ docker pull gcr.io/flowing-garage-267211/nginx:v1
v1: Pulling from flowing-garage-267211/nginx
Digest: sha256:62f787b94e5faddb79f96c84ac0877aaf28fb325bfc3601b9c0934d4c107ba94
Status: Downloaded newer image for gcr.io/flowing-garage-267211/nginx:v1
gcr.io/flowing-garage-267211/nginx:v1
gcptutorialmail@instance-1:~$ docker images
REPOSITORY                            TAG        IMAGE ID          CREATED          SIZE
nginx                                 latest     2073e0bcb60e      10 days ago      127MB
gcr.io/flowing-garage-267211/nginx    v1         2073e0bcb60e      10 days ago      127MB
gcptutorialmail@instance-1:~$ █
```

Figure 3-29. *Pulling image*

Managing and Securing the GCP Container Registry

Copying Images to a New Registry

Let's imagine a scenario where user from another project needs to access the image in the project we have used in hands on exercise. To demonstrate this use case, we will first create another project using following steps.

> **Step 1:** Click the project name, as indicated in the following, to open the Select Project window. Click the New Project link. Enter the project name ("Tutorial Project," in this case) and click the Create button. A pop-up notification will display the message "Create Project: Tutorial Project" (Figure 3-30).

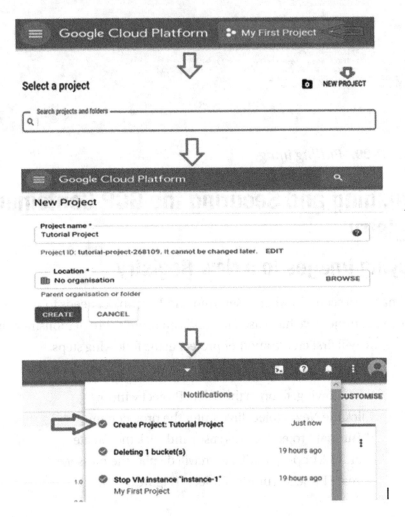

Figure 3-30. *Create new project*

> **Step 2:** Click the Project Name drop-down again, and the newly created project will be visible in the Select a project window (Figure 3-31).

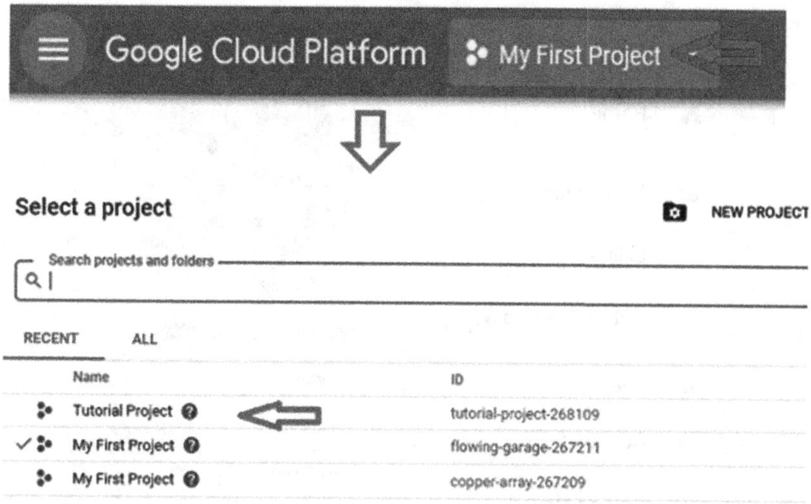

Figure 3-31. *New project list view*

> **Step 3:** An image can be copied from one registry to another, by using the command line, provided you have access to both registries. Now try to copy the nginx:v1 image present in the Container Registry of the project "My first Project" into the Container Registry of newly created project "Tutorial Project."
>
> To perform the copy operation, you must *enable* API Registry for the new project (Tutorial Project). To do this, go to the API dashboard screen, as shown in Figures 3-32, 3-33, and 3-34.

Figure 3-32. *API dashboard navigation*

Figure 3-33. *API dashboard navigation—continued*

Figure 3-34. *API dashboard navigation—continued*

Click the Enable button.

Now API services are enabled for the Tutorial
Project (Figure 3-35).

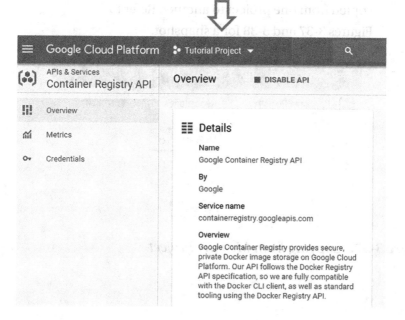

Figure 3-35. *API dashboard navigation—continued*

Step 4: After step 3, run the following command, to copy the image to the Tutorial Project Container Registry.

Command: `gcloud container images add-tag \`
`gcr.io/flowing-garage-267211/nginx:v1 \gcr.`
`io/tutorial-project-268109/nginx:v1`

Output: The result will be shown as follows (Figure 3-36).

```
gcptutorialmail@instance-1:~$ gcloud container images add-tag \gcr.io/flowing-garage-267211/nginx:v1 \gcr.io/tut
This will tag gcr.io/flowing-garage-267211/nginx:v1 with:
gcr.io/tutorial-project-268109/nginx:v1

Do you want to continue (Y/n)?  y

Created [gcr.io/tutorial-project-268109/nginx:v1].
Updated [gcr.io/flowing-garage-267211/nginx:v1].  []
```

Figure 3-36. *Copying image to repository output*

After the command is executed, the image gets copied from one project to another. Refer to Figures 3-37 and 3-38 for a snapshot.

Figure 3-37. *Copying from My First Project*

Figure 3-38. *Pasting to Tutorial Project*

Deleting Images from the Container Registry

To demonstrate image deletion from the GCP Container Registry, run the following command.

> **Command:** `gcloud container images delete`
> `gcr.io/tutorial-project-268109/nginx:v1`
>
> **Output:** The result will be as shown in Figure 3-39.

Figure 3-39. *Image deleted from registry*

> After deletion, you can check that the GCP Container Registry of the Tutorial Project will show no image (Figure 3-40).

Figure 3-40. *Blank image registry view*

Vulnerability Scanning an Image

Image vulnerability could have a huge impact on an existing system. It could lead to complete system failure or to a system being maliciously exploited. The Container Analysis service of GCP provides vulnerability scanning and storage of metadata of images. Container Analysis runs a scan on the image store in the Container Registry and monitors the scanned vulnerability report, to keep it updated. Container Analysis is a two-stage process.

1. Whenever a new image is pushed into the Container Registry, the Container Analysis service scans the image for vulnerabilities and stores the metadata, based on the container manifest. Each time the image is re-uploaded into the Container Registry, the same metadata is updated, thus keeping track of the image scan vulnerability report. This process is known as *incremental scanning.*

2. Next, it performs continuous monitoring of the metadata of the scanned images, to detect new vulnerabilities. It continuously checks and updates the vulnerability information, creates new

occurrences, and also deletes the occurrences
that are no longer valid. This process is called
continuous analysis.

The Vulnerability Result is the list of vulnerability occurrences for the image. It also contains the Severity level of the scan, which is classified as Critical, High, Medium, Low, and Minimal.

Now let's set up vulnerability scanning for a sample application image that is uploaded in the Container Registry.

Setting Up Vulnerability Scanning

Step 1: To enable the vulnerability scanning of an image,
you must enable the Container Scanning API for the
project. Follow these steps (Figures 3-41 and 3-42).

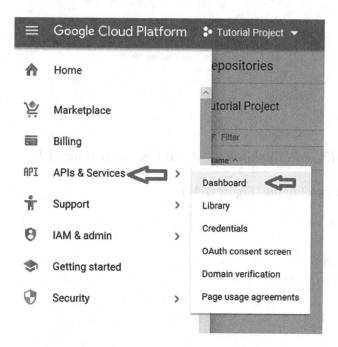

Figure 3-41. *API dashboard navigation*

Figure 3-42. *API dashboard navigation—APIs & Services*

Search for the Container Scanning API (Figure 3-43).

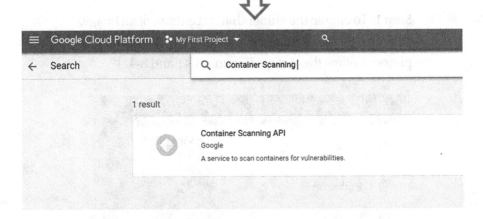

Figure 3-43. *API dashboard—Container Scanning API*

Click Enable (Figure 3-44).

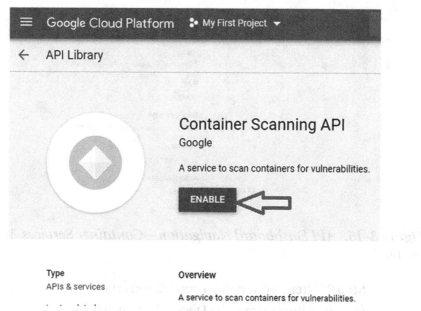

Figure 3-44. *API dashboard navigation—Container Scanning API—continued*

Now the Container Scanning API services are enabled for My First Project (Figure 3-45).

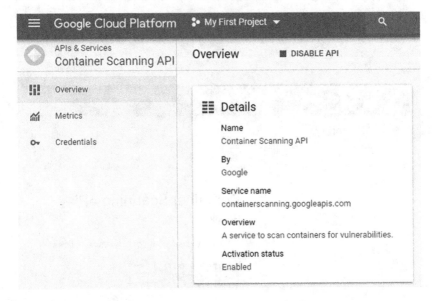

Figure 3-45.   *API Dashboard Navigation—Container Services API enabled*

Step 2: After step 1, pull an application image (e.g., wordpress) from the Docker Hub on which vulnerability scanning will be performed (Figure 3-46).

```
gcptutorialmail@instance-1:~$ docker pull wordpress
Using default tag: latest
latest: Pulling from library/wordpress
bc51dd8edc1b: Pull complete
a3224e2c3a89: Pull complete
be7a066df88f: Pull complete
bfdf741d72a9: Pull complete
a9e612a5f04c: Pull complete
c026d8d0e8cb: Pull complete
d94096c4941c: Pull complete
5a16031a7587: Pull complete
0cf1daf9efc0: Pull complete
b202acb13a6c: Pull complete
907001e30880: Pull complete
2e4b329c80b2: Pull complete
cd1ec92e7164: Pull complete
8cba435f5ca6: Pull complete
42d9ff86311d: Pull complete
4907cef4e3ab: Pull complete
d9efb2f24248: Pull complete
8301b0ae2103: Pull complete
a9e295ae3552: Pull complete
cd1a22f91cdc: Pull complete
f81677d558c1: Pull complete

Digest: sha256:ad6d2045079a9e8f0efw0adpdad320324868b8ff308e99ff1329ada8ce70abc
docker.io/library/wordpress:latest
gcptutorialmail@instance-1:~$
```

Figure 3-46. Pulling Docker image

> **Step 3:** Check for the image download on the local
> machine, tagging of the image, and pushing it into
> the Container Registry, which will auto-trigger the
> container image scanning, as follows:
>
> **Command:** 1) `docker images` 2) `docker tag
> wordpress gcr.io/flowing-garage-267211/
> wordpress:v1` 3) `docker push gcr.io/flowing-
> garage-267211/wordpress:v1`
>
> **Output:**
>
> a. Get the image list (Figure 3-47).

```
gcptutorialmail@instance-1:~$ docker images
REPOSITORY          TAG             IMAGE ID           CREATED           SIZE
wordpress           latest          0947f14b932b       11 days ago       540MB
gcptutorialmail@instance-1:~$
```

Figure 3-47. Image list

    b. Tag image (Figure 3-48).

```
gcptutorialmail@instance-1:~$ docker tag wordpress  gcr.io/flowing-garage-267211/wordpress:v1
gcptutorialmail@instance-1:~$ docker images
REPOSITORY                                TAG       IMAGE ID        CREATED        SIZE
wordpress                                 latest    0947f14b932b    11 days ago    540MB
gcr.io/flowing-garage-267211/wordpress    v1        0947f14b932b    11 days ago    540MB
```

Figure 3-48. *Image tag*

    c. Push the image in the repository (Figure 3-49).

```
gcptutorialmail@instance-1:~$ docker push gcr.io/flowing-garage-267211/wordpress:v1
The push refers to repository [gcr.io/flowing-garage-267211/wordpress]
228411ef795d: Layer already exists
ee32c4a0dbe6: Layer already exists
6e3f66c54cd7: Layer already exists
f5c0acf1a3a3: Layer already exists
96f756cdccab: Layer already exists
41aa04a6e525: Layer already exists
1c0be052db33: Layer already exists
b336af658a73: Layer already exists
2a76acb78f54: Layer already exists
3b6c67348df7: Layer already exists
5663f9ad09f4: Layer already exists
e6c3f6abe57c: Layer already exists
08ae91f65a25: Layer already exists
62b0e0531006: Layer already exists
63bdd471b6c2: Layer already exists
68ec2faa35f5: Layer already exists
1d9b8efc8fda: Layer already exists
f6240605700a: Layer already exists
e501e93022bc: Layer already exists
00ad11a7d941: Layer already exists
488dfecc21b1: Layer already exists

v1: digest: sha256:8dd489fe4$d22503d212cdafdf10ba612517ce995ddfc25ef2b951e040c57d3e size: 4708
gcptutorialmail@instance-1:~$
```

Figure 3-49. *Image pushed into the repository*

    Step 4: After step 3, check the image on the GCP
console. You can see that the "Vulnerabilities"
column appears in the wordpress image row. Click
the "fixes / total" link, to view details of the image
vulnerability scanning (Figures 3-50, 3-51, and 3-52).

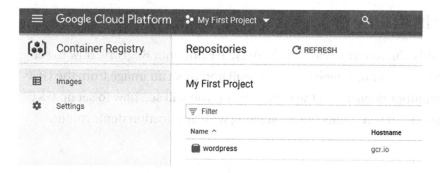

Figure 3-50. *Image check*

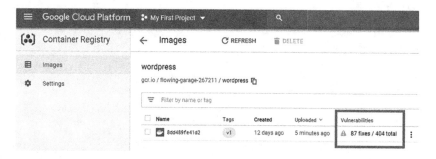

Figure 3-51. *Image vulnerabilities*

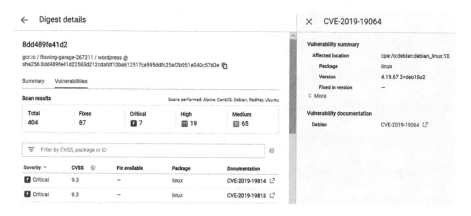

Figure 3-52. *Image vulnerabilities details*

Summary

In this chapter, you learned about GCP Container Registry, how to set up the Container Registry and to pull and push an image from the GCP Container Registry. In the next chapter, you will see how to set up GKE Networking elements before starting with application deployment.

CHAPTER 4

GKE Networking

This chapter explains how to set up a networking environment in GKE and it also covers various use cases for each of the sub components using various scenarios. The following topics are discussed:

- Introduction to Google Kubernetes Engine (GKE)
- GKE Network Terminologies
- Communication Among Containers
- Communication Between Pods on the Same Node
- Communication Between Pods on Different Nodes
- Communication of Pods with Services
- Communication of Pods with the Internet (Outside World)
- Load Balancing for Services
- Communication from an External Load Balancer to a Service
- Communication from an Internal Load Balancer to a Service
- Deployment of the GKE Cluster

© Navin Sabharwal, Piyush Pandey 2020
N. Sabharwal and P. Pandey, *Pro Google Kubernetes Engine*,
https://doi.org/10.1007/978-1-4842-6243-6_4

Introduction to Google Kubernetes Engine (GKE)

GKE is the platform as a service (PaaS) component of Google Cloud Platform (GCP) and is the managed version of Kubernetes hosted on GCP. It helps to manage the environments for deployment, including scaling and containerized applications.

GKE uses the Kubernetes open source cluster management system. The Kubernetes layer provides the mechanism with which to manage, such as performing administrative tasks, setting policies, and monitoring the health of deployed workloads. The GKE cluster is also used to deploy and manage applications.

Kubernetes on Google Cloud

GKE provides various advanced features for cluster management, including the following:

- A node pool feature to designate subsets of nodes within a cluster, for ease of management

- Automatic scaling of a cluster's node instance

- Automatic upgrades of a node cluster's software

- An auto-repair node to maintain its health and availability

- Logging and monitoring with GCP Stackdriver (Google Operations) for cluster visibility

The GKE cluster is required to have at least one master and worker component of Kubernetes. Following are the key components of the GKE cluster ecosystem:

- **Cluster master:** This component runs the Kubernetes control plane processes, including scheduler, API server, and other controllers. The cluster master life cycle is managed by GKE.

- **Cluster master and the Kubernetes API:** Any interaction with a cluster master is managed by Kubernetes API calls to perform read-only or read/write actions. Incoming API requests to a cluster master are managed via the Kubernetes API process running on the cluster master. End users can trigger Kubernetes API calls through Rest API calls, kubectl, or the GCP console.

- **Nodes:** Worker nodes of the Kubernetes cluster are commonly known as nodes. Nodes are individual Compute Engine VM instances created automatically by GKE, as per user-provided configurations at the time of provisioning. A node is leveraged to run services that are composed of one or more pods to run the application. A node typically includes the container runtime and the Kubernetes node agent (kubelet), which communicates with the cluster master to perform various administrative tasks.

  - **Types of node machines:** Nodes have different types of standard Compute Engine machine types. The default type is n1-standard-1, with one virtual CPU and 3.75GB of memory. From the following link, you can access details of the machine types available: https://cloud.google.com/compute/docs/machine-types.

- **Node OS images:** Nodes use specialized OS images, e.g., Linux RHEL and Ubuntu, for running containers. While creating a cluster, users can choose which types of OS images to use in node pools.

- **Node pools:** A group of nodes having the same types of configurations. Each node in the pool has a Kubernetes node label, `cloud.google.com/gke-nodepool`, which has the node pool's name as its value. A node pool can contain a single node or many nodes. While creating the cluster, the number and types of nodes can be specified, and this becomes the default node pool. We can add additional custom node pools of different sizes and types to a cluster. All nodes in any given node pool are identical to one another.

- **Node images:** While creating a GKE cluster or node pool, we must choose an operating system image that runs on each node. GKE offers the following node image options for clusters:

  - Ubuntu

  - Windows

  - Container-Optimized OS from Google

  - Container-Optimized OS with containerd

  - Ubuntu with containerd

GKE provides various types of clusters from which to choose while creating a cluster. Once created, the type of cluster cannot be changed. Following are the types of clusters that can be created using GKE:

- **Single-zone clusters:**

  A single-zone cluster uses a single master, also
  known as a control plane, running in a single zone
  and managing workloads on nodes running in
  the same zone. Based upon the availability and
  resiliency requirements for hosting application
  workloads any one of the following options can be
  leveraged while setting up GKE cluster.

- **Multi-zonal clusters:**

  A multi-zonal cluster uses a single replica of a
  control plane running in a single zone and has
  nodes running in multiple zones.

- **Regional clusters:**

  Within a given region, multiple replicas of control
  planes running in multiple zones and nodes also run on
  each zone in which the replica of the control plane runs.

Networking in GKE is similar to networking in virtualized and
cloud environments, but because containers are a different model
of deployment, the underlying networking elements also differ. The
purpose of GKE networking is to ensure that the communication occurs
between the various services running in Pods, and it should also enable
connectivity to other services outside the container ecosystem. When we
use GKE to deploy microservices-based applications, we must plan our
network on GCP, to ensure that all container-specific requirements are
fulfilled. Users must now design GKE networks, focusing on connectivity
between Pods, services, and external interfaces.

GKE's advanced software-defined networks enable a lot of
functionalities managed via declarative configurations, including routing,
IP filtering rules, firewall rules, etc. Let's start with some of the networking
concepts of GKE.

GKE Network Terminologies

Before discussing networking in GKE, readers should be aware of the various terms used to identify Google Kubernetes networking components.

Network Namespace

A network namespace provides a logical network isolated from the underlying host network interfaces. A network namespace acts as a copy of a network stack and gives the illusion of an independent environment to the process running under the namespace.

Virtual Ethernet Devices

A virtual Ethernet device is like a tunnel that connects the Pod to the node's real Ethernet. The two ends of this tunnel are denoted by vethX on the node side and ethX on the Pod side, where X corresponds to the number of the devices in place.

Bridges

A network bridge works on the principle of Layer 2 (L2)–level switching and transfers data from one Pod to another within a cluster. A bridge maintains a forwarding table, in which previously acquired mapping for MAC addresses and ports are kept and performs L2 transmissions using MAC addresses.

Iptables

Iptables is used to handle networking and port forwarding rulesets. It uses kernel-level "netfilter" rules to configure all routing for Kubernetes services.

Services

Services are a collection of Pods that serve a single purpose. For example, an application can have an Application and a DB tier that correspond to multiple Pods at the back end. These Pods will be grouped under different categories and will communicate via services.

In this way, if any Pod changes occur at the back end, the app-tier service will still be able to talk to the DB-tier service, as the point of interaction between the app environment and DB environment is via a service. App-Db interaction is depicted in Figure 4-1.

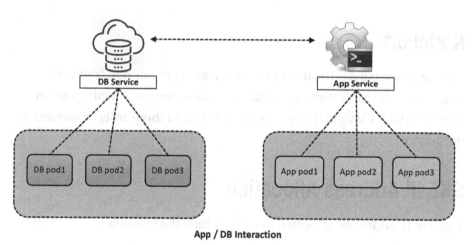

App / DB Interaction

Figure 4-1. *Application-database interaction*

Kube-proxy

Kube-proxy is an important binary in Kubernetes that runs on every node within the cluster and forms part of the Kubernetes control plane. It is responsible for routing the traffic from a service to a specific pod. It bifurcates all the traffic that goes in the service and routes it to the right node. In Kubernetes version 1.2, the kube-proxy now has rights to iptables and can insert netfilter rules into the node namespace. Netfilters, in turn, redirect traffic to the service.

HTTP(S) Load Balancer

Google Cloud's external HTTP(S) load balancer is a globally distributed load balancer for exposing applications publicly on the Internet. It is deployed across Google Points of Presence (PoPs) globally, providing low-latency HTTP(S) connections to users. Anycast routing is used for the load balancer IPs, allowing Internet routing to determine the lowest cost path to its closest Google load balancer.

GKE Ingress deploys the external HTTP(S) load balancer, to provide global load balancing natively for Pods as the back end.

NodePort

A NodePort service is the most primitive way to get external traffic directly to your service. NodePort, as the name implies, opens a specific port on all the nodes (the VMs), and any traffic that is sent to this port is forwarded to the service.

GKE IP Address Allocation

Types of IP addresses allocated in GKE include the following:

- **Node IP:** The IP address assigned to a given node is known as a node IP. Each node receives an IP address from the cluster's virtual private cloud (VPC) network. This IP address enables communication to the other nodes in the cluster. This IP address is also used by the control components kubelet and kube-proxy to connect to the control plane Kubernetes API server.

The node also receives a pool of IP addresses to be assigned to the Pods running on that node. By default, GKE assigns a /24 CIDR block for this.

- **Pod IP:** The IP address assigned to a given Pod is known as a Pod IP. This IP address is shared by all the containers running in that Pod, and it is used to connect these containers to other Pods in the cluster.

- **ClusterIP:** The IP address assigned to a service is known as a cluster IP. This address is allocated from the cluster's VPC network. Kubernetes assigns a stable IP address to each service from the cluster's pool of available service IP addresses. A cluster IP is unique within a cluster and does not change. The IP address is released only when the service is deleted from the cluster.

When Pods are deployed on nodes, GKE creates a network namespace for the Pod in the node's Linux kernel. The network namespace connects the node's physical network with the Pod, using a virtual network interface (VNI). This enables the communication flow from the Pod through the physical network of the host. This acts as a bridge for the Pods running on the same node and is also used by the Pods to send packets outside the node.

All containers running in a Pod use the network namespace of the Pod to access the network. All the containers connect to the same network interface.

By default, each Pod has access to connect to other Pods in the cluster. You can limit the same through configuration settings. Access to services is enabled by using the service IP and not the POD IP, because the Pods can be destroyed and created by GKE. A service has a stable IP address and port and provides load balancing across Pods.

The connectivity between Pods and services is managed with the kube-proxy component that runs on each node.

Communication Among Containers

In this section, we will cover how containers communicate with each other inside a Pod. On initialization, every Pod receives a unique IP and network namespace. As explained previously, the Pods share the same namespace and communicate with each other using localhost. Because the namespace is shared, communication occurs based on the different ports on which containers are configured. A multiple-container Pod is depicted in Figure 4-2.

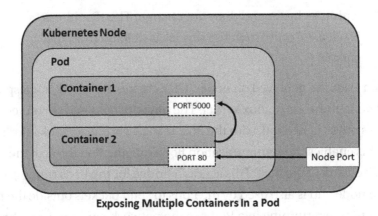

Figure 4-2. *Multiple-container Pod*

Communication Between Pods on the Same Node

Each Pod in Kubernetes is assigned an IP address, and communication among Pods occurs on that IP address. Every Pod in the cluster gets its own namespace, which interacts with the node root namespace to communicate with other Pods.

Each Pod receives a virtual Ethernet device called eth0. This eth0 is connected to a virtual Ethernet device in the host node (VM). Traffic from containers to Pods goes through this virtual connection.

When a Pod initiates communication with another Pod, it makes a request to its own eth0, which tunnels the message to the machine node's virtual Ethernet device.

Now that we know how requests reach the root namespace, the next question is how does data flow from the root namespace to another Pod. This is achieved via a network bridge.

A network bridge works on the same principle of providing an L2-level switch and using an Address Resolution Protocol (ARP) to discover MAC addresses. The bridge broadcasts the message received to all the connected devices and stores in a table the MAC addresses of devices that respond. The connectivity is done as follows:

1. A request is generated from a container to reach the Pod eth0.

2. This request is tunneled via a virtual Ethernet device to the respective virtual vethx interface.

3. From there, the request goes through a bridge that maintains the record for all the attached Pods within the node and transfers the request to the destination Pod.

4. The request goes to the virtual Ethernet device established with the destination Pod.

Connecting namespacing using a bridge is shown in Figure 4-3.

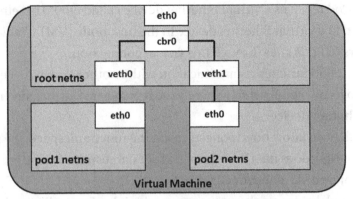

Connecting Namespacing Using a Bridge

Figure 4-3. *Connecting namespacing using a bridge*

Communication Between PODs on Different Nodes

In this section, we will use the knowledge gained from the "Communication Between Pods on the Same Node" section to see how a message request flows between two different Pods placed on two different nodes, as shown in the following packet-flow diagram (Figure 4-4).

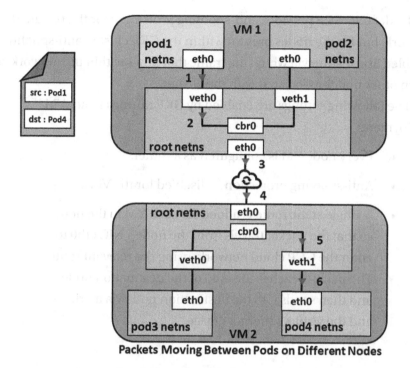

Packets Moving Between Pods on Different Nodes

Figure 4-4. *Packet movement between Pods on different nodes*

In Figure 4-4, pod1 is trying to communicate with pod4, located on a different node.

The request will be generated by a container in pod1, which will reach the virtual Ethernet eth0 of pod1 and be tunneled to reach the bridge present in the root namespace.

The bridge will follow the ARP to find the associated destination Pod. The request will fail, as the destination resides on a different node.

The bridge will eventually send the packet to the default gateway situated on the node of the VM network interface controller (NIC), eth0, from where the packet enters the underlying GKE network that spans the GKE cluster. This is the network that the underlying nodes or, say, the VM, reside on.

By default, GCP provides anti-spoofing protection for the private IP network, but for the nodes present within the GKE cluster, anti-spoofing is disabled as a feature via which the traffic that flows within the network can reach other nodes associated with the cluster.

The following settings are enabled by GKE during cluster VM deployment:

- Every node VM is configured as a router.

- Anti-spoofing protection is disabled for the VMs.

- A single static route is added for each VM in the node, so that the packet travels from the node's NIC eth0 to enter the GCP cloud network, using the relevant route. The packet reaches the eth0 of the destination node and then sends it to the destination pod4 via a bridge and the virtual Ethernet device.

Communication of PODs with Services

Services in Kubernetes play a pivotal role, as they provide an abstraction layer on top of the Pods. A cluster IP is provided to the service when it is initialized.

The communication between Pods and services follows a different approach than Pod-Pod communication (Figure 4-5).

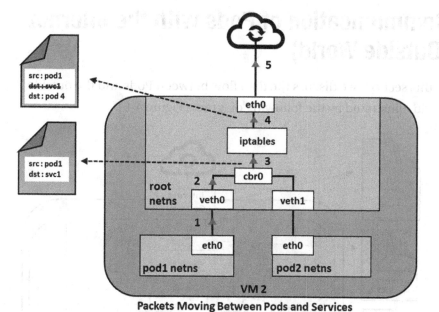

Packets Moving Between Pods and Services

Figure 4-5. Packet movement between Pods and services

The packet follows the same journey (as has been discussed in previous sections) until it reaches the bridge. For service-level event communications in Kubernetes, the packet, before going to the default gateway route from eth0, is filtered through the iptables, wherein the destination for the packet is changed to the relevant Pod in the back end.

Thus, via services, Kubernetes provides cluster load balancing to route the traffic to various Pods that are connected to the back end of services.

Communication of Pods with the Internet (Outside World)

In this section, we discuss the data flow between Pods and the outside world, illustrated by the following diagram (Figure 4-6).

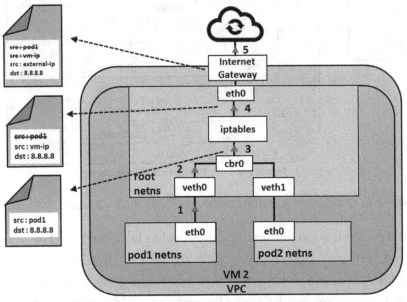

Routing Packets from Pods to Internet

Figure 4-6. *Routing packets from Pods to the Internet*

The path of the data packet is fairly the same, until it reaches the bridge, where the ARP will fail, and the data will be sent to the Ethernet end of the node, i.e., veth0. If we follow the traditional way of sending the packet out of the node Ethernet end into the outside world (Internet), the packet is bound to fail, as the Internet gateway network address translation (NAT) within the private cloud network can only understand VM addresses.

Before the data is passed on to the node Ethernet device, iptables does a source NAT and changes the packet source from Pod IP to node VM-IP, so it can be processed by the network gateway in a correct way. The data will reach the Internet gateway, where another NAT will be performed, to change the source from VM-IP to External IP, and, thus, the packet will reach the public Internet. The same reversed path will help the packet to reach the destination Pod. IP dismantling will be performed at each step, wherein the IP address will be translated, and the packet source and destination will be changed until the correct Pod is reached.

Load Balancing for Services

To make a service accessible from outside the network and/or cluster, and to get the data inside the service, GKE uses three types of load balancers to control the access. A single service can use multiple types of load balancers simultaneously.

External Load Balancer

An external load balancer manages traffic coming from outside the cluster and from outside the VPC environment and uses general GCP environment forwarding rules to route traffic to a designated node. The external load balancer can be initialized by setting the service's "type" field to a load balancer, in the service definition. When a service with a load balancer is initialized, a GCP cloud controller boots up to create a load balancer for that service and returns an *external IP* address, which can be given to the external systems to interact with the services via this load balancer.

Internal Load Balancer (TCP/UDP) Load Balancer

The internal load balancer manages traffic coming from outside the GKE cluster but from within the virtual cloud environments set up within GCP.

HTTP(s) Load Balancer (at Layer 7)

This is another type of external load balancer that manages traffic between the service and RESTful web service APIs–based applications, using ingress resources in GKE.

Communication from an External Load Balancer to a Service

The traffic from the IP advertised to the external network over the Internet is forwarded to the load balancer and then sent to all the nodes attached to the cluster, as it does not understand the container components and underlying networking (such as services).

Iptables rules on nodes will bifurcate the packet and send it across to the correct destination Pod, using internal load balancing rules set up by kube-proxy within the cluster. How packets are sent from the Internet to a service is depicted in Figure 4-7.

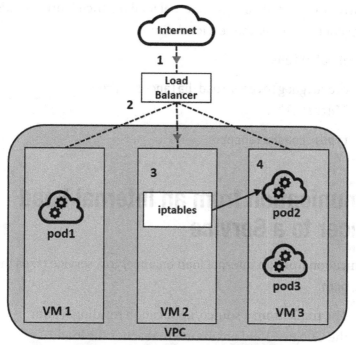

Packets Sent from Internet to a Service

Figure 4-7. *Packets sent from the Internet to a service*

Internal Load Balancer

An internal load balancer is initialized so as to provide a communication stream between an application that resides outside the cluster but on same Google cloud network as services within the cluster. The annotation and type specified within the service definition initializes an internal load balancer.

The internal load balancer receives an IP address from the cluster's VPC subnet, instead of an external IP address. Applications or services within the VPC network can use this IP address to communicate with services inside the cluster.

The syntax for initializing the internal load balancer corresponds to the following schema, within the service definition.

```
annotations:

cloud.google.com/load-balancer-type:
"Internal"

type: LoadBalancer
```

Communication from an Internal Load Balancer to a Service

Communication from an internal load balancer to a service takes the following path.

1. The traffic from a source/application residing within the Google Cloud environment reaches the load balancer.

2. As a GCP load balancer does not have visibility into the underlying Kubernetes components (such as services, Pods, etc.), the incoming traffic on the internal load balancer will be sent to a particular node.

3. When the traffic reaches a given node, that node uses its iptables NAT table to choose a Pod, even if the Pod is on a different node, and sends the packet to the destination node, as shown in Figure 4-8.

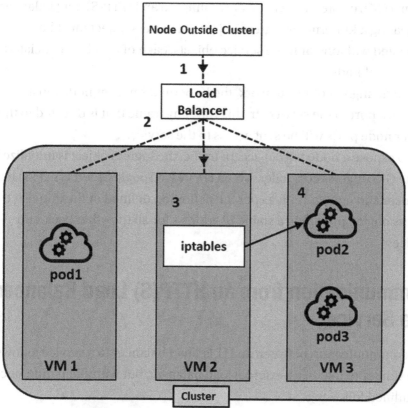

Packets Sent from Outside Node to a Service

Figure 4-8. Packets sent from an outside node to a service

HTTP(S) Load Balancer

To allow REST API–based applications to interact with services in a cluster, an HTTP(S) load balancer is used. It works on the HTTP/HTTPS protocol range of the network and exposes HTTP/HTTPS protocol routes from outside the cluster to services.

An HTTP(S) load balancer provides one stable IP address that you can use to route requests to a variety of back-end services.

In a GKE cluster, you create and configure an HTTP(S) load balancer by creating a Kubernetes ingress object. An ingress object must be associated with one or more service objects, each of which is associated with a set of Pods.

For an ingress object to work, the Kubernetes master node must allocate a port to the service. In this way, any traffic that is directed to the cluster node ports will be sent across to the service.

To expose a node port to accept traffic, the ingress object is initialized by the GKE ingress controller, which creates a Google Cloud HTTP(S) load balancer and configures it as per the definition defined in the initialized ingress object, providing a stable IP address for all the other back-end services.

Communication from an HTTP(S) Load Balancer to a Service

The communication between an HTTP load balancer to a service follows a path similar to that of an external load balancer, but with slight differences, as outlined following:

- The main difference is that the ingress will let you perform URL-based routing to services and associated Pods.

- Here, the source is the client IP that is trying to access the URL-based path, for example, /dryicelabs/ *. The traffic will land on the Google Cloud load balancer being initialized by the GKE ingress controller.

- From a load balancer (source), the traffic will be directed to one of the nodes (destination) ports, sitting behind a load balancer, as per the load-sharing configurations on the GCLB.

- When we declare a service definition, we specify a *NodePort*. This allocates a port on each node in the cluster, which will proxy requests to the service.

- At Node 3, the traffic is intercepted by the iptables, and the destination is changed to Pod3, located in a service that answers the correct NodePort request.

- The packet will eventually follow the internal route methods from Node 3 to the correct Pod3, as Pod4 and Pod5 belong to services that listen on a different port. (See Figure 4-9.)

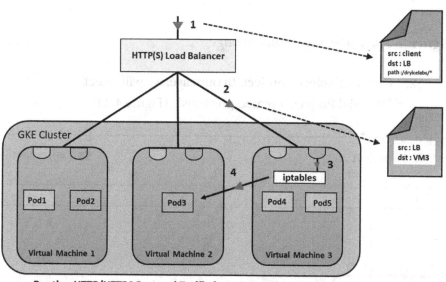

Routing HTTP/HTTPS Protocol Traffic from External to Service

Figure 4-9. *Routing HTTP/HTTPS protocol traffic from external to service*

Deployment of the GKE Cluster

In this section, you will learn how to create a GKE cluster and configure network options, while setting up a cluster, using the GCP console. In order to fulfill prerequisites for setting up a cluster, take the following steps.

1. Navigate to the Kubernetes Engine page in the Google Cloud console (Figure 4-10).

Figure 4-10. *Kubernetes Engine page*

2. Create or Select a project. In our case, we will select "Tutorial Project," created previously (Figure 4-11).

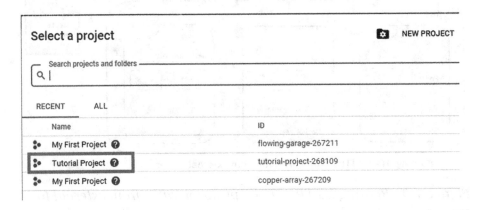

Figure 4-11. *Select a project*

3. In the GCP console, navigate to the Kubernetes Engine tab in the left column (Figure 4-12).

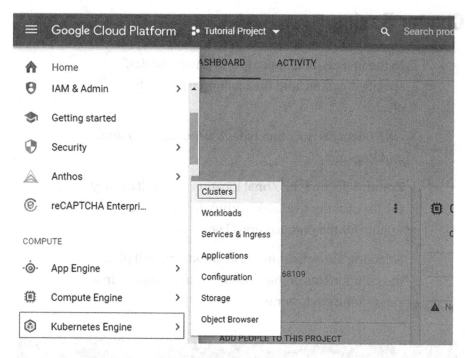

Figure 4-12. *Kubernetes Engine tab*

4. Click the Clusters tab and select Create cluster
    (Figure 4-13).

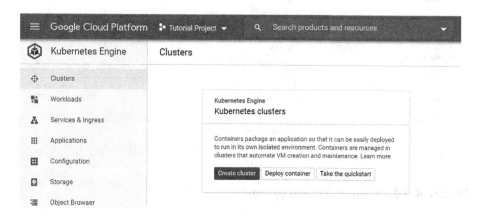

Figure 4-13. *Create cluster option*

Cluster Basics

1. In the first tab that appears for "Cluster basics," specify the name and the location type for the cluster.

   GKE offers two location types for the cluster: Zonal and Regional.

   Zonal: Selecting the Zonal location type will display the list of zones available within the Compute Engine for the organization (Figure 4-14).

   Selecting a zone within the location type will place the components of the cluster (master + nodes) in a single zone environment.

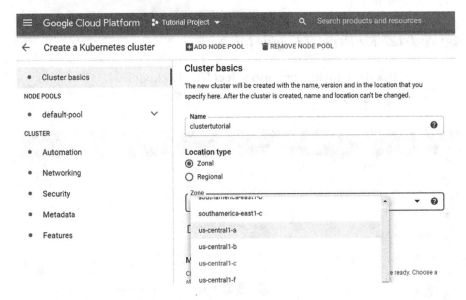

Figure 4-14. *Zone selection option*

Regional: A Regional location type signifies that the cluster components will span across a multi-zone environment (by default, a regional cluster creates three master controllers, spanning three different zones). If selected, the Regional location type will display the location of all available zones (Figure 4-15).

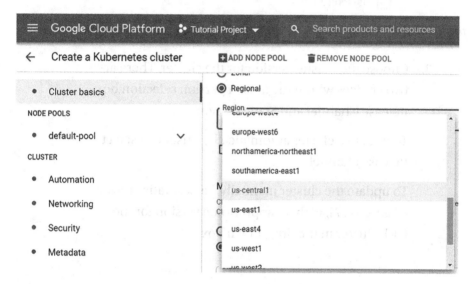

Figure 4-15. *Region selection option*

2. Specify node locations places the nodes in the selected location type.

Availability can be increased by selecting more than one zone (Figure 4-16).

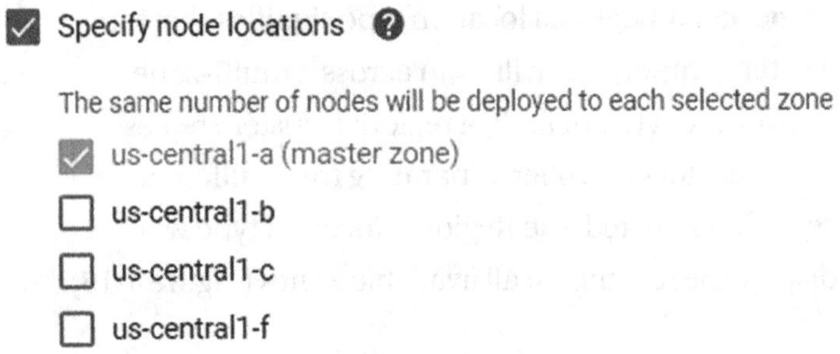

☑ Specify node locations ❓

The same number of nodes will be deployed to each selected zone

☑ us-central1-a (master zone)

☐ us-central1-b

☐ us-central1-c

☐ us-central1-f

Figure 4-16. *Node location selection options*

3. Choose the master version for the cluster. There are two choices within the Master version selection box: Release Channel and Static version.

    To update a cluster automatically, a user can select Release channel.

    To update the cluster manually, select Static version (Figure 4-17), with an appropriate version for the GKE cluster in the drop-down box.

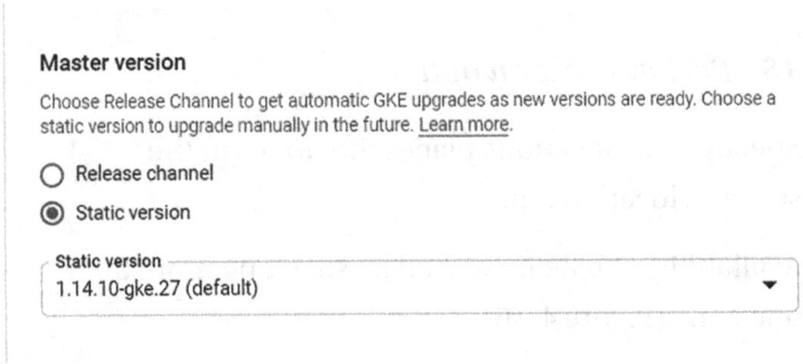

Master version

Choose Release Channel to get automatic GKE upgrades as new versions are ready. Choose a static version to upgrade manually in the future. Learn more.

◯ Release channel

◉ Static version

Static version
1.14.10-gke.27 (default)   ▼

Figure 4-17. *Master version selection options*

Node Pool

In GKE, by default, a new cluster will be created with at least one node pool. A node pool is a template for groups of nodes created in this cluster. More node pools can be added and removed after cluster creation, the procedure for which is explained following.

1. Specify the name and version of the nodes in the cluster (Figure 4-18).

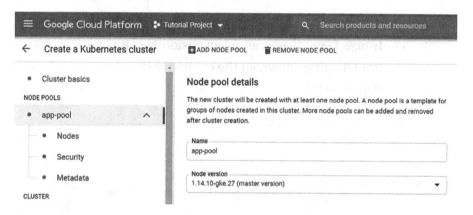

Figure 4-18. *Node pool details*

2. The next columns correspond to basic node settings within the cluster, namely

    - **Size**: Number of nodes in the cluster

    - **Enable auto-scaling**: If enabled, this feature will dynamically create or delete nodes.

    - **Enable auto-upgrade**: Automatic node upgrades help to keep the nodes up to date with the latest version of Kubernetes.

- **Enable auto-repair**: This setting, if checked, will monitor the nodes and start to repair the node if any errors are encountered.

- **Enable surge upgrade**: Surge upgrade creates additional nodes for short periods of time, to reduce disruption caused by upgrades.

- **Settings**: The next tab corresponds to settings when new nodes are created using the preceding node pool.

- **Image Type**: Users can select customized images from the drop-down for the created nodes (Figure 4-19).

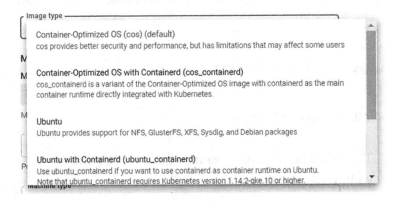

Figure 4-19. *Image type drop-down menu*

- **Machine family**: We will select a general-purpose machine from the relevant tab (Figure 4-20 & Figure 4-21).

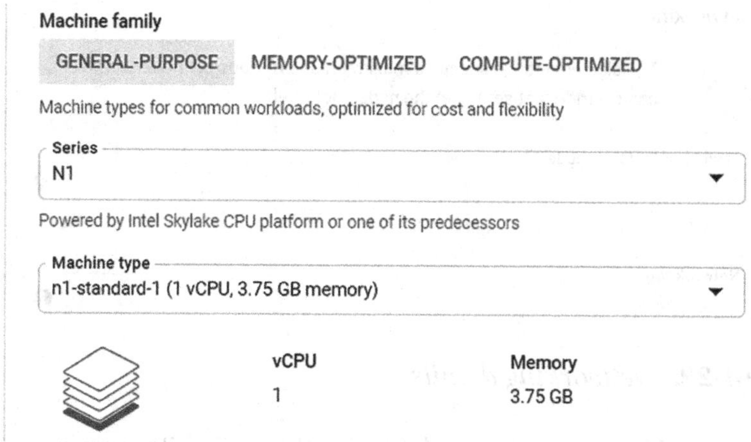

Figure 4-20. *Machine configuration details*

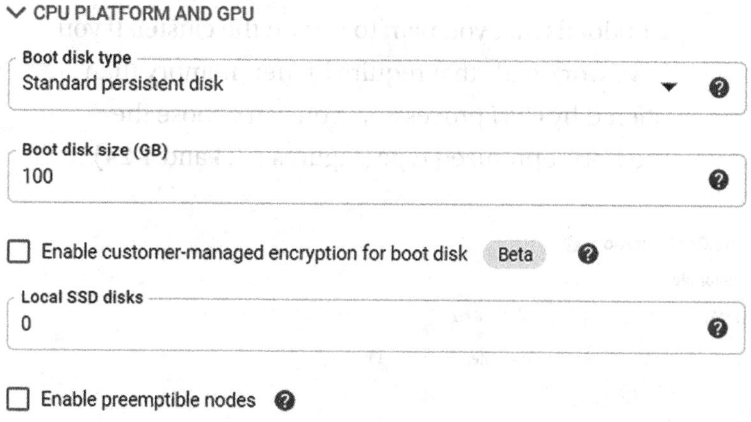

Figure 4-21. *CPU platform and GPU details*

- **Networking**: (See Figure 4-22.)

  - **Maximum Pods per node**: Specify the maximum pods per node. Default value is 110.

  - **Network tags**: Tags represent firewall rules applied to each node.

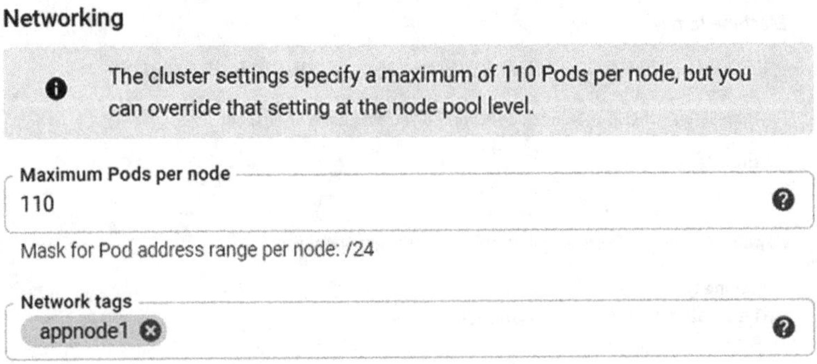

Networking

> ℹ️ The cluster settings specify a maximum of 110 Pods per node, but you
> can override that setting at the node pool level.

Maximum Pods per node
110   ❓

Mask for Pod address range per node: /24

Network tags
appnode1 ⊗   ❓

Figure 4-22. *Networking details*

- **Memory-optimized**: Choose this option if you want
  machines that have higher RAM. The selection
  of the type of machine depends on the types of
  workloads that you plan to run on the cluster. If you
  have workloads that require higher memory than
  offered by CPU processing, you can choose the
  memory-optimized type (Figures 4-23 and 4-24).

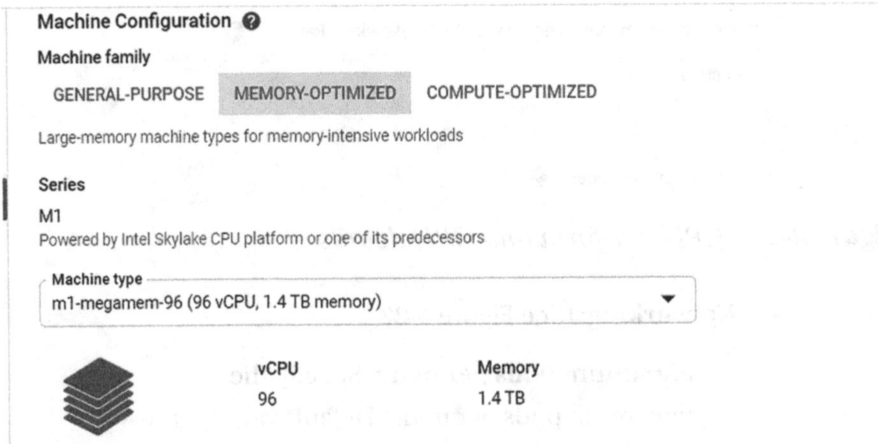

Machine Configuration ❓

Machine family

GENERAL-PURPOSE   MEMORY-OPTIMIZED   COMPUTE-OPTIMIZED

Large-memory machine types for memory-intensive workloads

Series

M1
Powered by Intel Skylake CPU platform or one of its predecessors

Machine type
m1-megamem-96 (96 vCPU, 1.4 TB memory)   ▼

	vCPU	Memory
	96	1.4 TB

Figure 4-23. *Memory optimization details*

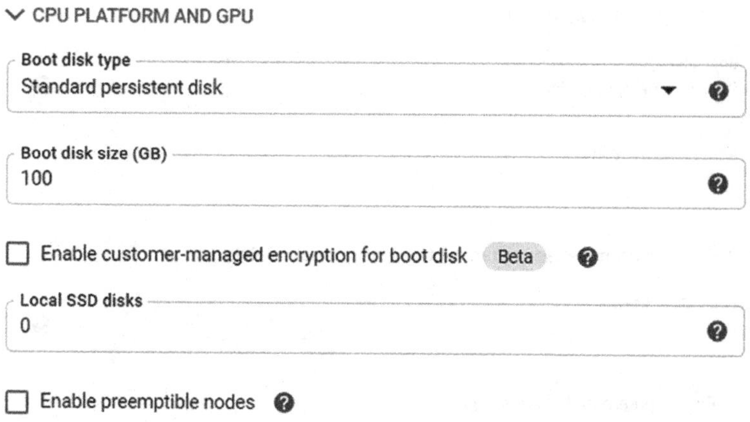

∨ CPU PLATFORM AND GPU

Boot disk type
Standard persistent disk

Boot disk size (GB)
100

☐ Enable customer-managed encryption for boot disk   Beta   ❓

Local SSD disks
0

☐ Enable preemptible nodes   ❓

Figure 4-24. *CPU platform and GPU details*

- **Compute-optimized**: Choose this option if your
  workloads require higher compute-processing
  capacity (Figures 4-25, 4-26, and 4-27).

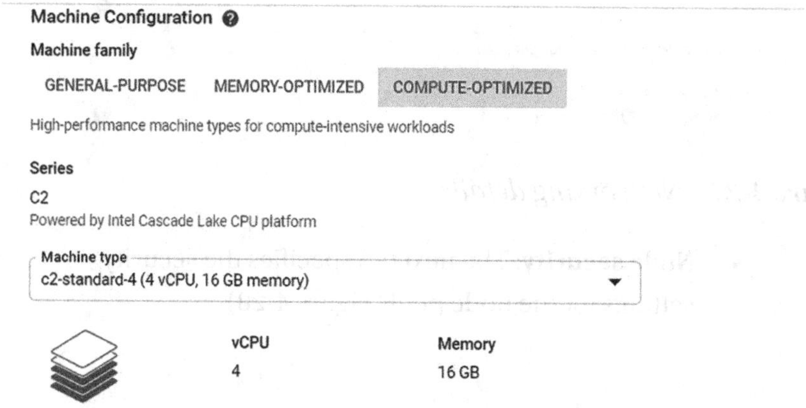

Machine Configuration ❓

Machine family

GENERAL-PURPOSE   MEMORY-OPTIMIZED   **COMPUTE-OPTIMIZED**

High-performance machine types for compute-intensive workloads

Series

C2
Powered by Intel Cascade Lake CPU platform

Machine type
c2-standard-4 (4 vCPU, 16 GB memory)

	vCPU	Memory
	4	16 GB

Figure 4-25. *Machine configuration details*

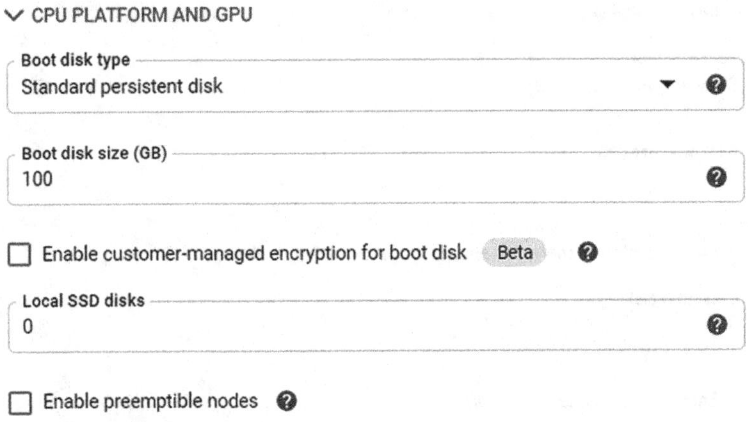

∨ CPU PLATFORM AND GPU

Boot disk type
Standard persistent disk   ▼   ❷

Boot disk size (GB)
100   ❷

☐ Enable customer-managed encryption for boot disk   Beta   ❷

Local SSD disks
0   ❷

☐ Enable preemptible nodes ❷

Figure 4-26. *CPU platform and GPU details*

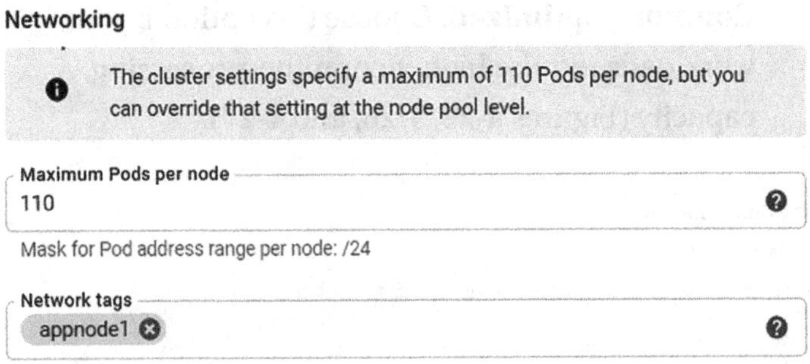

Networking

> ❶   The cluster settings specify a maximum of 110 Pods per node, but you
>   can override that setting at the node pool level.

Maximum Pods per node
110   ❷

Mask for Pod address range per node: /24

Network tags
appnode1 ✖   ❷

Figure 4-27. *Networking details*

- **Node security**: The next tab specifies the security
  settings for the node pool (Figure 4-28).

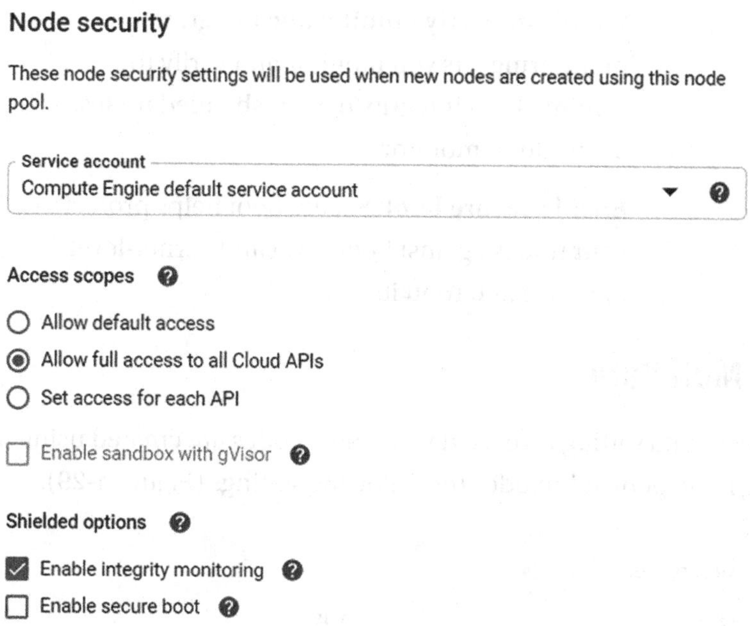

Node security

These node security settings will be used when new nodes are created using this node pool.

Service account
Compute Engine default service account   ▼   ❷

Access scopes ❷

○ Allow default access
◉ Allow full access to all Cloud APIs
○ Set access for each API

☐ Enable sandbox with gVisor ❷

Shielded options ❷

☑ Enable integrity monitoring ❷
☐ Enable secure boot ❷

Figure 4-28. *Node security details*

- **Service account**: Applications running on the VM use a service account to call Google Cloud APIs. Use Permissions on the console menu to create a service account, or use the default service account, if available.

- **Access scope**: Select the type and level of API access to the grant to the VM. The defaults are read-only access to Storage and Service Management, write access to Cloud Logging and Monitoring, and read/write access to Service Control.

- **Shielded options**: Shielded features include trusted UEFI firmware and vTPM and come with options for secure boot and integrity monitoring for your GKE nodes.

- **Enable integrity monitoring**: Integrity monitoring lets you monitor and verify the runtime boot integrity of your shielded nodes, using cloud monitoring.

- **Enable secure boot**: Secure boot helps protect your nodes against boot-level and kernel-level malware and rootkits.

Node Metadata

Node metadata settings are used when new nodes are created using the existing node pool. It includes the following settings (Figure 4-29).

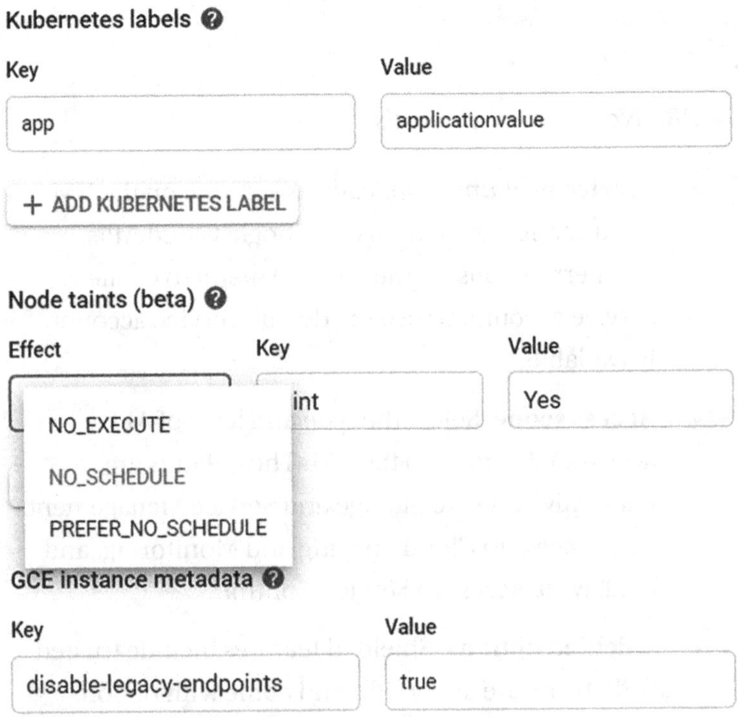

Figure 4-29. *Kubernetes labels*

- **Kubernetes labels**: These labels are applied to every Kubernetes node in this node pool. Kubernetes node labels can be used in node selectors to control how workloads are scheduled to your nodes.

- **Node taints**: These settings will be applied to every Kubernetes node in this node pool. Kubernetes taints can be used together with tolerations, to control how workloads are scheduled to your nodes.

- **GCE Instance metadata**: These items will appear in the Compute Engine instance metadata of every node in this node pool.

Automation

This setting sets cluster-level criteria for automatic maintenance, auto-scaling, and auto-provisioning. Edit the node pool for automation, such as for auto-scaling, auto-upgrades, and repairs (Figure 4-30).

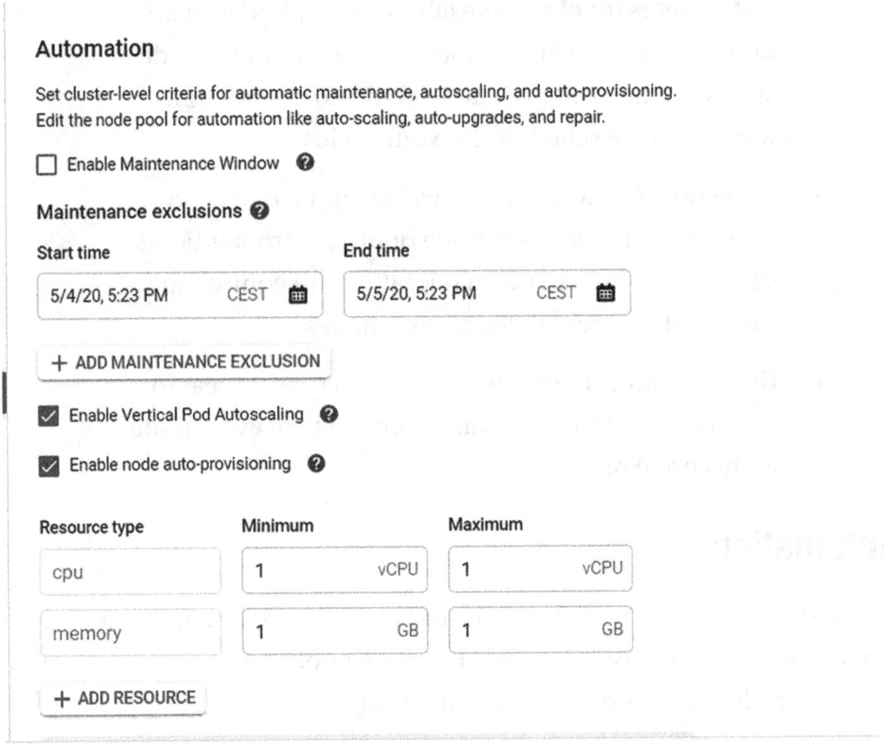

Figure 4-30. *Automation details*

- **Enable maintenance window**: To specify regular times for maintenance, enable maintenance windows. Normally, routine Kubernetes Engine maintenance may run at any time on your cluster.

- **Maintenance exclusions**: To specify times when routine, non-emergency maintenance won't occur, set up to three maintenance exclusions. Normally, routine Kubernetes Engine maintenance may run at any time on your cluster.

- **Enable vertical pod auto-scaling**: Vertical Pod auto-scaling automatically analyzes and adjusts your containers' CPU requests and memory requests.

- **Enable node auto-provisioning**: All nodes are used to compute the total cluster resources, including nodes in non-auto-scaling node pools. Limits are enforced for all auto-scaled node pools, including those you created manually.

Networking

The networking column within the console will correspond to how applications in Pods can communicate within and outside the cluster (Figure 4-31).

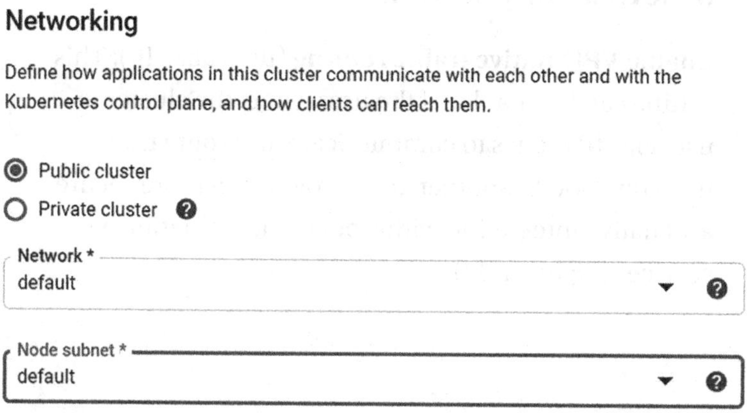

Networking

Define how applications in this cluster communicate with each other and with the Kubernetes control plane, and how clients can reach them.

⦿ Public cluster
◯ Private cluster ❷

┌ Network * ──────────────────────────────────┐
│ default   ▼ ❷ │
└──┘

┌ Node subnet * ──────────────────────────────┐
│ default   ▼ ❷ │
└──┘

Figure 4-31. *Networking detail*

The first check corresponds to the accessibility of the cluster in the environment and offers two choices:

- **Private Cluster**: Private cluster offers the ability to isolate nodes from connecting to the Internet/outside world. Nodes in a private cluster will not have public IPs.

- **Public cluster**: Nodes in the public cluster will have the public IPs associated with them.

- **Network and subnet**: Users can select the network and subnet details on which the cluster will be hosted. The network and subnet that the Kubernetes cluster is in determines what other Compute Engine resources it is able to communicate with.

Advance Networking Options

- **Enable VPC-native traffic routing** (uses alias IP): This setting can be enabled if the user wants the cluster to use alias IP ranges to communicate and route traffic from one pod to another, thus providing a more secure and native integration with Google Cloud Platform services (Figure 4-32).

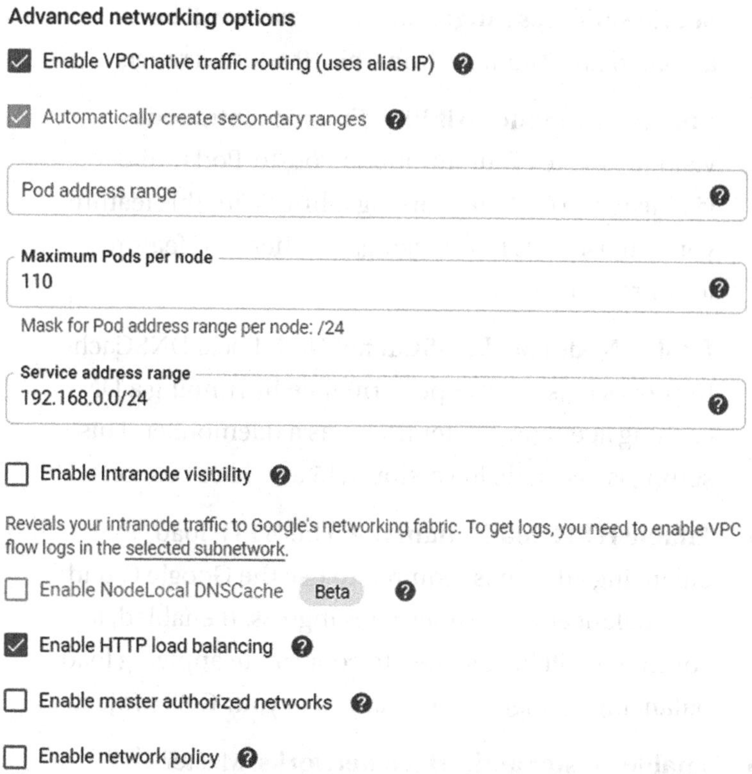

Advanced networking options

☑ Enable VPC-native traffic routing (uses alias IP) ❷

☑ Automatically create secondary ranges ❷

```
Pod address range                                              ❷
```

```
┌ Maximum Pods per node ────────────────────────────
│ 110                                                          ❷
```
Mask for Pod address range per node: /24

```
┌ Service address range ────────────────────────────
│ 192.168.0.0/24                                              ❷
```

☐ Enable Intranode visibility ❷

Reveals your intranode traffic to Google's networking fabric. To get logs, you need to enable VPC flow logs in the selected subnetwork.

☐ Enable NodeLocal DNSCache `Beta` ❷

☑ Enable HTTP load balancing ❷

☐ Enable master authorized networks ❷

☐ Enable network policy ❷

Figure 4-32. *Advance Networking detail*

- **Automatically create secondary ranges**: By default, the setting enables Kubernetes Engine to manage the secondary ranges used by the cluster.

- **Pod Address Range**: All Pods in the cluster are assigned an IP address from this range. Enter a range within a network range. If left blank, a default range will be picked up from the network

- **Maximum Pods per node**: This value is used to optimize the partitioning of a cluster's IP address range to subranges at node level.

- **Service address range**: Cluster services will be assigned an IP address from this IP address range.

- **Enable intranode visibility**: Enabling intranode visibility makes your intranode Pod-to-Pod traffic visible to the GCP networking fabric. With this feature, you can use VPC flow logging, or other VPC features, for intranode traffic.

- **Enable NodeLocal DNSCache**: NodeLocal DNSCache improves cluster DNS performance by running a DNS caching agent on cluster nodes as a daemonSet. This setting is available in version 1.15 and later versions.

- **Enable HTTP load balancing**: The HTTP load balancing add-on is required to use the Google Cloud load balancer with Kubernetes ingress. If enabled, a controller will be installed to coordinate applying load balancing configuration changes to your GCP project.

- **Enable master authorized networks**: Master authorized networks can be enabled to block untrusted non-GCP source IPs from accessing the Kubernetes master through HTTPS.

- **Enable network policy**: The Kubernetes Network Policy API allows the cluster administrator to specify what Pods are allowed to communicate with one another.

Security

Security includes cluster authentication handled by IAM and Google-managed encryption by default. It includes the following components (Figure 4-33).

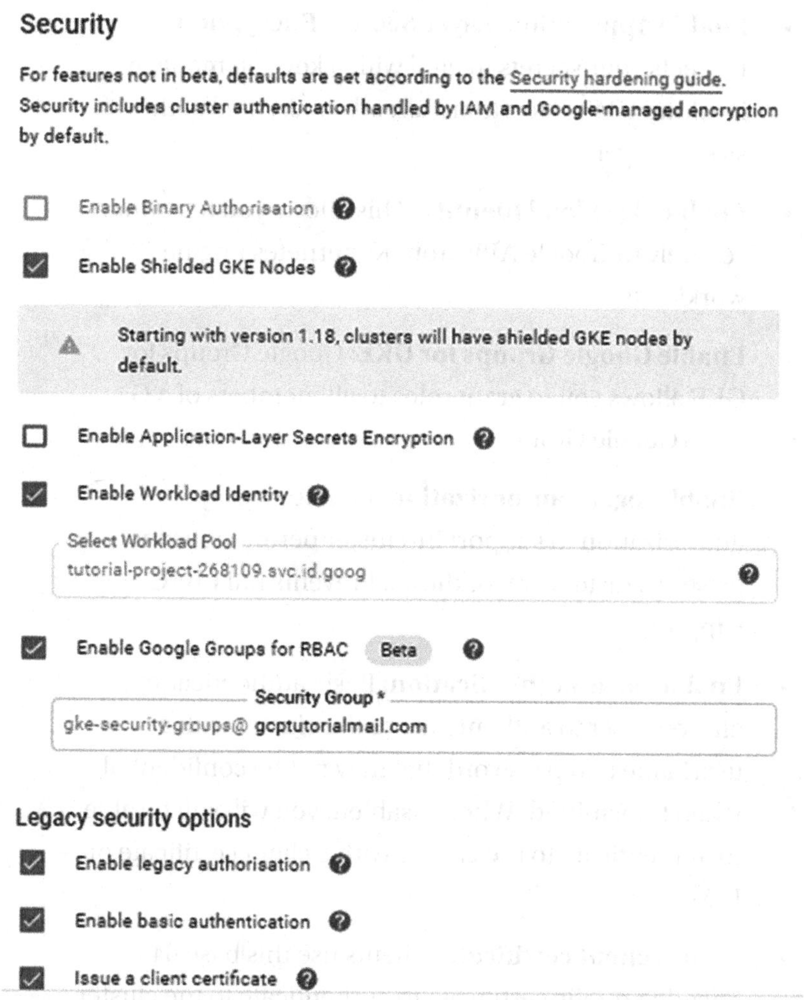

Security

For features not in beta, defaults are set according to the Security hardening guide. Security includes cluster authentication handled by IAM and Google-managed encryption by default.

☐   Enable Binary Authorisation   ❓

☑   Enable Shielded GKE Nodes   ❓

> ⚠   Starting with version 1.18, clusters will have shielded GKE nodes by default.

☐   Enable Application-Layer Secrets Encryption   ❓

☑   Enable Workload Identity   ❓

Select Workload Pool
tutorial-project-268109.svc.id.goog   ❓

☑   Enable Google Groups for RBAC   (Beta)   ❓

Security Group *
gke-security-groups@ gcptutorialmail.com

Legacy security options

☑   Enable legacy authorisation   ❓

☑   Enable basic authentication   ❓

☑   Issue a client certificate   ❓

Figure 4-33. *Security detail*

- **Enable Binary Authorization**: Binary authorization allows policy control over images deployed to the Kubernetes cluster.

- **Enable Shielded GKE Nodes**: Shielded GKE nodes provide strong cryptographic identity for nodes joining a cluster.

139

- **Enable Application-Layer Secrets Encryption**: Protects your secrets in etcd with a key you manage in Cloud KMS. Secrets are already encrypted at the storage layer.

- **Enable Workload Identity**: This allows you to connect securely to Google APIs from Kubernetes Engine workloads.

- **Enable Google Groups for GKE**: Google Groups for GKE allows you to grant roles to all members of a G Suite Google Group.

- **Enable legacy authorization**: Enables legacy authorization to support in-cluster permissions for existing clusters or workflows. Prevents full RBAC support.

- **Enable basic authentication**: Basic authentication allows a user to authenticate to the cluster with a username and password that may not be confidential when transmitted. When disabled, you will still be able to authenticate to the cluster with a client certificate or IAM.

- **Issue a client certificate**: Clients use this base 64–encoded public certificate to authenticate to the cluster end point. Certificates don't rotate automatically. They are difficult to revoke. To maximize security, leave this disabled. You are still able to authenticate to the cluster with basic authentication (not recommended) or IAM.

Metadata

This tab corresponds to data that can be added to organize your cluster (Figure 4-34).

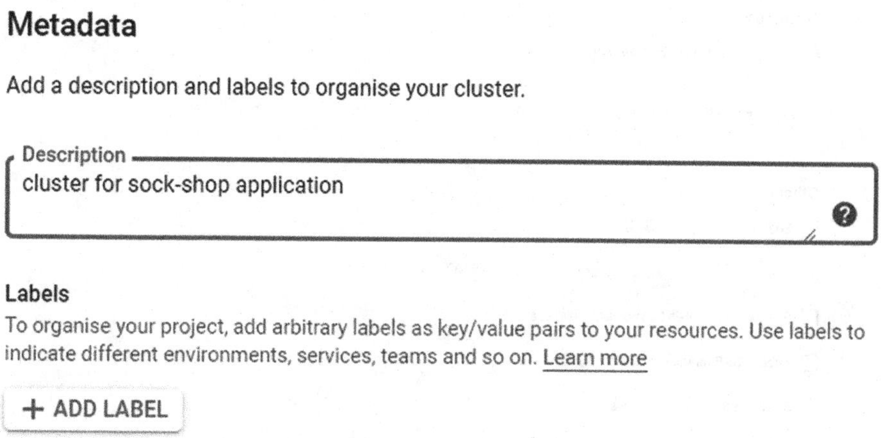

Metadata

Add a description and labels to organise your cluster.

```
Description
cluster for sock-shop application                                    ?
```

Labels

To organise your project, add arbitrary labels as key/value pairs to your resources. Use labels to indicate different environments, services, teams and so on. Learn more

Figure 4-34. *Metadata details*

Features

While creating a cluster, you can add various features for it, such as monitoring, metering, and dashboarding, for maintenance of the cluster (Figure 4-35).

Features

Serverless

☑ Enable Cloud Run for Anthos ❷

Telemetry

☑ Enable Kubernetes Engine Monitoring ❷

| System and workload logging and monitoring | ▼ |

Other

☐ Enable Cloud TPU ❷

☐ Enable Kubernetes alpha features in this cluster ❷

☐ Enable Kubernetes Dashboard (deprecated) ❷

☐ Enable GKE usage metering ❷

☐ Enable Istio (Beta) ❷

☐ Enable Application Manager (Beta) ❷

☐ Enable Compute Engine Persistent Disk CSI Driver (Beta) ❷

Figure 4-35. *Feature details*

- **Enable Cloud Run for Anthos**: Cloud Run for
  Anthos enables you to easily deploy stateless apps
  and functions to this cluster, using the Cloud Run
  experience. Cloud Run for Anthos automatically
  manages underlying resources and scales your app,
  based on requests.

- **Enable Kubernetes Engine Monitoring**: Kubernetes
  Engine Monitoring increases observability by
  aggregating incidents, system metrics, and logs into
  one single view.

- **Enable Cloud TPU**: This is used to accelerate machine
  learning workloads in your cluster.

- **Enable Kubernetes Dashboard (add-on)**: This is a web UI for Kubernetes clusters.

- **Enable GKE Usage Metering**: GKE usage metering allows you to see your cluster's resource usage broken down by Kubernetes namespaces and labels and to attribute usage to meaningful entities.

- **Enable Istio**: This is a service mesh that provides monitoring, traffic control, and security between the services running in Kubernetes Engine. If enabled, the Istio components will be installed in your cluster.

- **Enable Application Manager**: This is a GKE controller for managing the life cycle of applications.

- **Enable Compute Engine Persistent Disk CSI Driver**: Enables automatic deployment and management of the Compute Engine Persistent Disk CSI Driver. This feature is an alternative to using the gcePersistentDisk in-tree volume plug-in.

Cluster Management Dashboard

The cluster management dashboard gives a summary list of all the created clusters. A cluster created above can be viewed from below (Figure 4-36).

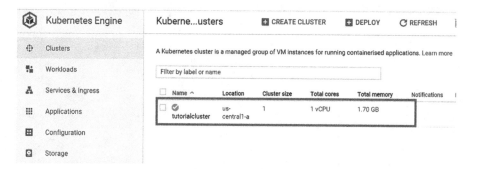

Figure 4-36. *Cluster management dashboard*

We will not delete the cluster created with the preceding configuration and will use the same cluster to deploy the sock-shop application in Chapter 5.

Summary

In this chapter we covered basics of GKE networking as well as learnt how to setup a GKE Cluster with various settings required as per best practice. In the next chapter we will cover application deployment on GKE.

CHAPTER 5

Deploying Containerized Applications with Google GKE

This chapter introduces readers with Application deployment approach on Google Kubernetes Engine (GKE) and includes the following:

- Introduction

- Simple Application Architecture Overview

- Introduction to the Sock Shop Microservice Application

- Application Deployment on GKE

- Deleting the Cluster

© Navin Sabharwal, Piyush Pandey 2020
N. Sabharwal and P. Pandey, *Pro Google Kubernetes Engine*,
https://doi.org/10.1007/978-1-4842-6243-6_5

Introduction

In this chapter, we will deploy a microservice architecture-based web application called sock-shop. We are providing only a brief introduction to the microservice architecture and its benefits, which will be sufficient to help you to understand the application behavior.

Simple Application Architecture Overview

Microservices are distributed and loosely coupled, independent, and deployable units, which means that if any individual service is down, this will not affect other services. Microservices communicate with one another through lightweight or language agnostic means, e.g., REST API, gRPC, or via queuing, such as RabbitMQ.

Advantages of Microservice Architecture

Following are the principal advantages of microservice architecture:

Easy and fast deployment: Microservices are often small in size, compared to monolithic applications, so their deployment is much faster and easier.

Faster release cycles: Every microservice is an independent deployable unit, which makes software release cycles shorter than with traditional applications, and agility, in terms of deployments and updates, is also supported.

Highly scalable: Microservices are often stateless and prefer deployment on a container. Whenever demand increases for specific services, growth can easily be scaled.

Accessible: As microservices are often small in size, developers can easily understand their functionality and how to update and enhance them efficiently, resulting in faster development cycles, with agile development methodologies.

Introduction to the Sock Shop Microservice Application

The Sock Shop application is an e-commerce-based microservice web application. It is a Docker-based application, and different components of the application can be represented, as shown in the following architecture diagram (Figure 5-1).

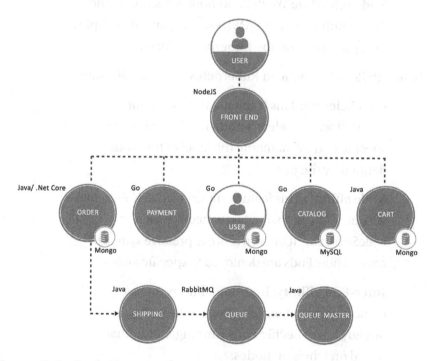

Figure 5-1. *Sock Shop application architecture*

The Sock Shop application is packaged as a Docker image. It uses a Docker file that contains instructions on how the image is built, using a Kubernetes-based deployment configuration file, `complete-demo.yaml`, created for this application.

The various components related to networking, persistence storage, and messaging queue that are used by the Sock Shop application are as follows:

> **Node pools selection:** For details on node pools, please refer to the relevant discussion under "Introduction to Google Kubernetes Engine (GKE)" in Chapter 1 & Chapter 4 "GKE Networking". The Sock Shop application uses default node pools already created in Chapter 4 at the time the Kubernetes cluster was created.

> **Node selection:** We defined node selection in the Pod definition of the YAML file that is used to deploy the application on the Kubernetes cluster.

To assign Pods to a node in Kubernetes, use the following:

> **nodeSelector:** This is the most popular and simplest way to select a node for deploying the specific Pod by matching the label of the Node defined by the user.

> **Node affinity:** This feature, introduced in Kubernetes version 1.4 version, is an enhanced version of `nodeSelector`. It offers a more expressive syntax to control how Pods are deployed to specific nodes.

> **Inter-Pod affinity:** Inter-Pod affinity allows colocation by scheduling Pods onto nodes that already have specific Pods running, rather than based on labels on nodes.

In our Sock Shop application, we are using nodeSelector to deploy Pods on a specific node. Refer to the following code snippet of the complete-demo.yaml file (Figure 5-2).

```
    nodeSelector:
        beta.kubernetes.io/os: linux
---
```

Figure 5-2. *nodeSelector*

Services

A service in Kubernetes is the logical set/group of Pods. Services are lightweight, so we can have many services within a Kubernetes cluster. Every service has a selector section that contains the Pod label to connect to. Refer to the following snippet of the complete-demo.yaml file to see the service definition for Sock Shop application (Figure 5-3).

```
apiVersion: v1
kind: Service
metadata:
  name: carts-db
  labels:
    name: carts-db
  namespace: sock-shop
spec:
  ports:
    # the port that this service should serve on
  - port: 27017
    targetPort: 27017
  selector:
    app: carts-db
---
```

Figure 5-3. *Service selector*

Following are the different types of Kubernetes services:

NodePort: This is a static port on each node on which a service is exposed that makes it available from outside the cluster.

ClusterIP (default): This exposes the service on an internal IP in the cluster, which makes that service only accessible from within the cluster.

LoadBalancer: This creates external load balancers in the current cloud, in our case, on GCP, and assigns a fixed external IP to the service.

In our Sock Shop application, we are exposing the front-end service as LoadBalancer and defining it as `type:LoadBalancer` in the `complete-demo.yaml` file. GKE will deploy an external network load balancer for accessing the sock shop application service using ports mentioned in configuration.

Other services of the Sock Shop application are exposed as internal services with in cluster and are exposed & accessible within the GKE cluster (Figure 5-4).

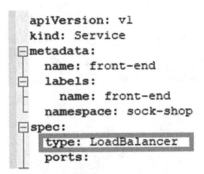

```
apiVersion: v1
kind: Service
metadata:
    name: front-end
    labels:
        name: front-end
    namespace: sock-shop
spec:
    type: LoadBalancer
    ports:
```

Figure 5-4. *LoadBalancer front-end service type*

Persistence storage database: This stores persistence data in the form of objects. For storing the data for our Sock Shop application, we use MongoDB and MySQL databases, running as a container under Pods and exposed internally in the Kubernetes cluster.

Messaging queue: A messaging queue is an asynchronous service-to-service communication widely used in microservice architectures. The Sock Shop application uses RabbitMQ, which is an open source messaging queue framework running as a container under Pods and also exposed internally in Kubernetes the cluster.

Application Deployment on GKE

The following steps install the Sock Shop application on the GKE cluster.

Step 1: Open the cloud shell. We will use the same cluster "clustertutorial" that we created in Chapter 4, to deploy an application by using the Google Cloud Shell that comes pre-installed with gcloud, docker, and kubectl command-line tools.

To open the cloud shell, do the following:

Go to the Google Cloud console.

Click the Active Cloud Shell button at the top of the console window, as shown in Figure 5-5.

Figure 5-5. *Cloud Shell link*

A cloud shell session will start, as shown in Figure 5-6.

```
🖿  ⚙️  (tutorial-project-268109) ✕  + ▾

Welcome to Cloud Shell! Type "help" to get started.
Your Cloud Platform project in this session is set to tutorial-project-268109.
Use "gcloud config set project [PROJECT_ID]" to change to a different project.
                                              []
gcptutorialmail@cloudshell:~ (tutorial-project-268109)$
```

Figure 5-6. *Cloud Shell session*

> **Step 2:** First, we will create the gcptutorialmail
> folder under the /home directory, then clone the
> complete-demo.yaml file from GitHub.
>
> Execute the following command to create
> gcptutorialmail under the /home directory.
>
> **Command:** mkdir gcptutorialmail
>
> **Output:** The output of the preceding command
> should resemble that shown in Figure 5-7.

```
gcptutorialmail@cloudshell:/home (tutorial-project-268109)$ mkdir gcptutorialmail
```

Figure 5-7. *Creating the gcptutorialmail directory*

> **Step 3:** Move into the gcptutorialmail folder by
> executing the following command.
>
> **Command:** cd /gcptutorialmail
>
> **Output:** The following should be the output of the
> preceding command (Figure 5-8).

```
gcptutorialmail@cloudshell:/home (tutorial-project-268109)$ cd gcptutorialmail/
gcptutorialmail@cloudshell:~ (tutorial-project-268109)$ pwd
/home/gcptutorialmail
gcptutorialmail@cloudshell:~ (tutorial-project-268109)$ 
```

Figure 5-8. *Moving to the gcptutorialmail directory*

Step 4: Now download the code base from Github,
by executing the following command.

Command: `git clone https://github.com/`
`dryice-devops/GCP.git`

Output: The result of the preceding command is
shown in Figure 5-9.

```
gcptutorialmail@cloudshell:~$ git clone https://github.com/dryice-devops/GCP.git
Cloning into 'GCP'...
remote: Enumerating objects: 3, done.
remote: Counting objects: 100% (3/3), done.
remote: Compressing objects: 100% (2/2), done.
remote: Total 3 (delta 0), reused 0 (delta 0), pack-reused 0
Unpacking objects: 100% (3/3), done.
```

Figure 5-9. *Downloaded code base*

Move to the GCP directory and list the code base
output, as follows.

Command: `cd GCP`

`ll - List directory`

Output: The result of the preceding command is
shown in Figure 5-10.

```
gcptutorialmail@cloudshell:~$ cd GCP
gcptutorialmail@cloudshell:~/GCP$ ll
total 28
drwxr-xr-x 3 gcptutorialmail gcptutorialmail  4096 Feb 17 16:34 ./
drwxr-xr-x 7 gcptutorialmail gcptutorialmail  4096 Feb 17 16:34 ../
-rw-r--r-- 1 gcptutorialmail gcptutorialmail 13112 Feb 17 16:34 complete-demo.yaml
drwxr-xr-x 8 gcptutorialmail gcptutorialmail  4096 Feb 17 16:34 .git/
```

Figure 5-10. *Moving the code base*

Step 5: Connect with the GKE cluster
`clustertutorial` by executing the following
command.

Command: `gcloud container clusters get-`
`credentials clustertutorial --zone us-`
`central1-a --project tutorial-project-268109`

Output: The result of the preceding command is
shown in Figure 5-11.

```
gcptutorialmail@cloudshell:~/GCP (tutorial-project-268109)$ gcloud container clusters get-credentials clustertut
orial --zone us-central1-a --project tutorial-project-268109
Fetching cluster endpoint and auth data.
kubeconfig entry generated for clustertutorial.
```

Figure 5-11. *Connecting to the* `clustertutorial` *cluster*

Step 6: Set up the project ID for the `gcloud` tool.

Command: `gcloud config set project`
`tutorial-project-268109`

Output: The result of the preceding command is
shown in Figure 5-12.

```
gcptutorialmail@cloudshell:~/GCP$ gcloud config set project tutorial-project-268109
Updated property [core/project].
gcptutorialmail@cloudshell:~/GCP (tutorial-project-268109)$ []
```

Figure 5-12. *Setting up the project Id*

Step 7: Create a namespace with the name *sock-shop*
that will serve as a placeholder for the application
deployment.

Command: `kubectl create namespace sock-shop`

Output: The result of the preceding command is
shown in Figure 5-13.

```
gcptutorialmail@cloudshell:~ (tutorial-project-268109)$ kubectl create namespace sock-shop
namespace/sock-shop created
```

Figure 5-13. *Creating a namespace*

Now check the namespace, by using the following command.

Command: kubectl get namespace | grep sock-shop

Output: The result of the preceding command is shown in Figure 5-14

```
gcptutorialmail@cloudshell:~ (tutorial-project-268109)$ kubectl get namespace | grep sock-shop
sock-shop        Active    2m18s
```

Figure 5-14. *List namespace*

Now check the cluster list, using the following command.

Command: gcloud container clusters list IP

Output: The result of the preceding command is shown in Figure 5-15.

```
gcptutorialmail@cloudshell:~/GCP (tutorial-project-268109)$ gcloud container clusters list
NAME            LOCATION       MASTER_VERSION  MASTER_IP      MACHINE_TYPE  NODE_VERSION
tutorialcluster us-central1-a  1.15.9-gke.8    34.66.82.249   g1-small      1.15.9-gke.8
```

Figure 5-15. *List Cluster*

Now, before deploying the application, the first requirement is to set up the credential, zone, and project for the container. To do this, use the following command.

Command: gcloud container clusters get-
credentials clustertutorial --zone us-
central1-a --project tutorial-project-268109

Output: The result of the preceding command is
shown in Figure 5-16.

```
gcptutorialmail@cloudshell:~/GCP (tutorial-project-268109)$ gcloud container clusters get
-credentials tutorialcluster --zone us-central1-a --project tutorial-project-268109
Fetching cluster endpoint and auth data.
kubeconfig entry generated for tutorialcluster.
```

Figure 5-16. *Getting a credential*

Step 8: Deploy the application. In Kubernetes,
Pods are the smallest unit, and an application
is represented as Pods. Pods are units that also
represent a container. The deployment manages
multiple copies of your application, called replicas,
and schedules them to run on individual nodes in
your cluster. In our case, deployment is performed
using the complete-demo.yaml configuration file
that contains details of the deployment. We will be
running only one Pod of the application.

complete-demo.yaml: A Brief Explanation

The different components of the complete-demo.yaml file can be
described as follows:

apiVersion: Defines the apiVersion of Kubernetes
to interact with the Kubernetes API server. When
creating an object, apiVersion will differ according
to the Kubernetes version.

kind: Defines the types of the Kubernetes object, e.g., ClusterRole, Deployment, Service, Pods, etc. For our application, kind is defined as Deployment and Service.

metadata: Defines an object, e.g., carts-db

namespace: Defines the namespace name that the Kubernetes object will create, e.g., sock-shop

replicas: Replicates a Pod

selector: Allows the client/user to identify a set of objects

template: Definitions of objects to be replicated— objects that might, in other circumstances, be created on their own

containers: Defines the characteristics of a container

Name: The name of the container

Image: Specifies what Docker image will be used to create the container.

Ports: The port on which the Docker container runs

env: Variable used by the Docker image to run the container

securityContext: The securityContext field is a SecurityContext object.

Security settings are specified for a container:

volumeMounts: This is the path in the container along which mounting will take place.

volume: This defines the volume definition that we are going to use.

Step 9: Run the following command to deploy the application.

Command: kubectl apply -f complete-demo. yaml

Output: The result of the preceding command is shown in Figure 5-17.

```
gcptutorialmail@cloudshell:~/GCP (tutorial-project-268109)$ kubectl apply -f complete-demo.yaml
deployment.apps/carts-db created
service/carts-db created
deployment.apps/carts created
service/carts created
deployment.apps/catalogue-db created
service/catalogue-db created
deployment.apps/catalogue created
service/catalogue created
deployment.apps/front-end created
service/front-end created
deployment.apps/orders-db created
service/orders-db created

deployment.apps/orders created
service/orders created
deployment.apps/payment created
service/payment created
deployment.apps/queue-master created
service/queue-master created
deployment.apps/rabbitmq created

deployment.apps/shipping created
service/shipping created
deployment.apps/user-db created
service/user-db created
deployment.apps/user created
service/user created
```

Figure 5-17. Output of the command to deploy the application

In GKE, containers are not accessible from the Internet by default, as they do not have external IP addresses. To explicitly expose our application to traffic from the Internet, we must define the type as LoadBalancer in the complete-demo.yaml file, as shown in Figure 5-18.

```
apiVersion: v1
kind: Service
metadata:
  name: front-end
  labels:
    name: front-end
  namespace: sock-shop
spec:
  type: LoadBalancer
  ports:
  - port: 80
    targetPort: 8079
    nodePort: 31010
  selector:
    app: front-end
```

Figure 5-18. *YAML code snippet*

Step 10: Validate the deployment by running the following command.

Command: kubectl get services -n sock-shop

Output: The result of the preceding command is shown in Figure 5-19.

```
gcptutorialmail@cloudshell:~/GCP (tutorial-project-268109)$ kubectl get services -n sock-shop
NAME          TYPE           CLUSTER-IP      EXTERNAL-IP      PORT(S)        AGE
carts         ClusterIP      10.81.7.91      <none>           80/TCP         9m57s
carts-db      ClusterIP      10.81.8.83      <none>           27017/TCP      9m58s
catalogue     ClusterIP      10.81.5.42      <none>           80/TCP         9m54s
catalogue-db  ClusterIP      10.81.6.238     <none>           3306/TCP       9m55s
front-end     LoadBalancer   10.81.2.86      35.188.192.249   80:31010/TCP   9m53s
orders        ClusterIP      10.81.8.59      <none>           80/TCP         9m50s
orders-db     ClusterIP      10.81.2.44      <none>           27017/TCP      9m52s
payment       ClusterIP      10.81.4.16      <none>           80/TCP         9m49s
queue-master  ClusterIP      10.81.10.18     <none>           80/TCP         9m48s
rabbitmq      ClusterIP      10.81.12.53     <none>           5672/TCP       9m47s
shipping      ClusterIP      10.81.11.36     <none>           80/TCP         9m45s
user          ClusterIP      10.81.11.29     <none>           80/TCP         9m43s
user-db       ClusterIP      10.81.10.199    <none>           27017/TCP      9m44s
```

Figure 5-19. *List app deployment*

Step 10: Once the external IP address of the application has been determined, copy the IP address. Point the browser to a URL (such as http://35.188.192.249), to check if your application is accessible (Figure 5-20).

Figure 5-20. *Deployed application*

Deleting the Cluster

Now that you have seen how to deploy an application onto a GKE cluster, we can delete the application, as well as the cluster, to clean up the GCP environment, as running a cluster has a price tag attached. To perform the clean-up activity, we can simply delete the cluster from the GCP console, which will eventually also delete the application. Follow these steps to delete the cluster:

Step 1: Click Kubernetes Engine ➤ Clusters, on the Kubernetes console page, as shown in Figure 5-21.

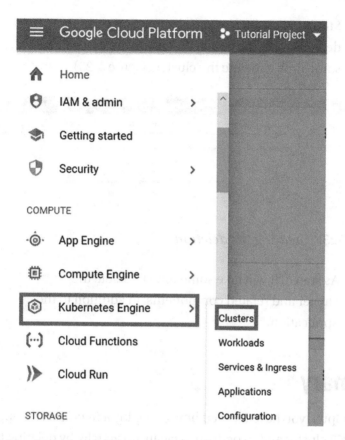

Figure 5-21. *Creating a list*

Step 2: Clusters will list the cluster created, as shown in Figure 5-22.

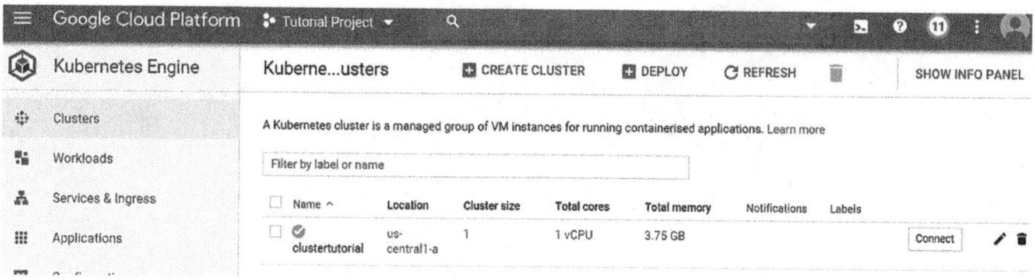

Name ^	Location	Cluster size	Total cores	Total memory	Notifications	Labels
clustertutorial	us-central1-a	1	1 vCPU	3.75 GB		

Figure 5-22. *Creating the list view*

Step 3: Click the cluster selection and press the delete icon at the end of the row. Wait, as it will take some time to delete the cluster (Figure 5-23).

Figure 5-23. *Creating the deletion*

As stated, it will take some time to delete the cluster and related components, in addition to the application.

Summary

In this chapter, you have learned how to deploy a microservice application on the GKE cluster and to perform a clean-up activity by deleting the cluster. In the next chapter, we will cover security controls provided by GCP specific to GKE.

CHAPTER 6

GKE Security

In this chapter, you will learn best practices to secure the GKE cluster. The following topics will be discussed:

- Google Cloud Shared Responsibility Model (GCSRM)
- Infrastructure Security
- Application Development and Release Security

Introduction

IT security is an overall strategy to prevent unauthorized access to various assets, such as applications and network, data, and hardware resources. It also preserves sensitive data, maintains data integrity, and guards the entire ecosystem of an organization from malicious hackers. Security in Google Cloud is a shared responsibility between the cloud provider and the customer. Google provides a model, the Google Cloud Shared Responsibility Model (GCSRM), to provide guidance on how security needs should be handled.

© Navin Sabharwal, Piyush Pandey 2020
N. Sabharwal and P. Pandey, *Pro Google Kubernetes Engine*,
https://doi.org/10.1007/978-1-4842-6243-6_6

Google Cloud Shared Responsibility Model (GCSRM)

GCSRM defines the responsibilities that Google and its customers have to manage the security of the various GCP components and services. GCSRM depends on the workload and starts from the bottom of the layer i.e. hardware and covers all areas up to the application layer. For the infrastructure as a service (IaaS) layer, Google is responsible for providing security at hardware, storage, and network levels, and for the software as a service (SaaS) layer, it is responsible for everything except access policies and content. For platform as a service (PaaS) layers such as GKE, Google's responsibility lies somewhere between that for IaaS and SaaS. Figure 6-1 shows Google Cloud's shared responsibility model and details Google's and customers' responsibilities in terms of IaaS, PaaS, and SaaS.

IaaS	PaaS	SaaS
Content	Content	Content
Access Policies	Access Policies	Access Policies
Usage	Usage	Usage
Deployment	Deployment	Deployment
Web Application Security	Web Application Security	Web Application Security
Identity	Identity	Identity
Operations	Operations	Operations
Access and Authentication	Access and Authentication	Access and Authentication
Network Security	Network Security	Network Security
Guest OS, Data & Content	Guest OS, Data & Content	Guest OS, Data & Content
Audit Logging	Audit Logging	Audit Logging
Network	Network	Network
Storage + Encryption	Storage + Encryption	Storage + Encryption
Hardened Kernel + IPC	Hardened Kernel + IPC	Hardened Kernel + IPC
Boot	Boot	Boot
Hardware	Hardware	Hardware

☐ Google's responsibility   ☐ Customer's responsibility

Figure 6-1. *Google Cloud's shared responsibility model*

GKE components come under the PaaS category.

Following are the components of GKE, managed by Google under its shared responsibility model (Table 6-1).

Table 6-1. *Google-Managed Kubernetes Components*

Components	Description
Underlying h/W\w infrastructure	Google is responsible for hardware, firmware, kernels, storage, OSs, networks, etc. Security of these components is maintained through encryption of data, highly secure datacenters, and use of secure software development patterns.
Kubernetes distribution	Google is responsible for patch updates on the Kubernetes versions and also provides the latest upstream versions of Kubernetes, under the shared responsibility model.
Cluster node OS	Cluster node OS images are managed by Google, e.g., Container-Optimized OS (COS) and Ubuntu. If a user opts for the auto-upgrade option, GKE will perform the upgrade on behalf of the user.
Control plane	Upgrades and management of the control plane is a Google responsibility. This includes Kubernetes master VMs, scheduler, API server, cluster CA, Identity and Access Management (IAM) authenticator and authorizer, audit logging configuration, etcd, and other controllers, such as the replication controller.

GKE uses the certified Kubernetes version that ensures smooth migration of applications between on-premise and GKE environments and enables customers to split a single workload across multiple GKE environments. GKE is also responsible for providing consistent upgrades of the Kubernetes versions.

According to the shared responsibility model, customers' responsibility is to manage the worker nodes that run the workloads. Customers must also define rules for deployments of Pods, services, and configurations, including setting up a network policy to restrict Pod-to-Pod traffic and define Pod security policy. The customer is also responsible for managing the applications deployed on the worker nodes.

Google is responsible for developing and releasing patches for container runtime and such Kubernetes components as kubelet and kube-proxy. The customer's responsibility is to apply these patches, by choosing either manual mode or by selecting the auto-upgrade option, using the cluster management feature of GKE.

The worker node auto-upgrade option applies updates to worker nodes on a regular basis, including updates to the worker node operating system and Kubernetes components, as per the latest stable version. This also includes security patches. For vulnerability management of container images, the customer is responsible for patching and hardening. GKE provides native features for detecting image vulnerabilities, using Google Container Registry. Additionally, customers can also use popular third-party products, such as Twistlock (Palo Alto), AquaSec, and Sysdig, for securing their container images.

Container-based applications can be compromised by misconfiguration and software bugs. Breaches can result in unauthorized access to workload and compute resources. Following are categories of container security in GCP.

- Infrastructure Security

- Application Development Security

- Application Release Security

In this chapter we will cover these categories. Additionally readers will also learn the best practices and methods to secure containerized applications, workloads, and the clusters running on GCP.

Infrastructure Security

Google provides various security features to protect the platform. GKE uses Google Cloud native functionalities, such as identity and access management, audit logging, application layer secrets encryption, and Workload Identity. GCP also leverages the Kubernetes native security features such as role-based access control (RBAC) for regulating access to network resources based on the roles of individual users.

Following are categories of infrastructure security in GCP:

> **Identity and access management:** GKE leverages
> GCP-provided IAM to manage access on project-
> level resources and uses Kubernetes native RBAC
> to manage the access on Kubernetes clusters and
> namespaces.
>
> **Audit logging:** GKE captures Kubernetes logs,
> which can be used by security administrators for
> further analysis and to generate alerts on specific
> security events. GKE automatically records the
> Kubernetes audit log via cloud audit logs.
>
> **Networking:** To secure Pod-to-Pod communication,
> GKE leverages network policies. By network policies,
> users can control the communication between
> the GKE cluster's Pods and services. Through
> Kubernetes's network policy API, we can create
> Pod-level firewall rules to control communication
> between Pods and services within the GKE cluster.
>
> Additionally, network policy also helps to define
> the rules of scenarios in which a single GKE cluster
> is serving multiple application tiers. For example,
> you can create a network policy to ensure that

a front-end service in a web application cannot communicate directly with a payment service (application tier). You can also restrict Pods and services in a particular namespace from accessing other Pods or services in a different namespace.

Compliance and minimal host OS: GKE supports compliance certifications, including ISO 27001, ISO 27017, ISO 27108, HIPAA, and PCI-DSS. It is the customer's responsibility to ensure that compliance controls are implemented at the GCP services level (using console, gcloud shell, or APIs) and at the application level.

Auto-upgrade components: Google is responsible for patching the Kubernetes master with the latest Kubernetes version. Patching/upgrading of worker nodes is a user responsibility. A user can apply the patches either manually or select the auto-upgrade option. Under the auto-upgrade scenario, GKE is responsible for doing patch management at the operating system layer.

Encryption keys and secrets encryption: GKE supports using GCP KMS with GCP-managed keys, or customer-managed encryption keys, for data encryption. GCP Secret Manager provides functionality for storing and management of secrets, as binary blobs or text strings. The GCP IAM service is used to control access to Secret Manager. This service can be used for securing information, such as database passwords, keys, or TLS certificates required by an application. GCP Secret Manager can be used for storing sensitive data, such as passwords, OAuth tokens, and SSH keys, in your GKE clusters.

Cluster hardening: In terms of cluster security, GKE recommends cluster hardening based on CIS GKE Kubernetes Benchmark, which is a subset of CIS Kubernetes Benchmark.

Workload identity: Containerized applications may use the other GCP services, for example, GCP Storage or Cloud SQL. In order to connect with these services, the application should authenticate and access the services using the GCP IAM service. Workload Identity uses a Google-managed service account to share credentials for authentication, following the principles of least privilege for application authentication.

Managed SSL certificates: Containerized applications may require access over the Internet, using HTTPS to ensure secure access to the system. One can obtain and manage these certificates directly from third-party vendors or use the Google-provided certificates, where certificate management and renewal are handled by Google itself.

Identity and Access Management

In this section, you will learn about authentication types and authorization options provided by GCP to secure the GKE infrastructure. Google provides the following ways of authenticating users to a GCP Service:

Google Sign-in: Google Sign-in provides Gmail and G Suite accounts to log in to the GCP console.

OAuth 2.0: GCP supports the OAuth 2.0 protocol, with OpenID Connect to authenticate users.

Firebase authentication: This provides user authentication through Facebook, Twitter, and Google accounts.

User API: Uses Google App Engine's built-in Users API service to authenticate Google and G Suite accounts.

Following are the channels that interact with GKE services:

- Google Cloud Platform console, i.e., web interface
- Cloud SDK and Cloud Shell, which provide a command-line interface
- REST API interface for custom applications
- Kubernetes native kubectl utility

The GCP Console

The GCP console is a web-based user interface that is used to create a project and manage the GCP resources, e.g., compute resources, storage, GKE clusters, etc.

GCP Console Features

- The GCP console provides an intuitive interface to manage GCP projects and underline services.

- The console provides easy access to all GCP services and APIs, with a dashboard specific to all GCP services and APIs and access to management resources for each service.

Accessing the GCP Console

Step 1: To access GCP Console, click the following link: https://console.cloud.google.com

The link will open the Sign-in page, as shown in Figure 6-2.

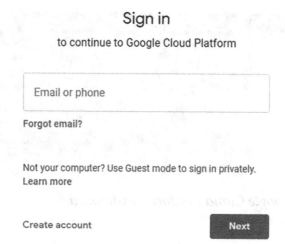

Figure 6-2. *Google Cloud Platform Sign in*

Step 2: Enter the email address, then click the Next button.

Now enter your password and click the Next button, as illustrated in Figure 6-3.

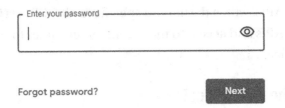

Figure 6-3. *Google Cloud Platform password*

After a successful login, you will see the GCP dashboard, from which you can access various GCP services, including Storage, IAM & Admin, Compute Engine, and Kubernetes Engine (Figure 6-4).

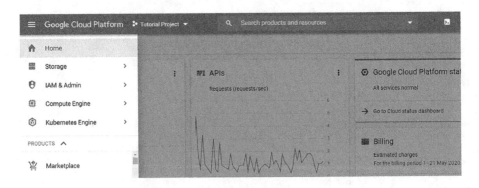

Figure 6-4. *Google Cloud Platform dashboard*

Cloud SDK

Cloud SDK is a set of command-line tools developed by Google for such popular programming languages as Java, Python, GO, etc. Users can employ these tools to interact with Storage, Compute Engine, BigQuery, GKE cluster, and other GCP services. Cloud SDK is free for users with a Google Cloud account.

gcloud

Cloud SDK provides a command-line interface known as gcloud shell. For GKE management, gcloud shell can be used to create a GKE cluster and manage GKE authentication and GKE Cluster Management.

kubectl

kubectl provides commands for control over Kubernetes clusters. It allows for deploying applications, inspecting and managing cluster resources, and viewing logs.

Install Cloud SDK

In this section, you will learn how to install Cloud SDK in Red Hat and CentOS. Google Cloud Compute instances already come bundled with Cloud SDK. If you are using Google Compute Instance, you can skip the following steps.

Prerequisites:

- Sign in to your Google account.

- Billing should be enabled for your Google Cloud project.

- Navigate to the project selector page and select either the existing project, or create a new project, as shown in Figure 6-5.

Figure 6-5. *Google Cloud Platform Create Project*

Take the following steps to install Cloud SDK in your Red Hat Enterprise Linux (RHEL) machine (for non-GCP-based VMs).

Step 1: Update the yum configuration with the Cloud SDK repository by executing the following code.

```
sudo tee -a /etc/yum.repos.d/google-cloud-sdk.repo << EOM
[google-cloud-sdk]
name=Google Cloud SDK
baseurl=https://packages.cloud.google.com/yum/repos/cloud-sdk-
el7-x86_64
enabled=1
gpgcheck=1
repo_gpgcheck=1
gpgkey=https://packages.cloud.google.com/yum/doc/yum-key.gpg
       https://packages.cloud.google.com/yum/doc/rpm-package-
       key.gpg
EOM
```

Step 2: Execute the following command to install the Cloud SDK.

Command: `yum install google-cloud-sdk`

Step 3: Execute the following command to trigger the authentication process.

Command: `gcloud init`

After executing the preceding command, the result shown in Figure 6-6 will be displayed.

```
Welcome! This command will take you through the configuration of gcloud.

Your current configuration has been set to: [default]

...

To continue, you must login. Would you like to login (Y/n)?  y

Your browser has been opened to visit:

https://accounts.google.com/o/oauth2/auth?scope=https%3A%2F%2Fwww.googleapis.co%2
Fauth%2Fappengine.admin+https%3A%2F%2...
```

Figure 6-6. *Result of gcloud init command*

Copy the authentication URL and paste it into your browser. The browser page will display the verification code. Paste the verification code back into the terminal, as shown in the Figure 6-7.

```
Your browser has been opened to visit:

https://accounts.google.com/o/oauth2/auth?scope=https%3A%2F%2Fwww.googleapis.co%2
Fauth%2Fappengine.admin+https%3A%2F%2...
```

Figure 6-7. *gcloud init authentication URL*

Step 4: In the browser window, review the application permissions and click Accept and copy and paste the returned code on the command line after Enter verification code. Otherwise, the code is automatically sent to the command-line tool.

Step 5: Choose the credentials for this configuration.

After setting up your credentials, gcloud prompts for a default project for this configuration. Select a project ID from the list.

Kubernetes supports two types of accounts. The first type is a user account, that is, for normal users, which is not managed by Kubernetes and cannot be created or deleted through a kubectl command. The second type is a service account, which is created and managed by Kubernetes. A service account can be used only by Kubernetes objects, e.g., Pods.

In GKE, Google manages the Kubernetes user accounts that can be either Google Cloud service accounts or Google accounts. Kubernetes service accounts and Google Cloud service accounts are different in nature. Kubernetes service accounts belong to the cluster in which they are defined, whereas Google Cloud service accounts are part of the Google Cloud project itself. Google Cloud service accounts can easily be granted access permissions for GKE clusters, as well as Google Cloud resources using Cloud Identity and Access Management. In keeping with CIS GKE Benchmark Recommendation 6.2.1: "Prefer not running GKE clusters using the Compute Engine default service account."

After authentication, we must provide authorization to these identities, to create, update, read, or delete operations on the Kubernetes cluster.

Best Practices for Authentication and Authorization:

- **Disable legacy authorization:** RBAC and Cloud IAM should be used to define the policies that allow user and service accounts to perform actions on the Kubernetes cluster. To ensure that RBAC limits permissions according to the least privilege model, we must disable the legacy authorization. The following command can be used to disable the legacy authorization while creating the Kubernetes cluster.

  Command: `gcloud container clusters create CLUSTER_NAME -no-enable-legacy-authorization`

  Disable basic authentication: Basic authentication authenticates a user by username and password, which, when stored in plain text with no encryption, can lead to brute force attack. In order to prevent such scenarios, basic authentication must be disabled. From GKE version 1.2 and above, basic authentication is disabled by default for a cluster.

  Disable client certificate: Client certificate issuance is disabled by default for clusters created with GKE version 1.12 and above.

Cloud IAM Policies

This section will describe how to create cloud-access and -management policies to allow authorized user and service accounts to interact with GKE. Through Cloud IAM polices, we can restrict who can access our project and what action they can perform. Cloud IAM works along with Kubernetes RBAC to provide authorization to user and service accounts at the project level, and RBAC controls access to Kubernetes object or namespace levels.

Types of Cloud IAM Roles

GCP provides the following types of IAM roles:

- Predefined

- Primitive

- Custom

Predefined GKE Role

GKE provides predefined roles that provide access to specific Google Cloud resources.

Following are the predefined roles for GKE:

- roles/container.admin

- roles/container.viewer

- roles/container.hostServiceAgentUser

- roles/container.clusterAdmin

- roles/container.clusterViewer

- roles/container.developer

To view predefined permissions, take the following steps:

Step 1: Click IAM & Admin, shown in Figure 6-8.

Figure 6-8. *IAM & Admin*

Step 2: Click the Roles option, as shown in Figure 6-9.

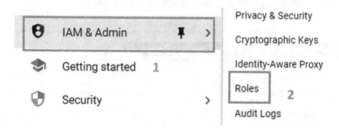

Figure 6-9. *Roles*

Step 3: On the Roles page, click Filter table, as shown in Figure 6-10.

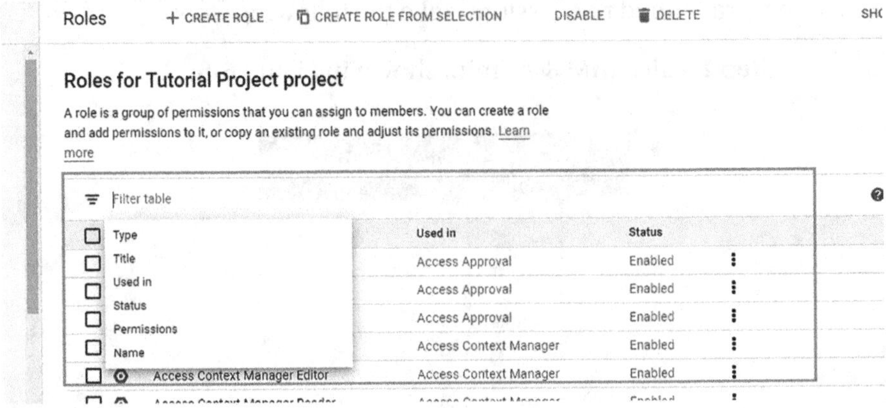
Roles
+ CREATE ROLE
CREATE ROLE FROM SELECTION
DISABLE
DELETE
Roles for Tutorial Project project
A role is a group of permissions that you can assign to members. You can create a role and add permissions to it, or copy an existing role and adjust its permissions. Learn more
Filter table
Type
Title
Used in
Status
Permissions
Name
Used in
Status
Access Approval
Enabled
Access Approval
Enabled
Access Approval
Enabled
Access Context Manager
Enabled
Access Context Manager Editor
Access Context Manager
Enabled

Figure 6-10. *Filter table*

Step 4: Now filter the roles, as follows (Figure 6-11):

Type: Pre-defined

Used in: Kubernetes Engine

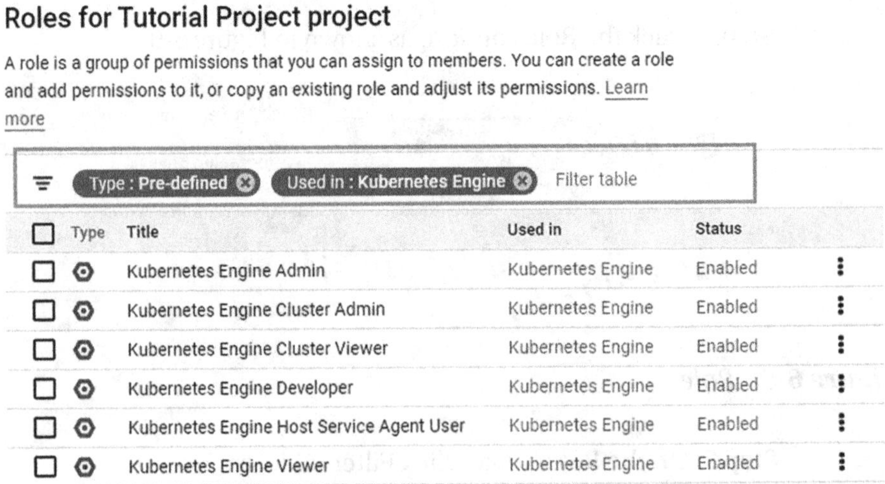
Roles for Tutorial Project project
A role is a group of permissions that you can assign to members. You can create a role and add permissions to it, or copy an existing role and adjust its permissions. Learn more
Type : Pre-defined
Used in : Kubernetes Engine
Filter table
Type
Title
Used in
Status
Kubernetes Engine Admin
Kubernetes Engine
Enabled
Kubernetes Engine Cluster Admin
Kubernetes Engine
Enabled
Kubernetes Engine Cluster Viewer
Kubernetes Engine
Enabled
Kubernetes Engine Developer
Kubernetes Engine
Enabled
Kubernetes Engine Host Service Agent User
Kubernetes Engine
Enabled
Kubernetes Engine Viewer
Kubernetes Engine
Enabled

Figure 6-11. *Filter table by Type and Used in*

Step 5: Select any option, e.g., Kubernetes Engine Admin, as shown in Figure 6-12.

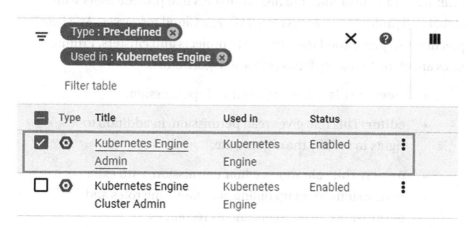

Figure 6-12. *Kubernetes Engine Admin*

Step 6: Once you select the Kubernetes Engine Admin option, you can see its description in the panel at the right of screen, as shown in Figure 6-13.

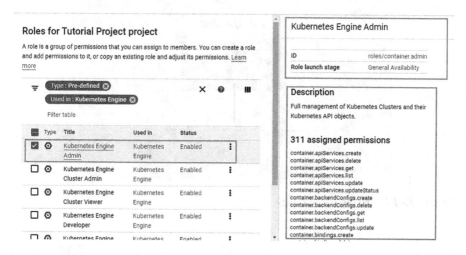

Figure 6-13. *Kubernetes Engine Admin description*

Primitive Roles

Primitive Cloud IAM roles are historical roles that provide users with global and project-level access to all Google Cloud resources. As a best practice, use predefined roles to secure projects and clusters. Primitive roles are of the following types (see also Figure 6 14):

- **viewer**: This role grants read-only permission.

- **editor**: This role gives read permission, in addition to rights to modify the object state.

- **owner**: This role allows editor permission, with extra permissions to set up billing and managing roles and permissions for a project and its resources.

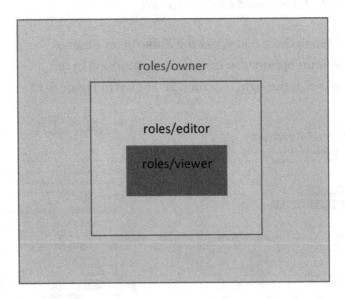

Figure 6-14. Primitive roles

Service Account User Role

A service account user role (`roles/iam.serviceAccountUser`) can be assigned either to all service accounts in a project or at a particular service account level. Users granted the service account user role on a service account can use it to access indirectly all the resources to which the service account has access. For example, if a service account has been granted the Kubernetes Engine Cluster Admin (`roles/Kubernetes Engine Cluster Admin`) role, a user who has been granted the service account users role (`roles/iam.serviceAccountUser`) on that service account can act as the service account to start a GKE cluster. In this flow, the user impersonates the service account, to perform tasks, using the granted roles and permissions.

Now let's review the roles available in GCP for GKE.

> **Step 1:** Click the IAM & Admin section, as per Figure 6-15.

Figure 6-15. *IAM & Admin*

Step 2: Click the Roles option, as shown in Figure 6-16.

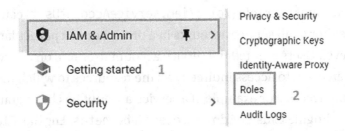

Figure 6-16. Roles

Step 3: On the Roles page, click Filter table, as per Figure 6-17.

Roles   + CREATE ROLE   ⟡ CREATE ROLE FROM SELECTION   DISABLE   🗑 DELETE   SH(

Roles for Tutorial Project project

A role is a group of permissions that you can assign to members. You can create a role and add permissions to it, or copy an existing role and adjust its permissions. Learn more

▼	Filter table			❷
☐	Type		Used in	Status
☐	Title		Access Approval	Enabled ⋮
☐	Used in		Access Approval	Enabled ⋮
☐	Status		Access Approval	Enabled ⋮
☐	Permissions		Access Context Manager	Enabled ⋮
☐	Name		Access Context Manager	Enabled ⋮
☐	⊙	Access Context Manager Editor	Access Context Manager	Enabled ⋮
☐	⊙	Access Context Manager Reader	Access Context Manager	Enabled ⋮

Figure 6-17. Filter table

Step 4: Now filter the roles, by selecting Service Account Admin and then the Service Account Admin option, as shown in Figure 6-18.

Roles for Tutorial Project project

A role is a group of permissions that you can assign to members. You can create a role and add permissions to it, or copy an existing role and adjust its permissions. Learn more

Figure 6-18. *Filter table Service Account Admin option*

> **Step 5:** Once you select the Service Account Admin option, you will see the description and permissions under the panel at the right of the page (Figure 6-19).

Figure 6-19. *Service Account Admin description*

The Service Account Admin Permissions are as follows:

- `iam.serviceAccounts.create`
- `iam.serviceAccounts.delete`
- `iam.serviceAccounts.get`
- `iam.serviceAccounts.getIamPolicy`
- `iam.serviceAccounts.list`
- `iam.serviceAccounts.setIamPolicy`
- `iam.serviceAccounts.update`
- `resourcemanager.projects.get`
- `resourcemanager.projects.list`

Custom Roles

If predefined roles are not sufficient, we can define our own custom roles.

Role-Based Access Control

Kubernetes's native RBAC is a method of regulating access to cluster resources, based on the roles of individual users.

Through RBAC, we can define the actions (i.e., get, update, delete) that Kubernetes subjects (software, kubelets, users) are allowed to perform over Kubernetes entities (Pods, nodes).

RBAC is used to provide access to Kubernetes resources at the cluster level or within Kubernetes namespaces. With RBAC, we can also control access to Google accounts, Google Cloud service accounts, and Kubernetes service accounts.

GKE follows the CIS GKE Benchmark Recommendation 5.6.1: "Create administrative boundaries between resources using namespaces." As per the least-privilege principle, it is recommended that teams be given limited access to Kubernetes, by creating separate namespaces or clusters. GCP Cloud IAM and Kubernetes RBAC work together to facilitate this.

Kubernetes provides the following types of RBAC permissions:

> **Role and ClusterRole:** A set of permissions over a user or group of users. Role is always confined to a single namespace, while ClusterRole is cluster-scoped.

> **RoleBinding and ClusterRoleBinding:** These grant permissions defined in a Role/ClusterRole, respectively, to a user or group of users. RoleBindings are bound to a certain namespace, and ClusterRoleBindings are cluster-global.

For example, in Figure 6-20, Role is defined for the namespace monitoring and provided read-only permission (get, watch, and list) for all the Pods in the monitoring namespace.

```
kind: Role
apiVersion: rbac.authorization.k8s.io/v1
metadata:
  namespace: monitoring
  name: podreader
rules:
- apiGroups: [""] # "" indicates the core API group
  resources: ["pods"]
  verbs: ["get", "watch", "list"]
```

Figure 6-20. *Kubernetes Role*

Users and groups of users are called as subjects or groups of subjects, respectively. Now, after creating Role/ClusterRole, we must assign these to a subject or group of subjects in RoleBinding/ClusterRoleBinding.

In GKE subjects are of the following types (Table 6-2):

Table 6-2. *GKE Subject Types*

Subjects	Value Type	Description
Kubernetes service account	Service account	The name of a Kubernetes service account
Google Cloud user account	User	Registered email address of Google Cloud
Cloud IAM service account	User	Auto-generated Cloud IAM service account email address
G Suite Google Group address (Beta) on a verified domain	Group	Email address of a Google group that is itself a member of the Google group gke-security-groups@customerdomain.com

We have defined RoleBinding, as shown in Figure 6-21, to grant the podreader Role to GKE subjects.

```
kind: RoleBinding
apiVersion: rbac.authorization.k8s.io/v1
metadata:
  name: podreaderbinding
  namespace: monitoring
subjects:
# Kubernetes service account
- kind: ServiceAccount
  name: user
# Google Cloud user account
- kind: User
  name: user@example.com
# Cloud IAM service account
- kind: User
  name: tutorial-project-268109889@appspot.gserviceaccount.com
# G Suite Google Group
- kind: Group
  name: monitoring-group@example.com
roleRef:
  kind: Role
  name: podreader
  apiGroup: rbac.authorization.k8s.io
```

Figure 6-21. Kubernetes RoleBinding

Audit Logging

A Kubernetes cluster generates the Kubernetes audit logs, which record all the API calls to the GKE cluster. Security administrators can further analyze these logs, to investigate for security auditing and monitoring. GKE automatically records the Kubernetes audit log via Cloud audit logs and Stackdriver (now called Google Operations) logging. As a best practice, Google enables Cloud operations or Stackdriver logging by default, at the time of creating the GKE cluster.

Operating system logs are different from Cloud audit logs and Kubernetes audit logs. In order to access Kubernetes worker node (VM) OS-level logs, users can enable Linux audit logging using the GCP console.

Following are the types of audit logs:

Admin Activity log: This log contains those related to API calls and other administrator activities, such as modifying the GKE configuration, GKE resource metadata, etc. Whenever users create any object or change the access-management permissions, logs are recorded under the Admin Activity log. To view an Admin Activity log, users must have the following Cloud IAM roles: Logging/Logs Viewer or Project/Viewer. Admin Activity logging is enabled by default and at no extra cost.

Data Access log: This log records the logs of API calls for reading the configuration or metadata of GKE resources. Data-access operations performed on publicly shared resources are not recorded as logs by the Data Access log. To view the Data Access log, users must have the following Cloud IAM roles: Logging/Private Logs Viewer or Project/Viewer. The Data Access log should be enabled explicitly, and it's chargeable by GCP.

Viewing the Admin Activity Log Through the Google Cloud Console

Taking the following steps allows you to view the Admin Activity log.

Step 1: Log in to the GCP console page with your credentials, as mentioned in the "Accessing the GCP Console" section.

Step 2: Navigate to the Logs Viewer page in the Logging menu (Figure 6-22).

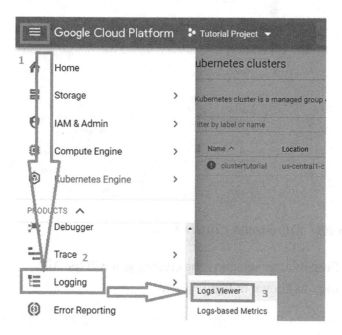

Figure 6-22. *Logs Viewer option*

Step 3: Near the top of the page, locate the drop-down menu for selecting a resource type. From the drop-down menu, select Kubernetes Cluster, then specify the Location or choose All locations. If you select a location, then select a specific cluster. In our case, we select the location as us-central1-c and select clustertutorial as a specific cluster, as shown in Figure 6-23.

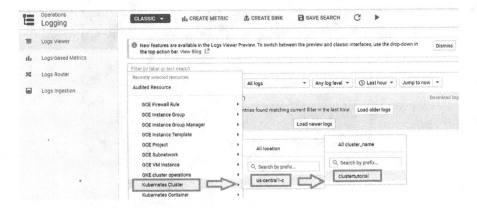

Figure 6-23. *Kubernetes Cluster logs*

Step 4: After selecting the cluster, you will see All logs, as shown in Figure 6-24.

Figure 6-24. *Kubernetes Cluster, All logs*

Step 5: The next menu to the right is for selecting a log. From the drop-down menu, select activity, then click OK, as shown in Figure 6-25.1.

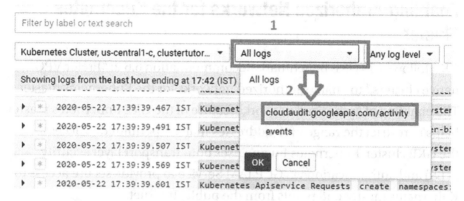

Figure 6-25.1. *Selecting the activity log*

After selecting "activity," you will see the relevant details, as shown in Figure 6-25.2. The display shows all log levels by default.

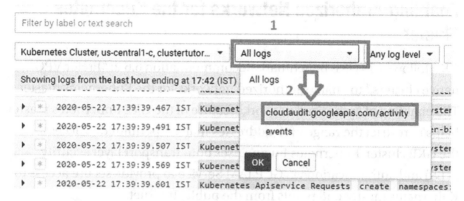

Figure 6-25.2. *Kubernetes Cluster, activity log*

Network Security

Following are best practices and recommendations for network security.

Enabling Authorized Networks for the Kubernetes Master

GKE follows CIS GKE Benchmark Recommendation 6.6.2: "Prefer VPC-native clusters," to enable authorized networks for the Kubernetes master. The enabling of authorized networks feature of the GKE Kubernetes master helps to restrict the range of IP addresses that are permitted to access the GKE cluster. Kubernetes Engine uses both transport layer security (TLS) and authentication via GCP IAM Service to provide secure access to Kubernetes master end points from the public Internet.

Authorized networks provide an additional layer of security, by limiting external, non-GCP network access to a specific set of network addresses, for example, your datacenter IP ranges.

Node Firewall

A node firewall mechanism helps to implement stateful firewall rules between GKE nodes that are based on the Compute Engine instance. Firewall rules restrict or allow traffic to a network. Firewall rules are applied to instances by using tags within the network. Tagging a network is a useful method with which to apply firewall rules and route to a specific VM instance. Tags don't have to be unique across multiple VPC networks. Users can create a network tag while creating the compute instance and edit later.

The following steps will add a tag in the existing compute instance:

> **Step 1:** Log in to the Google console, as described earlier in this chapter.

> **Step 2:** Navigate to VM instances page, as show in Figure 6-26.

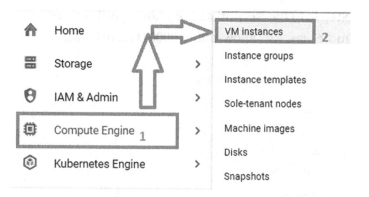

Figure 6-26. *VM instances page*

Step 3: Select an instance, as shown in Figure 6-27.

	Name ^	Zone	Recommendation	In use by	Internal IP	External IP	Connect	
	instance-1	us-central1-a			10.128.0.5 (nic0)	35.223.212.124	SSH ▾	⋮

Figure 6-27. *Selecting a VM instance*

Step 4: On the VM instance details page, click the Edit option, shown in Figure 6-28.

← VM instance details	✏ EDIT	⏻ RESET

✅ instance-1

Details   Monitoring

Remote access

SSH ▾ | Connect to serial console ▾

▢ Enable connecting to serial ports ❓

Figure 6-28. *Editing a VM instance*

Step 5: In the Network tags section, specify one or more tags, e.g., allow-traffic-9000 (Figure 6-29).

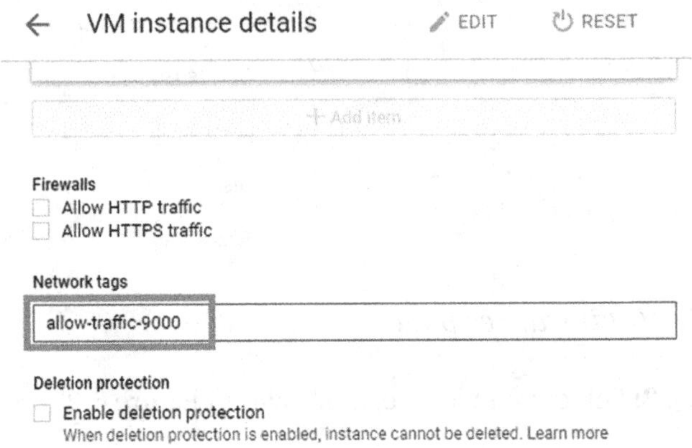

←   VM instance details   ✏ EDIT   ⏻ RESET

┼ Add item

Firewalls
☐ Allow HTTP traffic
☐ Allow HTTPS traffic

Network tags
allow-traffic-9000

Deletion protection
☐ Enable deletion protection
    When deletion protection is enabled, instance cannot be deleted. Learn more

Figure 6-29. *VM instance network tags*

Step 6: Finally, click Save (Figure 6-30).

Cloud API access scopes
You must stop the VM instance to edit its API access scopes
Allow default access
≫ Details

Save   Cancel

Figure 6-30. *VM instance network tags—Save*

In GKE, every node pool has its own set of tags, which can be used to manage firewall rules. By default, each compute instance of a node pool has a tag that identifies a specific Kubernetes Engine cluster (to which node pool it belongs). This tag is used in firewall rules that Kubernetes Engine creates automatically. Users can create custom tags at either cluster or node pool creation time, using the --tags flag in the gcloud command line, as follows.

In command 1, we create a firewall rule named `allow-9000-fwr`, to allow an internal load balancer to access port 9000, by specifying an — **allow** flag on all nodes that have the `allow-9000` tag.

Command 2 applies this firewall rule, while creating a Kubernetes cluster `clustertutorial` that has a custom `allow-9000` tag in the `---tag` flag, as follows.

Command 1:

```
gcloud compute firewall-rules create allow-
9000-fwr --target-tags allow-9000 --allow
tcp:9000 \

--network gke --source-range 130.211.0.0/22
```

Command 2:

```
gcloud container clusters create
clusterturorial --tags allow-9000
```

Enabling Network Policy for Pods' Secure Communication

GKE follows CIS GKE Benchmark Recommendation 6.6.7: "Ensure Network Policy is Enabled and set as appropriate." By default, all Pods in a Kubernetes cluster can communicate with one another. Users can control Pod-to-Pod communication through a network policy.

A network policy is a specification of how groups of Pods are allowed to communicate with one another and other network end points. Pods within a cluster connect over the network by using their allocated IP address (also known as a Pod IP address). A cluster administrator can restrict Pod-to-Pod communication by using network policy.

Network policy resources use *labels* to identify and select specific Pods and define rules that define what traffic is allowed to the selected Pods.

Once network policy is attached to a namespace in the GKE cluster for selecting a specific pod, it will accept or reject any connections as per the network policy.

We can define a network policy by using the Kubernetes NetworkPolicy API to create Pod-level firewall rules. These firewall rules decide which Pods and services can access one another inside the GKE cluster.

In GKE, we can enable network policy enforcement either while creating the Kubernetes Cluster or later.

GKE provides the following ways to enable network policy enforcement:

By gcloud tool

By console

By API

In this chapter, we cover two ways (gcloud and console) to enable network policy enforcement.

Enabling Network Policy Enforcement by the gcloud Command

Execute the following command, to enable network policy enforcement while creating a new cluster, by using the –enable-network-policy flag. Run the following command from Cloud SDK.

Command:

```
gcloud container clusters create cluster-
name --enable-network-policy
```

To enable network policy enforcement for an existing cluster, execute the following commands.

Command: Run the following gcloud command to enable the add-on by using flag --update-addons=N etworkPolicy=ENABLED.

```
gcloud container clusters update cluster-
name --update-addons=NetworkPolicy=ENABLED
```

Execute the following gcloud command, to enable network policy enforcement on an existing cluster, which in turn re-creates the cluster's node pools, with network policy enforcement enabled.

Command:

```
gcloud container clusters update cluster-
name --enable-network-policy
```

Enabling Network Policy Through the Google Console

Step 1: Navigate to the Google Kubernetes Engine menu in the Cloud console, as shown in Figure 6-31.

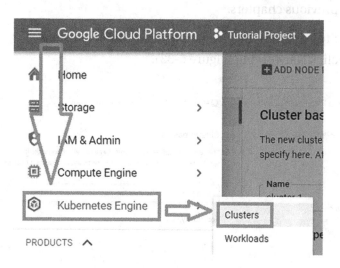

Figure 6-31. GKE cluster

Step 2: Click the Create cluster button (Figure 6-32).

Figure 6-32. *GKE Create cluster button*

Step 3: Configure your cluster, as explained in the previous chapters.

Step 4: From the navigation pane, under Cluster, click Networking (Figure 6-33).

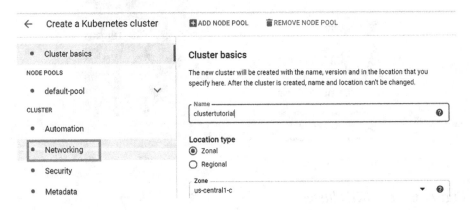

Figure 6-33. *GKE Cluster Networking option*

Step 5: Select the Enable network policy check box
(Figure 6-34).

● Networking		Reveals your intranode traffic to Google's networking f flow logs in the selected subnetwork.
● Security		☐ Enable NodeLocal DNSCache **Beta** ❷
● Metadata		☑ Enable HTTP load balancing ❷
● Features		☐ Enable master authorised networks ❷
		☑ Enable network policy ❷

Figure 6-34. *GKE Cluster Enable network policy option*

Step 6: Click the Create button, as shown in
Figure 6-35.

Figure 6-35. *GKE Cluster Create option*

Enabling Network Policy Enforcement for an Existing Cluster Through the Google Console

Step 1: Navigate to the Google Kubernetes Engine
menu in the Cloud console, as shown in the
preceding "Enabling Network Policy Through the
Google Console" section.

Step 2: Click the cluster for which you want to
enforce network policy and Click Edit, next to the
pencil icon (Figure 6-36).

Figure 6-36. *GKE Cluster Edit*

> **Step 3:** From the Network policy for master drop-
> down menu, select Enabled (Figure 6-37).

Figure 6-37. *GKE Cluster Edit drop-down Enabled option*

> **Step 4:** Click Save, and then click Edit again, once
> the cluster is updated (Figure 6-38).

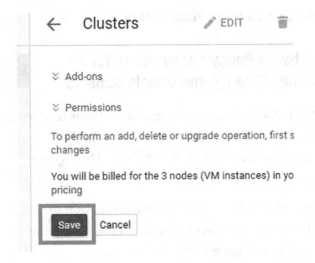

Figure 6-38. *GKE Cluster Edit—Save*

Step 5: From the Network policy for nodes drop-down menu, select Enabled (Figure 6-39).

Figure 6-39. *GKE Cluster Network policy for nodes drop-down Enabled option*

Step 6: Click Save, as shown in Figure 6-38, Step 4.

Creating a Network Policy

After enabling network policy enforcement for the cluster, we must define the actual network policy, using the Kubernetes NetworkPolicy API.

Figure 6-40 is an example of how network policy is defined through YAML in Kubernetes.

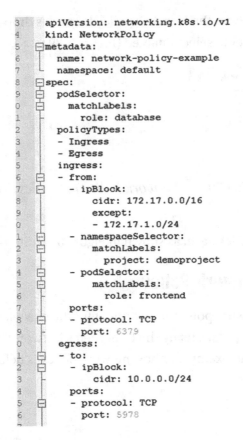

```
3    apiVersion: networking.k8s.io/v1
4    kind: NetworkPolicy
5    metadata:
6        name: network-policy-example
7        namespace: default
8    spec:
9        podSelector:
0          matchLabels:
1            role: database
2        policyTypes:
3        - Ingress
4        - Egress
5        ingress:
6        - from:
7          - ipBlock:
8              cidr: 172.17.0.0/16
9              except:
0              - 172.17.1.0/24
1          - namespaceSelector:
2              matchLabels:
3                project: demoproject
4          - podSelector:
5              matchLabels:
6                role: frontend
7          ports:
8          - protocol: TCP
9            port: 6379
0        egress:
1        - to:
2          - ipBlock:
3              cidr: 10.0.0.0/24
4          ports:
5          - protocol: TCP
6            port: 5978
```

Figure 6-40. *Network policy YAML*

Following are the mandatory fields to define NetworkPolicy:

- apiVersion

- kind

- metadata

- spec

The apiVersion, kind, and metadata fields have already been explained in earlier chapters of this book.

The spec field contains all those settings that define network restrictions within a given namespace.

podSelector selects a group of pods for which the policy applies.

In this sample policy, select pods with the label role= database. If you do not specify a value in podSelector, it considers all pods in the specified namespace defined under the metadata section.

policyTypes defines the type of traffic to be restricted (inbound as ingress, outbound as egress, or both). If we do not specify any policyTypes, Ingress will always be set by default, and egress will be set if the NetworkPolicy has any egress rules.

ingress includes inbound traffic whitelist rules.

This sample policy contains a single rule, which matches traffic on a single port from one of the following three sources:

- ipBlock

- namespaceSelector

- podSelector

ingress allows connections to all Pods in the default namespace with the label role=database on TCP port 6379, from any Pod in the default namespace with the label role=frontend, and from any Pod in a namespace with the label project= demoproject.

IP addresses allowed access are in the ranges 172.17.0.0–172.17.0.255 and 172.17.2.0–172.17.255.255 (i.e., all of 172.17.0.0/16, except 172.17.1.0/24), as shown in Figure 6-40.1.

```
ingress:
- from:
  - ipBlock:
      cidr: 172.17.0.0/16
      except:
      - 172.17.1.0/24
  - namespaceSelector:
      matchLabels:
          project: demoproject
  - podSelector:
      matchLabels:
          role: frontend
  ports:
  - protocol: TCP
    port: 6379
```

Figure 6-40.1. *Network policy with* ingress *YAML*

egress includes outbound traffic whitelist rules.

In this example, egress allows connections from any Pod in the default namespace with the label role=database to CIDR 10.0.0.0/24 on TCP port 5978, as shown in Figure 6-40.2.

```
egress:
- to:
  - ipBlock:
      cidr: 10.0.0.0/24
  ports:
  - protocol: TCP
    port: 5978
```

Figure 6-40.2. *Network policy with egress YAML*

Filtering Traffic Through a Load Balancer

GCP provides various types of load balancers for filtering incoming traffic. For example, the HTTP/HTTPS-based load balancer will terminate unauthorized requests and execute context-aware load balancing decisions. When we define a Kubernetes service type as a load balancer, GCP will create an external network load balancer and attach it with that Kubernetes service. The Kubernetes service connects with the various Pods, using their label to pass the request. Through kube-proxy, we can

filter the request at the node level. You need to provide the CIDR range
for whitelisting the ranges of IP address, to get access to the service, by
defining the loadBalancerSourceRanges configuration in the service.

In the following example, a load balancer will be created that is
only accessible to clients with IP addresses from 130.210.207.1 and
130.210.207.2, as illustrated in Figure 6-41.

```
apiVersion: v1
kind: Service
metadata:
  name: your_app_name
spec:
  ports:
  - port: 8736
    targetPort: 9346
  selector:
    app: test
  type: LoadBalancer
  loadBalancerSourceRanges:
  - 130.210.207.1/32
  - 130.210.207.2/32
```

Figure 6-41. loadBalancerSourceRanges

Creating a Private Kubernetes Cluster in GKE

Kubernetes nodes of private clusters are not accessible from the public
Internet. The workload (Pods and controllers) that are running in this
environment are also isolated from the public Internet. Kubernetes master
and its nodes communicate with each other privately, using VPC peering.
Private enabled Kubernetes cluster networks provide maximum security,
as services are not exposed to the public Internet.

Compliance and Minimal Host OS

Compliance consists of a set of rules, policies, specifications, or law defined according to the relevant industry or institution, e.g., health care, finance, government, etc. GCP products regularly undergo independent verification of their security, privacy, and compliance controls, certifications, verifications of compliance, or audit reports against standards.

GCP offers compliance by region, e.g., EMEA, United States, Asia Pacific, offering compliance by industry or agency.

GCP compliance offerings even go beyond the reports and certifications. They also provide documentation, guidelines, and legal assurances to the users, to align with laws, regulations, and frameworks. Google Kubernetes Engine compliance certifications include ISO 27001, ISO 27017, ISO 27108, HIPAA, and PCI-DSS.

By default, GKE uses COS images for configuring GKE nodes, and it has pre-installed Docker runtime and cloud-init, ensuring secure and fast deployment of GKE nodes. It is an open source project, maintained by Google under Chromium OS. Google implements several security design principles to construct COS.

Enabling COS provides the following security benefits:

- **Smaller attack surface:** COS has a smaller footprint, reducing instances' potential attack surface.

- **Locked-down:** COS instances include a locked-down firewall and other security settings by default.

- **Kernel hardening:** COS is enabled with many security hardening features for kernels, such as audit, kernel page table isolation, IMA, etc., to enforce security policies.

- **Automatic updates:** COS instances are configured to automatically download weekly updates as background. To use the latest updates, a reboot is required.

- **Access restriction:** By default, COS does not contain any accessible user account. It manages the user account and SSH keys by instance or project metadata. Since milestone 66 and later versions, it also supports access through IAM. Password-based login is disabled, and root logins are not allowed.

Auto-upgrade Components

CIS GKE Benchmark 6.5.3 recommends that users "Ensure Node Auto-Upgrade is enabled for GKE nodes." Node auto-upgrades keep nodes and node pools of the Kubernetes cluster updated with the latest and most stable version of Kubernetes. It also ensures new binaries of the operating system the nodes are fixed with and security issues are resolved without manual interference.

Enable Automatic Upgrades Through the Cloud Console

To enable auto-upgrades for the node pool, perform the following steps:

Step 1: Navigate to the Google Kubernetes Engine menu in the Cloud console, as shown in Figure 6-42.

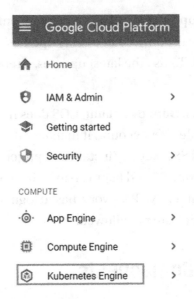

Figure 6-42. *Enabling auto-upgrade—Kubernetes Engine menu*

Step 2: Select the cluster option, as shown in
Figure 6-43.

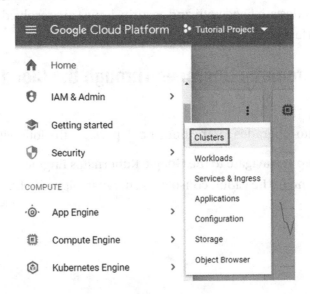

Figure 6-43. *Enabling auto-upgrade*

Step 3: Select your cluster and Click the cluster Edit button (pencil icon), as shown in Figure 6-44.

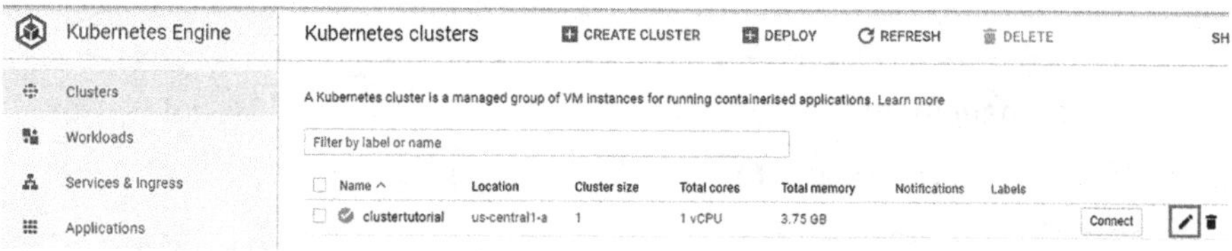

Figure 6-44. *Enabling auto-upgrade—Edit button*

Step 4: In the Node pools section, click the relevant node pool, as shown Figure 6-45.

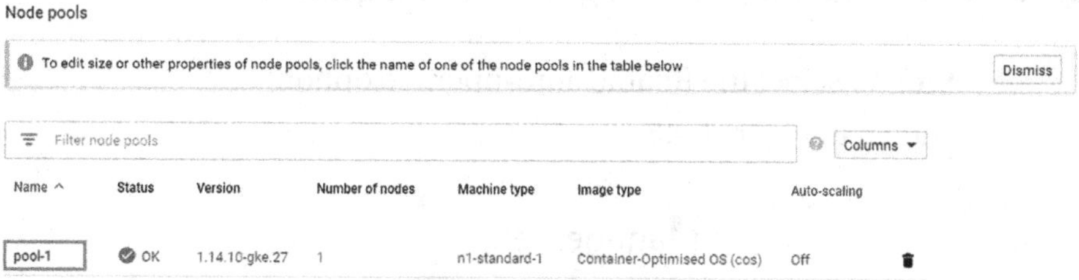

Figure 6-45. *Enabling auto-upgrade—Node pools*

Step 5: Click the Edit option, as shown in Figure 6-46.

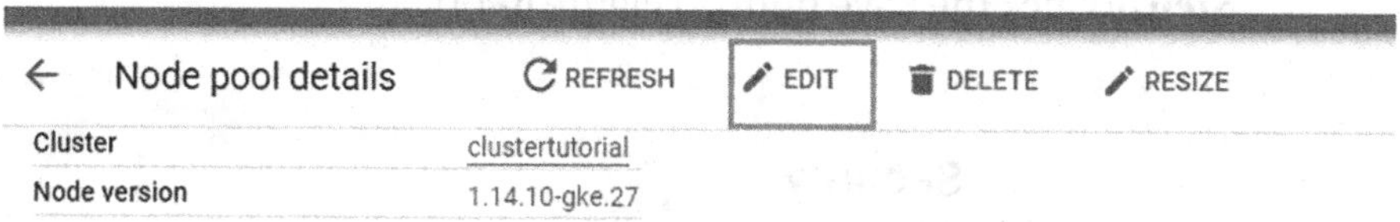

Figure 6-46. *Enabling Auto Upgrade—Edit option*

Step 6: Navigate to the Management section, shown in Figure 6-47.

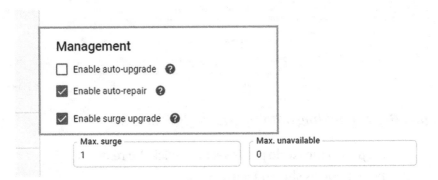

Figure 6-47. *Enabling auto-Upgrade—Management*

Step 7: Select the Enable auto-upgrade option, shown in Figure 6-48.

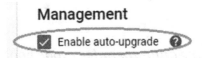

Figure 6-48. *Enabling auto-upgrade option*

Step 8: Click the Save button (Figure 6-49).

Figure 6-49. *Enabling auto-upgrade—Save button*

Step 9: After saving the changes, you will see that auto-upgrade options have been enabled, under the Management section of the Node pool details form, shown in Figure 6-50.

← Node pool details	C REFRESH	✎ EDIT
Boot disk size (per node)	100 GB	
Boot disk encryption	Google-managed	
Pre-emptible nodes	Disabled	
Maximum pods per node	110 (inherited from clustertutorial)	

Management

Auto-upgrade ❔	Enabled
Auto-repair ❔	Enabled

Figure 6-50. *Enabled auto-upgrade options*

When we create a cluster using the gcloud command, node auto-upgrade is currently enabled by default, and in case of default, node pool auto-upgrade is also enabled.

Enabling Automatic Node Repair

The node auto-repair feature keeps nodes in the Kubernetes cluster healthy and in running order. Enabling the automatic node repair feature helps GKE to perform health checks of cluster nodes on a regular basis and initiate repair processes, in case of consecutive health-check failure.

You can enable the automatic node repair option by executing the gcloud command or through the Cloud console.

Enabling Automatic Node Repair Through gcloud

Execute the following command to create a cluster with autorepair enabled.

Command:

```
gcloud container clusters create cluster-
name --zone compute-zone --enable-autorepair
```

The preceding command passes the cluster name in the cluster-name variable and the zone name in the compute-zone variable where you want to create your cluster.

Enabling Automatic Node Repair Through the Cloud Console

To enable automatic node repair through the Cloud console, perform the same steps in the "Enabling Automatic Upgrades Through the Cloud Console" section, up to step 5, and then, for additional changes, take the following steps:

Step 1: Go to the Management section, as shown in Figure 6-51.

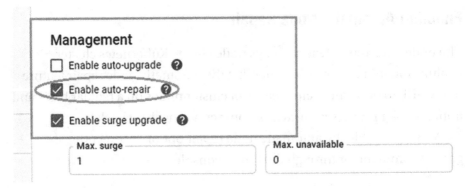

Figure 6-51. Enabling auto-repair—Management

Step 2: Click the Save button (Figure 6-52).

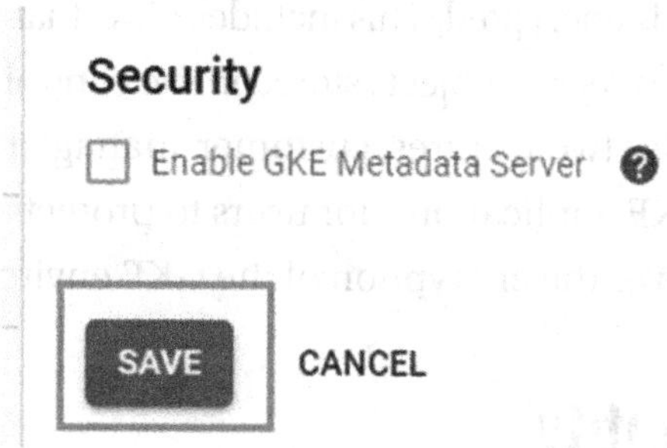

Security

☐ Enable GKE Metadata Server ❓

SAVE   CANCEL

Figure 6-52. *Enabling auto-repair—Save button*

Step 3: After you save the changes, you will be able to see, under the Management section of the Node pool details form, that the auto-repair option has been enabled, as shown in Figure 6-53.

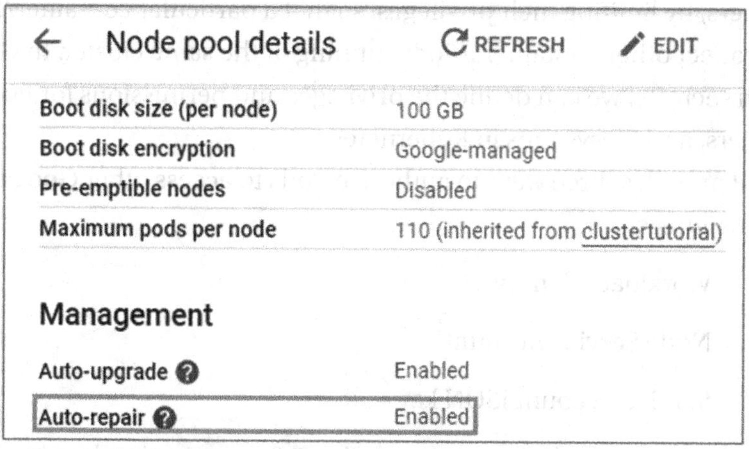

← **Node pool details**   ↻ REFRESH   ✎ EDIT

Boot disk size (per node)	100 GB
Boot disk encryption	Google-managed
Pre-emptible nodes	Disabled
Maximum pods per node	110 (inherited from clustertutorial)

Management

Auto-upgrade ❓	Enabled
Auto-repair ❓	Enabled

Figure 6-53. *Enabling auto-repair—Node pool details*

Encryption Keys and Secrets Encryption

By default, GKE data is encrypted. This includes disks that are attached to GKE nodes and Kubernetes secrets objects stored in the control plane database.

GCP also provides two features, customer-managed encryption keys(CMEK) and GKE applications, for users to protect and have additional control over the encryption of the GKE environment.

Workload Identity

Workloads are objects that define the rules according to which Pods in a Kubernetes cluster are deployed. In this section, you will see the best practices with which to secure workloads.

Defining Privileges and Access Control for Pods

For overall security of the cluster, we have to secure the Pods and containers, by limiting their privileges, so that a particular container/Pod cannot affect other containers/Pods running in the same cluster. In GKE, through security, we can define the privileges and permissions for Pods, containers, and filesystems in Kubernetes.

GCP provides three ways to authorize Pods to access other Google Cloud resources.

- Workload Identity

- Node Service Account

- Service Account JSON key

CIS GKE Benchmark Recommendation 6.2.2 recommends using dedicated Google Cloud Service Accounts and Workload Identity. For more information on this benchmark, visit the relevant site from the following link: https://cloud.google.com/kubernetes-engine/docs/how-to/hardening-your-cluster.

To access Google Cloud services from within the GKE cluster in a secure manner, GCP recommends using the Workload Identity feature. Workload Identity enables mapping of the Google service account to the Kubernetes Pod, which facilitates the elimination of the potential overload of managing the service account credential JSON file within the Pod or cluster. Now let's follow the steps to create a Workload Identity that connects the Google service account with the GKE service account.

> **Step 1:** Enable the Google Kubernetes Engine API by accessing the website from the following link: https://console.cloud.google.com/apis/library/container.googleapis.com.

> **Step 2:** Click the Activate Cloud Shell icon at the extreme right corner of the Google Cloud console as shown in (Figure 6-54).

Figure 6-54. *Activate Cloud Shell icon*

> **Step 3:** After Cloud Shell opens, execute the gcloud config command, to set project ID.

> **Command:**

> gcloud config set project tutorial-project-268109

In our case, tutorial-project-268109 is our project ID (Figure 6-55).

```
gcptutorialmail@cloudshell:~ (tutorial-project-268109)$ gcloud config set project tutorial-project-268109
Updated property [core/project].
```

Figure 6-55. gcloud config set ProjectID *command*

Step 4: Execute the following command, to set the zone (see also Figure 6-56).

Command:

```
gcloud config set compute/zone us-central1-c
```

```
gcptutorialmail@cloudshell:~ (tutorial-project-268109)$ gcloud config set compute/zone us-central1-c
Updated property [compute/zone].
```

Figure 6-56. gcloud config set compute/zone command

Step 5: Execute the following command, to set the region (Figure 6-57).

Command:

```
gcloud config set compute/region us-central1
```

```
gcptutorialmail@cloudshell:~ (tutorial-project-268109)$ gcloud config set compute/region us-central1
Updated property [compute/region].
```

Figure 6-57. gcloud config set compute/region command

Step 6: Enable the Cloud IAM Service Account Credentials API by clicking the following link: https://console.cloud.google.com/apis/api/iamcredentials.googleapis.com/.

Step 7: Create a cluster with Workload Identity enabled, by executing the following command.

Command:

```
gcloud beta container clusters create
cluster-name --release-channel regular \
--workload-pool=project-id.svc.id.goog
```

Replace cluster-name and project-id with your cluster name and project ID, respectively.

Our cluster name is `clustertutorial`, and `tutorial-project-268109` is our project ID.

`gcloud` beta container clusters create `clustertutorial --release-channel regular \`

`--workload-pool=tutorial-project-268109.svc.id.goog`

The preceding is illustrated in Figure 6-58.

```
gcptutorialmail@cloudshell:~(tutorial-project-268109)$ gcloud beta container clusters create clustertu
orial \
>    --release-channel regular \
>    --workload-pool=tutorial-project-268109.svc.id.goog
```

Figure 6-58. *Creating a cluster with Workload Identity*

It will take several minutes to create the cluster. Wait until you receive the details highlighted in Figure 6-59.

```
Created [https://container.googleapis.com/v1beta1/projects/flowing-garage-267211/zones/us-central1-c/
lusters/clustertutorial].
To inspect the contents of your cluster, go to: https://console.cloud.google.com/kubernetes/workload_
gcloud/us-central1-c/clustertutorial?project=flowing-garage-267211
kubeconfig entry generated for clustertutorial.
NAME             LOCATION       MASTER_VERSION  MASTER_IP      MACHINE_TYPE   NODE_VERSION   NUM_NODE
  STATUS
clustertutorial  us-central1-c  1.16.8-gke.15   34.72.172.220  n1-standard-1  1.16.8-gke.15  3
  RUNNING
```

Figure 6-59. *The created cluster*

Step 8: Execute the following command, to configure the kubectl to communicate with the cluster (Figure 6-60).

Command:

`gcloud container clusters get-credentials clustertutorial`

```
gcptutorialmail@cloudshell:~(tutorial-project-268109)$ gcloud container clusters get-credentials clust
rtutorial
Fetching cluster endpoint and auth data.
kubeconfig entry generated for clustertutorial.    _
```

Figure 6-60. *Configure kubectl*

Step 9: Create the Google service account by
executing the following command (Figure 6-61).

Command:

```
gcloud iam service-accounts create workload-
service-account-name
```

```
gcptutorialmail@cloudshell:~(tutorial-project-268109)$ gcloud iam service-accounts create workload-serv
ice-account-name
Created service account [workload-service-account-name].
```

Figure 6-61. *Creating a Google service account*

Step 10: Create the namespace, k8s-service-
account-namespace, to use for the Kubernetes
service account, by executing the following
command (Figure 6-62).

Command:

```
kubectl create namespace k8s-service-
account-namespace
```

```
gcptutorialmail@cloudshell:~(tutorial-project-268109)$ kubectl create namespace k8s-service-account-nam
espace
namespace/k8s-service-account-namespace created
```

Figure 6-62. *Creating the namespace to use the Kubernetes service
account*

Step 11: Create the Kubernetes service account
(k8s-service-account-name), by executing the
following command (Figure 6-63).

Command:

```
kubectl create serviceaccount --namespace
k8s-service-account-namespace k8s-service-
account-name
```

k8s-service-account-namespace is the Kubernetes
namespace created in step 10.

k8s-service-account-name is the Kubernetes
service account name.

```
gcptutorialmail@cloudshell:~(tutorial-project-268109)$ kubectl create serviceaccount --namespace k8s-s
rvice-account-namespace  k8s-service-account-name
serviceaccount/k8s-service-account-name created
```

Figure 6-63. *Output of the Kubernetes service account creation*

Step 12: Execute the following command, to allow
the Kubernetes service account to be mapped to the
Google service account, by creating a Cloud IAM
policy binding between the two accounts.

Command:

```
gcloud iam service-accounts add-iam-policy-
binding \ --role roles/iam.workloadIdentityUser
\ --member "serviceAccount:tutorial-
project-268109.svc.id.goog[k8s-service-account-
namespace/k8s-service-account-name]" \
workload-service-account-name@tutorial-
project-268109.iam.gserviceaccount.com
```

tutorial-project-268109 is the project ID.

k8s-service-account-namespace is the Kubernetes
namespace.

k8s-service-account-name is the Kubernetes
service account.

`workload-service-account-name` is the name of the Google service account.

Figure 6-64 shows the output of the commands linking the Google and Kubernetes service accounts.

```
gcptutorialmail@cloudshell:~(tutorial-project-268109)$gcloud iam service-accounts add-iam-policy-bind:
ng \
>   --role roles/iam.workloadIdentityUser \
>   --member "serviceAccount:flowing-garage-267211.svc.id.goog[k8s-service-account-namespace/k8s-serv:
ce-account-name]" \
>   workload-service-account-name@flowing-garage-267211.iam.gserviceaccount.com
Updated IAM policy for serviceAccount [workload-service-account-name@flowing-garage-267211.iam.gservi(
eaccount.com].
bindings:
- members:
  - serviceAccount:flowing-garage-267211.svc.id.goog[k8s-service-account-namespace/k8s-service-account
-name]
  role: roles/iam.workloadIdentityUser
etag: BwWmd6174xE=
version: 1
```

Figure 6-64. *Output of the command linking the Google and Kubernetes service accounts*

Step 13: Add the `iam.gke.io/gcp-service-account=`**gsa-name@project-id** annotation to the Kubernetes service account, using the email address of the Google service account, by executing the following command (Figure 6-65).

Command:

`kubectl annotate serviceaccount \`
`--namespace k8s-service-account-namespace`
`\ k8s-service-account-name \ iam.gke.io/gcp-`
service-account=workload-service-account-name@
projectid.iam.gserviceaccount.com

```
gcptutorialmail@cloudshell:~ (tutorial-project-268109)$ kubectl annotate serviceaccount \
>   --namespace k8s-service-account-namespace \
>   k8s-service-account-name \
>   iam.gke.io/gcp-service-account=workload-service-account-name@project-id.iam.gserviceaccount.com
serviceaccount/k8s-service-account-name annotated
```

Figure 6-65. *Adding the `iam.gke.io/gcp-service-account` annotation to the Kubernetes service account*

Step 14: Verify that the service accounts are configured correctly, by executing following command (Figure 6-66).

Command:

```
kubectl run -it \--generator=run-pod/
v1 \--image google/cloud-sdk:slim
\--serviceaccount k8s-service-account-name \
--namespace k8s-service-account-namespace \
workload-identity-test
```

```
gcptutorialmail@cloudshell:~ (tutorial-project-268109)$  kubectl run -it \
>    --generator=run-pod/v1 \
>    --image google/cloud-sdk:slim \
>    --serviceaccount k8s-service-account-name \
>    --namespace k8s-service-account-namespace \
>    workload-identity-test
Flag --generator has been deprecated, has no effect and will be removed in the future.
```

Figure 6-66. *Verifying the service accounts*

It may take few minutes to download the `cloud-sdk` image. After the download is complete, the interactive shell is launched automatically. Execute the following command, to verify the active service account.

Command:

```
gcloud auth list
```

If the service accounts are correctly configured, the Google service account email address is listed as the active (and only) identity (Figure 6-67).

```
root@workload-identity-test :/# gcloud auth list
                        Credentialed Accounts
ACTIVE   ACCOUNT
*          workload-service-account-name@project-id.iam.gserviceaccount.com

To set the active account, run:
    $ gcloud config set account `ACCOUNT`
```

Figure 6-67. *Verifying the active service accounts*

Managed SSL Certificates

Kubernetes provides ingress objects to route the HTTPS-based traffic to applications running in the GKE cluster. The GKE ingress controller creates the Google Cloud HTTP(S) Load Balancer, which can be either external or internal, depending on the configuration of the Kubernetes service. To make a secure connection between a load balancer and a Kubernetes service, GKE recommends the HTTPS load balancer with an SSL certificate.

GCP supports the following types of SSL certificates.

> **Self-Managed Certificates**: Self-managed certificates are those that can be obtained by customers from any certificate authority. Managing and renewing self-managed certificates is the customer's responsibility.

> **Google-Managed Certificates**: Google-managed SSL certificates are obtained and managed for the customer by Google Cloud and renewed automatically. Google-managed SSL certificates are based on customer-specific domains. They are available in beta versions for all GKE versions, at the time of writing this book.

Application Development and Release Security

Application development and release security are broadly classified under three major phases:

- Development phase
- Build phase
- Deployments phase

The security activities that are performed during the containerized application development and release life cycle on GKE are illustrated in Figure 6-68.

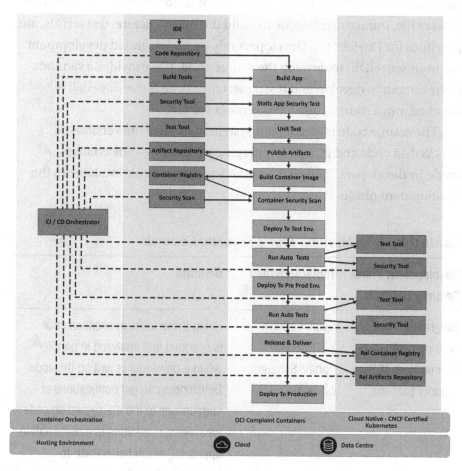

Figure 6-68. *Application development and release security controls in CI/CD*

Development Phase

In the development phase, the application code is developed by developers according to the business requirement. A typical code for a containerized application includes the application code, unit testing code, Docker file, infrastructure code to build the infrastructure, test scripts, and pipelines for DevSecOps. Developers rely on an integrated development environment (IDE) to develop the source code. IDE provides a sandbox environment to develop and test code. Once code is developed, it is checked into a source code management system.

The source code management system maintains the versions of checked-in code and is used for merging and tracing code changes made by developers. Table 6-3 lists the security controls available in the development phase.

Table 6-3. *Development Phase Security Controls*

Development Phase Security Controls	Tools/Activities	Benefits
Integrated development environment (IDE) security plug-ins	Synk, CodeDX, Whitesource, Fortify, Sonarlint, binskim	Using these tools, application code is scanned and analyzed in parallel when a developer is writing the code. Developers can get notifications or suggestions in the IDE regarding code weakness, in addition to a remediation approach, which helps them to improve their coding skills and code quality. This practice is known as shift-left testing.

(continued)

Table 6-3. (*continued*)

Development Phase Security Controls	Tools/Activities	Benefits
Source code repository security plug-in	Gitrob, gitleaks, Google Cloud Source Repositories	Applications that use tokens or private keys to communicate with an external service.
		As a best practice, tokens and secrets should not be saved in a source code management system. Secrets and tokens should be saved in a secret vault, e.g., a HashiCorp vault or GCP-provided Cloud KMS service.
		GCP provides Cloud Source Repositories with inbuilt security features to detect security keys and prohibit git push action, in the case of a policy violation.

Build Phase

Once the code is checked into SCM, a build phase is triggered, either manually or automatically, via the web hook REST API call to the CI/CD pipeline. In the build phase, the first step is to perform open source compliance and license scanning, to determine any security vulnerabilities in open source libraries used by the developers. Once completed, the code is compiled, and unit test cases are executed, as per the build tools, e.g., Maven. If no errors occur during the build phase, static code analysis is kicked off, to uncover security vulnerabilities, e.g., use of broken or risky cryptographic algorithms, SQL injection in application code that makes applications susceptible to attack. Popular tools to detect such vulnerabilities include SonarQube, Veracode, and Appscan.

The last step of the build phase is to create the deployable unit known as artifacts and stored in a repository like Artifactory. If the build fails, owing to any reason, e.g., a code compile issue or unit test failure, the build process stops, and notifications are sent to the team, to rectify the issue. Table 6-4 lists the security controls available in the build phase.

Table 6-4. Build Phase Security Controls

Build Phase Security Controls	Tools/Activities	Benefits
Open source compliance and licensing	Blackduck, Whitesource	These tools help to identify any security vulnerabilities in open source libraries used by the developer and ensure that the developer does not violate any open source licensing.
Static code analysis (SAST)	SonarQube, Veracode, Checkmarx	Static code analysis tools scan the source code and binaries against the security rules defined by OWSAP or CVS, to detect security vulnerabilities, e.g., use of a broken or risky cryptographic algorithm, SQL injection, etc., and provide recommendations to resolve them.

(continued)

Table 6-4. (*continued*)

Build Phase Security Controls	Tools/Activities	Benefits
Artifacts security scanning	Artifacts repository tools, such as JFrog Artifactory, Nexus	Artifact repositories are used to store version-controlled binaries with role-based access to authorized users. This provides improved build stability, by reducing reliance on external repositories. Auditing on stored artifacts is also performed. JFrog provides Xray. It scans all the stored artifacts and dependencies. This provides unprecedented visibility, enabling Xray to determine the impact of any vulnerability or issues discovered in artifacts.

Development and Release Phase

Development and release is the final phase, in which artifacts are deployed on various environments, e.g., development, testing, and production. Promotion of build artifacts depends on such factors as passing tests (for function, performance, load, and stress) and security scans, e.g., Docker image and Container scanning, dynamic application security. Additionally, security monitoring is enabled, to promote security incident detection and management. Reporting and dashboard are used to show the aggregate metrics from multiple tools, to create a monitoring interface for software development teams.

Table 6-5 lists the security controls used in the deployment and release.

Table 6-5. *Deployment and Release Phase Security Controls*

Deployment and Release Phase	Tools/Activities	Benefits
Container Image security tool	AquaSec, TwistLock, Sysdig Secure. GCP provides container analysis to scan the vulnerabilities in containers.	These solutions ease the container hardening process and provide vulnerabilities reports and recommendations.
Container enforcement policy	Black Duck, WhiteSource	These help to identify any security vulnerabilities in open source libraries used by a developer and ensure that the developer does not violate any open source licensing.
Dynamic application security test (DAST)	Appscan, OWSAP ZAP, Fortify	DAST analysis tools try to hack an application, by SQL injection, cross-site scripting, etc. DAST identifies vulnerabilities earlier in the software development life cycle.
Monitoring, dashboarding, and reporting	Stackdriver (now Google Operations), GCP Security Command Center, Sysdig, Prometheus, Splunk, Kibana, Grafana, GCP Data Studio	These solutions simplify operations of containerized applications, by providing monitoring and dashboarding and help operations teams in the regular maintenance of the GKE infrastructure and deployed applications.

(continued)

Table 6-5. (*continued*)

Deployment and Release Phase	Tools/Activities	Benefits
Continuous compliance and runtime security	AppArmor, Seccomp, Twistlock, AquaSec, Sysdig Secure	These solutions perform security scans on running Docker containers, to determine security vulnerabilities and safeguard the Linux kernel from kernel-level service attacks.

Summary

In this chapter, you learned about the various security and compliance controls provided by GCP to manage security aspects of GKE. You also learned how security must be integrated in the software development life cycle while developing applications for the GKE platform. In the next chapter, we will learn about the Grafana dashboards and Stackdriver (now Google Operations) tools that can help us to monitor and manage our GKE infrastructure.

## CHAPTER 7

GKE Dashboarding Using Stackdriver (Google Operations) and Grafana

In this chapter, you will learn how to create dashboards for GKE, using Stackdriver (Google Operations) and Grafana. Following are the topics covered:

- Introduction to Google Stackdriver (Cloud Operations)
- Setting Up Google Stackdriver (Google Operations) with Grafana

Introduction to Google Stackdriver (Google Operations)

Google Stackdriver (Google Operations) is a monitoring service that provides IT teams with performance data about applications and virtual machines (VMs) running on the GCP and the Amazon Web Services (AWS) public cloud. It is based on collectd, an open source daemon that collects system and application performance metrics. It includes capabilities that

© Navin Sabharwal, Piyush Pandey 2020
N. Sabharwal and P. Pandey, *Pro Google Kubernetes Engine*,
https://doi.org/10.1007/978-1-4842-6243-6_7

focus especially on Kubernetes operators and other features of Kubernetes, such as CPU and memory utilization. Cluster information can be viewed by its infrastructure, workloads, and containers.

Grafana is an open observability platform that can be used with Google Operations as a visualization layer.

In this chapter, you will learn how to install Grafana, using Helm templates. We will use the Sock Shop application that we deployed on a GKE cluster in Chapter 5 and configure Google Operations as a back end with which Grafana can create dashboards displaying key observability details about the cluster and applications running on it.

Setting Up Google Stackdriver (Google Operations) with Grafana

In this section, we will deploy Grafana in a dedicated namespace in the cluster (created in Chapter 6), using a Helm chart and template. Helm is an open source package manager for Kubernetes. Grafana ships with built-in support for Google Operations (Stackdriver).

Setting Up the Environment

Step 1: The first step in using Google Operations is to enable the Cloud Resource Manager API on your project ("Tutorial Project"). To do this, go to the API dashboard screen (Figures 7-1 and 7-2).

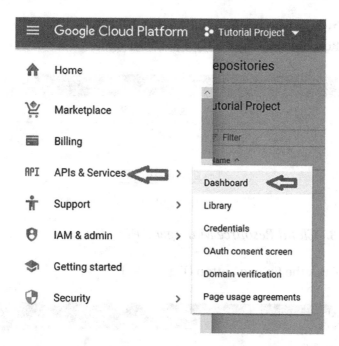

Figure 7-1. *API dashboard navigation*

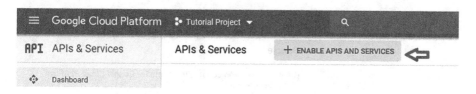

Figure 7-2. *API Dashboard Navigation*

Step 2: Search for cloud resource API and click Cloud Resource Manager API on the link (Figure 7-3).

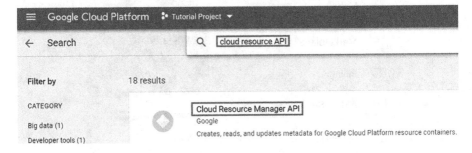

Figure 7-3. *Cloud Resource Manager API*

Click the Enable button (Figure 7-4).

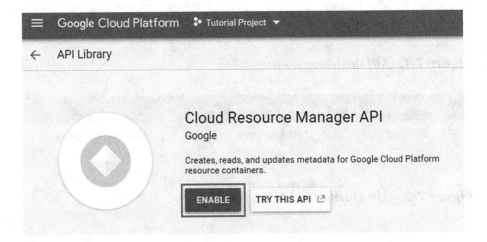

Figure 7-4. *Enabling the Cloud Resource Manager API*

Step 3: Clicking the Enable button will lead to the page shown in Figure 7-5. Now the Cloud Resource Manager driver is enabled for the project.

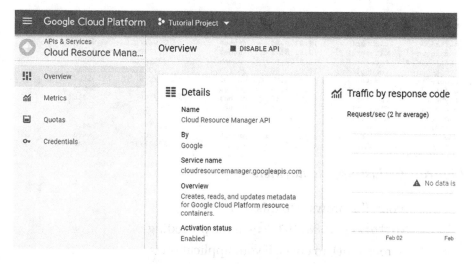

Figure 7-5. *Enabled Cloud Resource Manager driver*

Deploying and Validating Application Deployment on the GKE Cluster

As we deleted the deployed application at the end of Chapter 6, repeat the earlier steps to deploy the Sock Shop application. In this section, we validate the deployment of the Sock Shop application on the GKE Cluster by running the following command:

> **Command:** `kubectl get services -n sock-shop`

> **Output:** The following output (Figure 7-6) will be the result of executing the preceding command.

```
gcptutorialmail@cloudshell:~/GCP (tutorial-project-268109)$ kubectl get services -n sock-shop
NAME            TYPE           CLUSTER-IP      EXTERNAL-IP       PORT(S)          AGE
carts           ClusterIP      10.81.7.91      <none>            80/TCP           9m57s
carts-db        ClusterIP      10.81.8.83      <none>            27017/TCP        9m58s
catalogue       ClusterIP      10.81.5.42      <none>            80/TCP           9m54s
catalogue-db    ClusterIP      10.81.6.238     <none>            3306/TCP         9m55s
front-end       LoadBalancer   10.81.2.86      35.188.192.249    80:31010/TCP     9m53s
orders          ClusterIP      10.81.8.59      <none>            80/TCP           9m50s
orders-db       ClusterIP      10.81.2.44      <none>            27017/TCP        9m52s
payment         ClusterIP      10.81.4.16      <none>            80/TCP           9m49s
queue-master    ClusterIP      10.81.10.18     <none>            80/TCP           9m48s
rabbitmq        ClusterIP      10.81.12.53     <none>            5672/TCP         9m47s
shipping        ClusterIP      10.81.11.36     <none>            80/TCP           9m45s
user            ClusterIP      10.81.11.29     <none>            80/TCP           9m43s
user-db         ClusterIP      10.81.10.199    <none>            27017/TCP        9m44s
```

Figure 7-6. *List App deployment*

> Point the browser to this URL
> (http://35.188.192.249 in the preceding
> screenshot), to check if your application is
> accessible (Figure 7-7).

Figure 7-7. *Deployed application*

Deploying Grafana

In this section, we deploy Grafana in a dedicated namespace in our cluster, using a Helm chart and template. Helm is an open source package manager for Kubernetes.

Step 1: Execute the following command to initialize Helm.

Command: `helm init`

Output: The following output will result after the preceding command is executed (Figure 7-8).

```
gcptutorialmail@cloudshell:~ (tutorial-project-268109)$ helm init
Creating /home/gcptutorialmail/.helm
Creating /home/gcptutorialmail/.helm/repository
Creating /home/gcptutorialmail/.helm/repository/cache
Creating /home/gcptutorialmail/.helm/repository/local
Creating /home/gcptutorialmail/.helm/plugins
Creating /home/gcptutorialmail/.helm/starters
Creating /home/gcptutorialmail/.helm/cache/archive
Creating /home/gcptutorialmail/.helm/repository/repositories.yaml
Adding stable repo with URL: https://kubernetes-charts.storage.googleapis.com
Adding local repo with URL: http://127.0.0.1:8879/charts
$HELM_HOME has been configured at /home/gcptutorialmail/.helm.

Tiller (the Helm server-side component) has been installed into your Kubernetes Cluster.

Please note: by default, Tiller is deployed with an insecure 'allow unauthenticated users' policy.
To prevent this, run `helm init` with the --tiller-tls-verify flag.
For more information on securing your installation see: https://docs.helm.sh/using_helm/#securing-your-helm-ins
allation
```

***Figure 7-8.** Helm initialization*

Step 2: Execute the following command to update the local Helm repository.

Command: `helm repo update`

Output: The following output will result after the preceding command is executed (Figure 7-9).

```
gcptutorialmail@cloudshell:~ (tutorial-project-268109)$ helm repo update
Hang tight while we grab the latest from your chart repositories...
...Skip local chart repository
...Successfully got an update from the "stable" chart repository
Update Complete.
gcptutorialmail@cloudshell:~ (tutorial-project-268109)$ []
```

***Figure 7-9.** Helm repo update*

Step 3: Execute the following command to download Grafana.

Command: `helm fetch stable/grafana --untar`

Output: Figure 7-10 shows the output that results after the preceding command is executed.

```
gcptutorialmail@cloudshell:~ (tutorial-project-268109)$ helm fetch stable/grafana --untar
gcptutorialmail@cloudshell:~ (tutorial-project-268109)$ []
```

Figure 7-10. *Downloading Grafana*

Step 4: Create a namespace dedicated to Grafana that will be deployed in the same cluster, by executing the following command.

Command: `kubectl create ns grafana`

Output: The following output will result after the preceding command is executed (Figure 7-11).

```
gcptutorialmail@cloudshell:~ (tutorial-project-268109)$ kubectl create ns grafana
namespace/grafana created
gcptutorialmail@cloudshell:~ (tutorial-project-268109)$ []
```

Figure 7-11. *Creating a namespace in Grafana*

Step 5: Now we will use a Helm chart to create the `.yaml` file. Execute the following commands:

Command: (1) `helm template grafana – namespace grafana grafana > grafana.yaml`

Command: (2) `ll`

Run the preceding command to list the `grafana. yaml` file created.

Output: Figure 7-12 shows the output from the first of the preceding commands.

```
gcptutorialmail@cloudshell:~$ helm template grafana --namespace grafana grafana > grafana.yaml
```

Figure 7-12. *Creating a namespace in Grafana*

Figure 7-13 shows the resulting output from executing the second of the preceding commands.

```
gcptutorialmail@cloudshell:~$ ll
-rw-r--r-- 1 gcptutorialmail gcptutorialmail 12060 Feb 27 16:27 grafana.yaml
```

Figure 7-13. *Output of the Grafana .yaml file*

Step 6: Now that the .yaml file has been created, run the following command to deploy Grafana.

Command: kubectl apply -f grafana.yaml -n grafana

Output: Figure 7-14 shows the output after executing the preceding command.

```
gcptutorialmail@cloudshell:~$ kubectl apply -f grafana.yaml -n grafana
podsecuritypolicy.policy/release-name-grafana configured
podsecuritypolicy.policy/release-name-grafana-test configured
secret/release-name-grafana created
configmap/release-name-grafana created
configmap/release-name-grafana-test created
serviceaccount/release-name-grafana created
serviceaccount/release-name-grafana-test created
clusterrole.rbac.authorization.k8s.io/release-name-grafana-clusterrole configured
clusterrolebinding.rbac.authorization.k8s.io/release-name-grafana-clusterrolebinding unchanged
role.rbac.authorization.k8s.io/release-name-grafana created
role.rbac.authorization.k8s.io/release-name-grafana-test created
rolebinding.rbac.authorization.k8s.io/release-name-grafana created
rolebinding.rbac.authorization.k8s.io/release-name-grafana-test created
service/release-name-grafana created
pod/release-name-grafana-test created
deployment.apps/release-name-grafana created
```

Figure 7-14. *Deploying Grafana with a YAML configuration*

Step 7: After deployment, verify the installation, using the following command.

Command: `kubectl get pods -n grafana`

Output: Figure 7-15 shows the output of the preceding command.

```
gcptutorialmail@cloudshell:~ (tutorial-project-268109)$ kubectl get pods -n grafana
NAME                                      READY   STATUS    RESTARTS   AGE
release-name-grafana-6bc7fbfc47-bhgtn     1/1     Running   0          3d22h
release-name-grafana-test                 0/1     Error     0          3d22h
```

Figure 7-15. *List of Pods for Grafana*

Connecting with the Grafana Installation

The preceding steps will execute the installation of Grafana in the same cluster in which the Sock Shop application is deployed. Following are the steps used to connect with the Grafana installation.

Step 1: To connect with Grafana, first get the password, using the following command, and copy the output.

Command: `kubectl get secret --namespace grafana release-name-grafana -o jsonpath= "{.data.admin-password}" | base64 --decode ; echo`

Output: Figure 7-16 shows the output of the preceding command.

```
gcptutorialmail@cloudshell:~ (tutorial-project-268109)$ kubectl get secret --namespace grafan
a release-name-grafana -o jsonpath="{.data.admin-password}" | base64 --decode ; echo
MWQ7yUKCKT4uSS12eP7eOYmEOC10I5423oxdyzU9
```

Figure 7-16. *Secret key for Grafana installation*

After running the command, the following is the output sample generated. (Check your specific setup values before moving to next step.)

MWQ7yUKCKT4uSSl2eP7eOYmEOC10I5423oxdyzU9

Step 2: To use the Pod name in the current session, employ the following command, to capture the name of the Grafana Pod as a variable.

Command: export GRAFANA_POD=$(kubectl get pods --namespace grafana -l "app=grafana,release=grafana" -o jsonpath="{.items[0].metadata.name}")

Output: Figure 7-17 illustrates the output of the preceding command.

```
gcptutorialmail@cloudshell:~ (tutorial-project-268109)$ export GRAFANA_POD=$(kubectl get pods
 --namespace grafana -l "app=grafana,release=grafana" -o jsonpath="{.items[0].metadata.name}"
)
error: error executing jsonpath "{.items[0].metadata.name}": Error executing template: array
index out of bounds: index 0, length 0. Printing more information for debugging the template:
        template was:
                {.items[0].metadata.name}
        object given to jsonpath engine was:
                map[string]interface {}{"apiVersion":"v1", "items":[]interface {}{}, "kind":"
List", "metadata":map[string]interface {}{"resourceVersion":"", "selfLink":""}}
```

Figure 7-17. *Setting the Grafana Pod details into a variable*

Step 3: To enable access to the Grafana UI, use the port forwarding command. Before running the port forwarding command, get the name of the Grafana Pod name, using the first command, and copy the name into the second command.

Command: (1) kubectl get pods -n grafana

Command: (2) kubectl port-forward release-name-grafana-6bc7fbfc47-bhgtn 3000 -n grafana

Output: Figure 7-18 shows the output of the code to name the Grafana Pod.

```
gcptutorialmail@cloudshell:~$ kubectl get pods -n grafana

NAME                                  READY   STATUS    RESTARTS   AGE
release-name-grafana-6bc7fbfc47-bhgtn 1/1     Running   0          4d18h
release-name-grafana-test             0/1     Error     0          4d18h
```

Figure 7-18. *Getting the Grafana Pod name*

Figure 7-19 is the output of the port forwarding. It will set Grafana to run on port 3000.

```
gcptutorialmail@cloudshell:~ (tutorial-project-268109)$ kubectl port-forward release-name-gra
fana-6bc7fbfc47-bhgtn 3000 -n grafana
Forwarding from 127.0.0.1:3000 -> 3000
```

Figure 7-19. *Port forwarding details for accessing Grafana*

Step 4: Now navigate to the web preview in Cloud Shell, to access the UI, after changing the port to 3000. Navigate to web preview icon at the top right ➤ Change port ➤ 3000 (Figure 7-20).

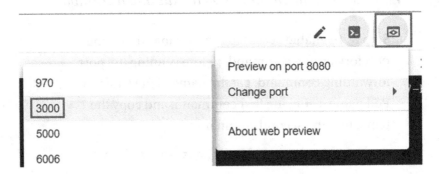

Figure 7-20. *Accessing Grafana*

Step 5: Step 4 will display the Grafana dashboard
in the browser. enter "admin" as the username, and
enter your setup-specific password (the password
following is used in the authors' setup), generated in
step 1, as shown in Figure 7-21.

`MWQ7yUKCKT4uSSl2eP7eOYmEOC10I5423oxdyzU9`

Figure 7-21. *Grafana login page*

After entering the username and password, the
dashboard will be displayed, as shown in Figure 7-22.

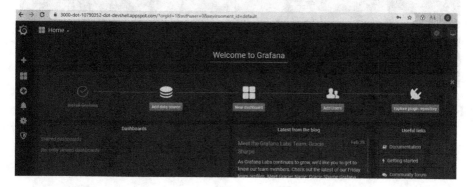

Figure 7-22. *Grafana main page*

Data Source Configuration

Step 1: Click the Add data source icon (Figure 7-23).

Figure 7-23. Add data source icon

Step 2: Search for Stackdriver (Google Operations) data source by typing "Stack" in the search text box. This will display the list including the Stackdriver (Google Operations) data source. Click the Select button (Figure 7-24).

Figure 7-24. Search data source

Step 3: Upon selecting the data source, the Stackdriver (Google Operations) Authentication screen will appear (Figure 7-25).

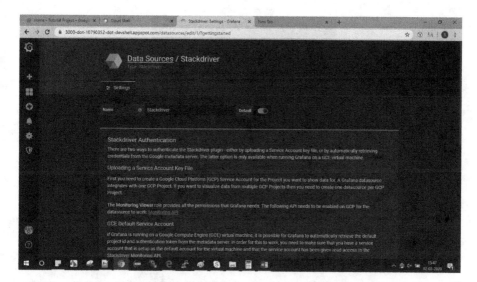

Figure 7-25. *Stackdriver (Google Operations) Authentication screen*

Step 4: On this screen, upload the service account
key file that can be downloaded from the service, as
shown in Figure 7-26.

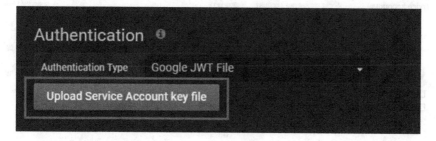

Figure 7-26. *Uploading the account key file*

To download the service account key file, take the following steps.

Step 1: Click the Service accounts link under the
IAM & Admin menu (Figure 7-27).

Figure 7-27. *Service accounts*

> **Step 2:** The previous step will redirect users to the
> following screen, which lists all the service accounts
> created in this project, as seen in Figure 7-28.

Figure 7-28. *Service accounts screen*

> **Step 3:** Click the three dots in the Actions column
> and click the Create key link in the drop-down, as
> shown in Figure 7-29.

Key ID
Actions
7ebc5047bb053955f10ff22efb63c5c
1dec7ca5c7772ce3c6410
0415f1d88a437f962ff0d9
Edit
Disable
Create key
Delete

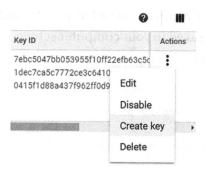

***Figure 7-29.** Create key*

Step 4: Clicking Create key will display the following screen. Select the JSON Key type and click the Create button (Figure 7-30).

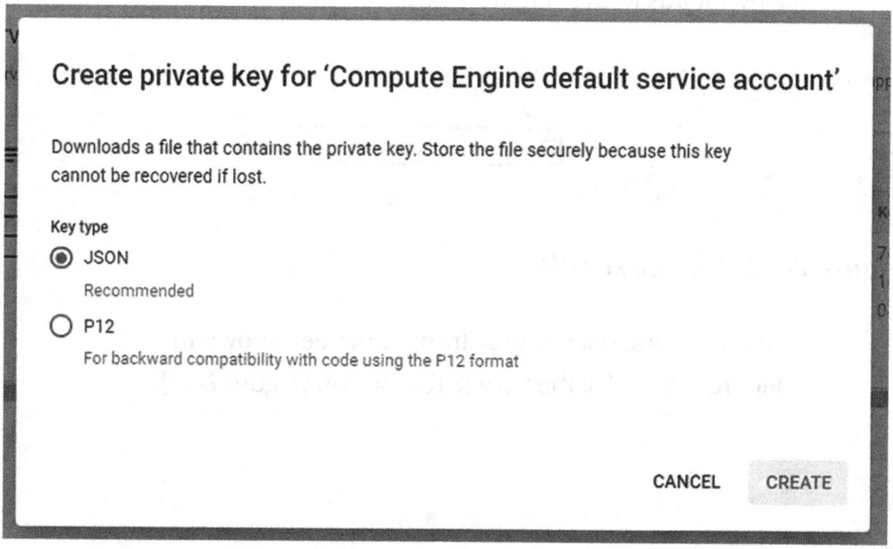

Create private key for 'Compute Engine default service account'
Downloads a file that contains the private key. Store the file securely because this key cannot be recovered if lost.
Key type
JSON
Recommended
P12
For backward compatibility with code using the P12 format
CANCEL
CREATE

***Figure 7-30.** Create private key screen*

Step 5: The Create button will display the following Private key saved to your computer screen (Figure 7-31).

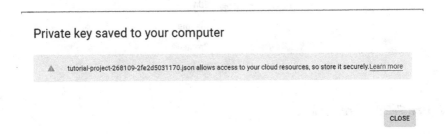

Figure 7-31. Private key screen

Step 6: The file will be saved to the computer in the Downloads folder (Figure 7-32).

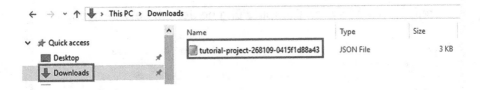

Figure 7-32. Service key file

Upload this service key file from the screen shown in Figure 7-26. Click the Save & Test button (Figure 7-33).

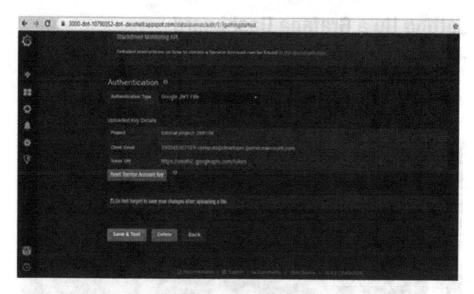

Figure 7-33. *Authentication Save & Test screen*

On successful authentication, the following screen
will be displayed (Figure 7-34).

Authentication ⓘ

Authentication Type	Google JWT File

Uploaded Key Details

Project	tutorial-project-268109
Client Email	353345307101-compute@developer.gserviceaccount.com
Token URI	https://oauth2.googleapis.com/token
Private Key	configured

Reset Service Account Key ⓘ

✔ Successfully queried the Stackdriver API.

Save & Test   Delete   Back

Figure 7-34. *Authentication success screen*

Setting Up a Grafana Dashboard

The following steps will set up the Grafana dashboard for our project.

> **Step 1:** Click Create and then Dashboard, as shown in Figure 7-35.

Figure 7-35. *Grafana Dashboard screen*

> If required, the Grafana dashboard can be downloaded from the following link: https://grafana.com/grafana/dashboards.

> **Step 2**: On Clicking Dashboard, the following screen will be displayed. Select Add Query (Figure 7-36).

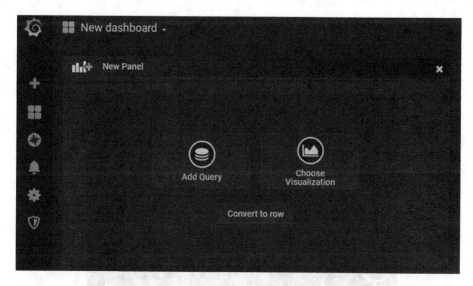

Figure 7-36. Grafana Dashboard New Panel screen

> **Step 3**: From the New Dashboard screen select the
> desired Service, Metric, and other settings to get the
> data (Figure 7-37).

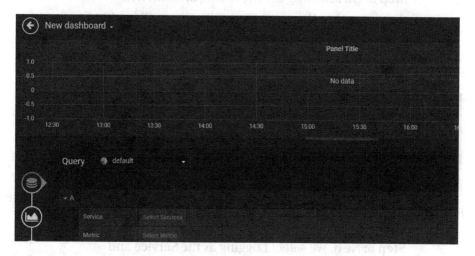

Figure 7-37. Grafana New dashboard screen

Step 4: For our purposes, the Service we select is Compute, and the Metric is CPU utilization (Figure 7-38).

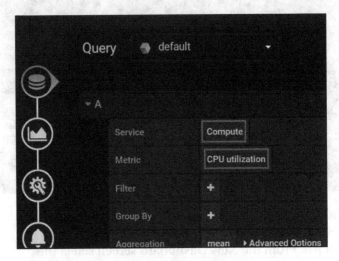

Figure 7-38. *Grafana Dashboard query selection screen*

Step 5: On selecting the preceding options, live data related to Compute CPU utilization will begin to come, as shown in Figure 7-39. This data can be customized, as required.

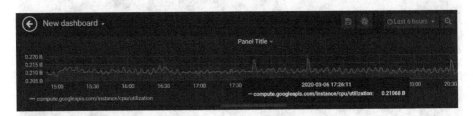

Figure 7-39. *Data related to Compute CPU utilization*

Step 6: Next, we select Logging as the Service and Log bytes ingested as the Metric (Figure 7-40).

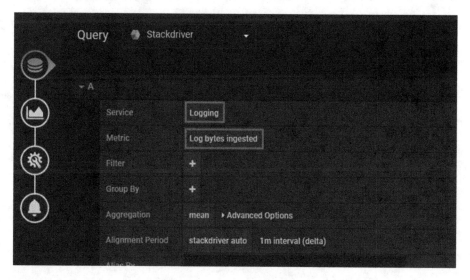

Figure 7-40. *Service and Metric selection*

> **Step 7:** After selecting our options, live data related to our log will begin to come (Figure 7-41). This can be customized, as required.

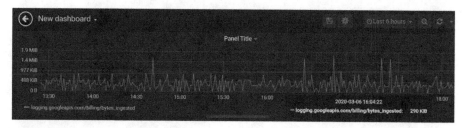

Figure 7-41. *Log-related data*

Summary

In this chapter, we have learned about how to set up Grafana and use Grafana dashboards to display Google Stackdriver (Google Operations) metrics. In the next chapter, we will learn about GKE monitoring using Sysdig.

CHAPTER 8

Monitoring GKE Using Sysdig

This chapter provides readers hands-on steps for container application monitoring using Sysdig, covering the following topics:

- Introduction to the Sysdig Monitoring Solution
- Container Application Monitoring

Introduction to the Sysdig Monitoring Solution

Sysdig Monitor is a powerful container monitoring solution that provides comprehensive observability and also provides additional capabilities of security and compliance (using Sysdig Secure) with performance and capacity monitoring. It has out of the box capability of providing container visibility and integration with numerous platforms including, Kubernetes, Docker container, Google GKE, AWS EKS, and Azure AKS.

It is available as both software as service (SaaS) and on-premises software offerings.

© Navin Sabharwal, Piyush Pandey 2020
N. Sabharwal and P. Pandey, *Pro Google Kubernetes Engine*,
https://doi.org/10.1007/978-1-4842-6243-6_8

Following are the key features of Sysdig Monitor:

Simplifies discovery and metric collection: Sysdig provides capability of dynamically discovering applications, containers, hosts, networks, and custom metrics, such as Prometheus, JMX, and statsD, for deep insight into complex environments.

Visualizes service reliability: Sysdig provides a consolidated overview of service performance, capacity, and security risk profile, in order to help developers and DevOps teams quickly identify application issues and take action.

Monitors infrastructure and applications: Leveraging it's capability of exhaustive integrations with Kubernetes, OpenShift, Docker, Mesos, DC/OS, AWS, Google, IBM, Azure, etc., Sysdig provides visibility beyond infrastructure into how your apps and services are performing.

Dashboards: Sysdig provides out-of-the-box and customizable dashboards that enable at-a-glance views of your infrastructure, applications, compliance, and metrics and lets you visualize your environment the way you want.

Proactively alerts for faster response: Sysdig provides configurable alerts to enable proactive notification of any condition, including events, downtime, and anomalies, to help you get a handle on issues before they impact operations, as shown in Figure 8-1.

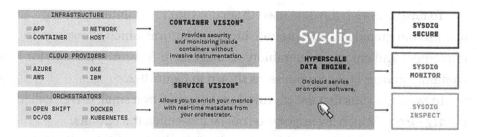

Figure 8-1. *Sysdig functional architecture*

Container Application Monitoring

Sysdig fetches monitoring metrics from kernel level by subscribing to tracepoints that many system kernels are already processing and publishing. This ability to see inside containers is known as container vision. It makes data capture a very lightweight exercise (typically 1–3% of CPU resources and 500M of system memory). Sysdig is based on the open source Linux troubleshooting and forensics project of the same name (`sysdig`). The open source project allows you to see every single system call, down to process, arguments, payload, and connection, on a single host. This data is dynamically mapped to containers, microservices, clouds, and orchestrators in a way that is at once powerful and simple to use.

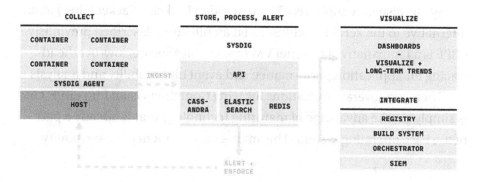

Figure 8-2. *Sysdig container monitoring architecture*

To further enrich the data used to secure your environment, Sysdig has also integrated Falco & Anchore into the platform which allows you to implement and enforce vulnerability-management & security policies for container images and containers, as shown in Figure 8-2.

In Sysdig, events first are captured in the kernel by a small driver, called `sysdig-probe`, which leverages a kernel facility called tracepoints.

Tracepoints make it possible to install a "handler," which is called from specific functions in the kernel. Currently, Sysdig registers tracepoints for system calls on entry and exit and for process-scheduling events. `sysdig-probe`'s handler is limited to copying the event details into a shared read-only ring buffer, encoded for later consumption. The reason to keep the handler simple, as you can imagine, is performance, because the original kernel execution is "frozen" until the handler returns. The freeze is on the order of nanoseconds.

The event buffer is memory-mapped into user space, so that it can be accessed without any copy, minimizing CPU usage and cache misses. Two libraries, libscap and libsinsp, then offer support for reading, decoding, and parsing events. Specifically, libscap offers trace file management functionality, while libsinsp includes sophisticated state tracking functionality (e.g., you can use a file name instead of an FD number) and also filtering, event decoding, a Lua JIT compiler to run plug-ins, and much more.

Sysdig also now supports eBPF (extended Berkeley Packet Filter) as an alternative to the kernel module-based architecture described previously. eBPF is a Linux-native in-kernel VM that enables secure, low-overhead tracing for application performance and event observability and analysis.

There are several motivations for tying ContainerVision into eBPF. One is simply to take advantage of maturing technology that is already a part of the base operating system. This makes management of observability that much easier and frictionless. Another reason why eBPF makes sense is the advent of container-optimized operating systems. These solutions, such as COS from GCP and Project Atomic Host led by Red Hat, feature an immutable infrastructure approach that disallows kernel modules altogether. By tapping into eBPF, users of these newer OS approaches achieve the same level of container observability Sysdig has delivered for some time with the kernel module, as shown in Figure 8-3.

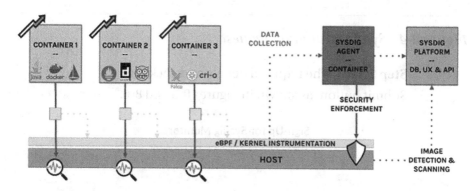

Figure 8-3. *Sysdig container monitoring architecture*

Now let's request an evaluation version of Sysdig Monitor and see how it monitors container applications.

> **Step 1:** Navigate to https://sysdig.com and
> request the evaluation version of Sysdig. Select
> Products and click the Sign-up today button, as
> shown Figure 8-4.

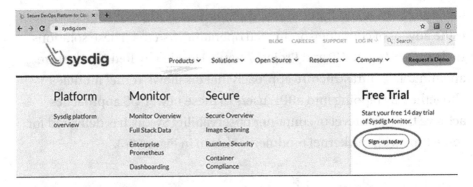

Figure 8-4. *Sysdig evaluation request*

Step 2: Fill in the required details and click the
Submit button, as shown in Figures 8-5 and 8-6.

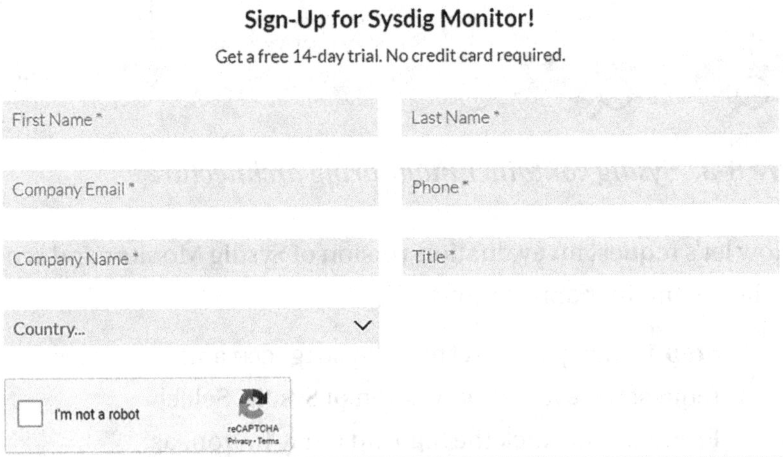

Sign-Up for Sysdig Monitor!

Get a free 14-day trial. No credit card required.

First Name *

Last Name *

Company Email *

Phone *

Company Name *

Title *

Country...

☐ I'm not a robot

reCAPTCHA
Privacy · Terms

Figure 8-5. *Sysdig evaluation request form*

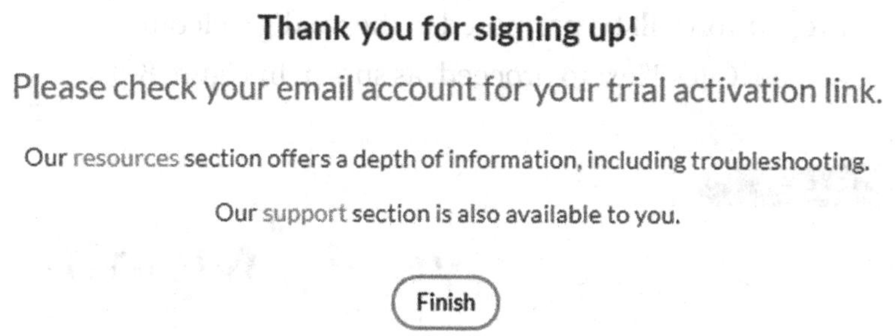

Thank you for signing up!
Please check your email account for your trial activation link.
Our resources section offers a depth of information, including troubleshooting.
Our support section is also available to you.
Finish

Figure 8-6. *Sysdig evaluation account activation*

Step 3: You will receive an activation link via the email address provided. It takes roughly 30 minutes to one hour to receive the email. Click the activation link in the email to complete the evaluation access request. You will be prompted to set up a new password for Sysdig. Click the Activate and login button to proceed, as shown in Figure 8-7.

SysdigMonitor
prashantkum@hcl.com
Enter new password
Confirm new password
Activate and login
Already registered? Login

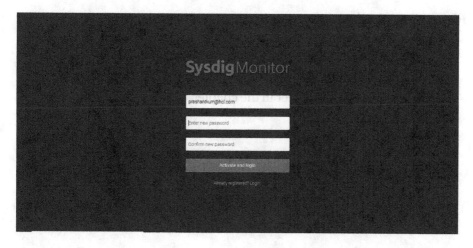

Figure 8-7. *Sysdig evaluation account password setup*

Step 4: You will be prompted to the Sysdig welcome screen. Click Next to proceed, as shown in Figure 8-8.

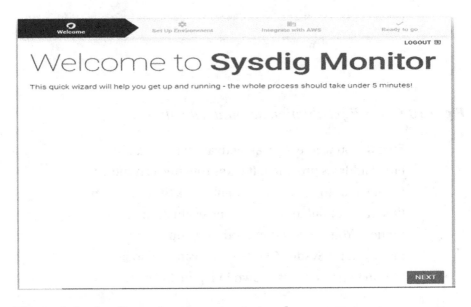

Figure 8-8. *Sysdig evaluation account welcome page*

Step 5: Select Kubernetes on the next screen (Figure 8-9). After selection, you will see a key (Figure 8-10). Copy the key. We will use it later in the chapter.

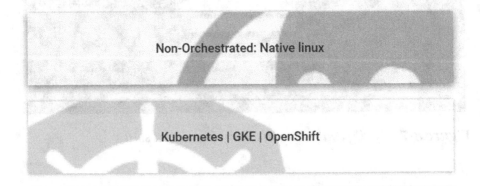

Figure 8-9. *Sysdig evaluation account setup for Kubernetes*

Waiting for first node to connect... Go ahead and follow the instructions below!

Kubernetes | GKE | OpenShift

You can find instructions to install and configure Sysdig Monitor on the support page.
Here is your Access Key you will need to use during the configuration:

b7f77372-0f4e-444a-b13a-c3818fd5c885   COPY

OPEN INSTRUCTIONS

Figure 8-10. Sysdig evaluation account Kubernetes integration key

Using GKE, we will now set up a cluster on GCP and integrate Sysdig
Monitor with the same, for container application monitoring. For this lab,
we will assume the reader has a working knowledge of GCP and a GCP
account.

Open Port 6443 for Agent Ingress and Egress

As GKE uses stateful firewalls, we must actively open port 6443 for the
Sysdig agent, for both inbound and outbound traffic.

> **Step 1:** Open the Firewall rules section in VPC
> network, to create the new rules for inbound and
> outbound traffic, as shown in Figure 8-11.

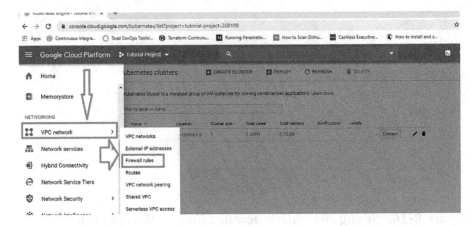

Figure 8-11. *GCP console Firewall rules*

> **Step 2:** Click Create Firewall Rule, to create inbound
> rules, as shown in Figure 8-12.

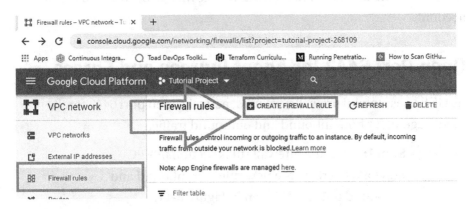

Figure 8-12. *GCP firewall rule creation*

> **Step 3:** Fill in the Create firewall rule form for
> inbound rules, as per the following:
>
> **Name:** Give an appropriate name
>
> **Logs:** Choose the Off option
>
> **Network:** default
>
> **Priority:** 1000

Direction of traffic: Ingress

Ingress is used for inbound traffic.

Action on match: Allow

Target tags: Provide the same target tag that you used on your cluster. In our case, it is gke-clustertutorial-cff607d3-node.

Source IP ranges: 10.16.0.0/14 (the same as on your cluster)

Protocols and ports: Check tcp and select port 6443.

Now click the Create button. Refer to Figures 8-13, 8-14, and 8-15.

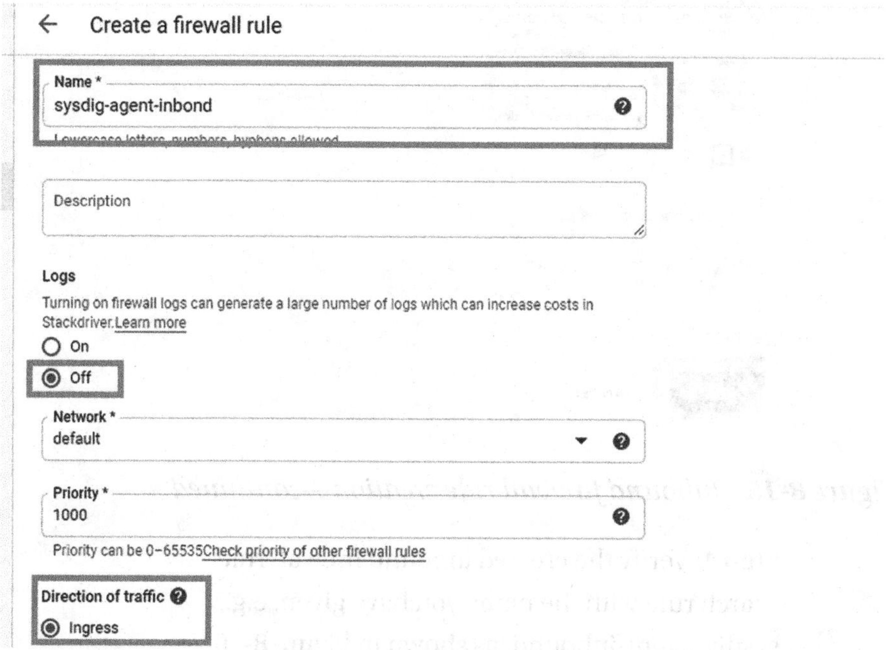

Figure 8-13. *Inbound firewall rule creation*

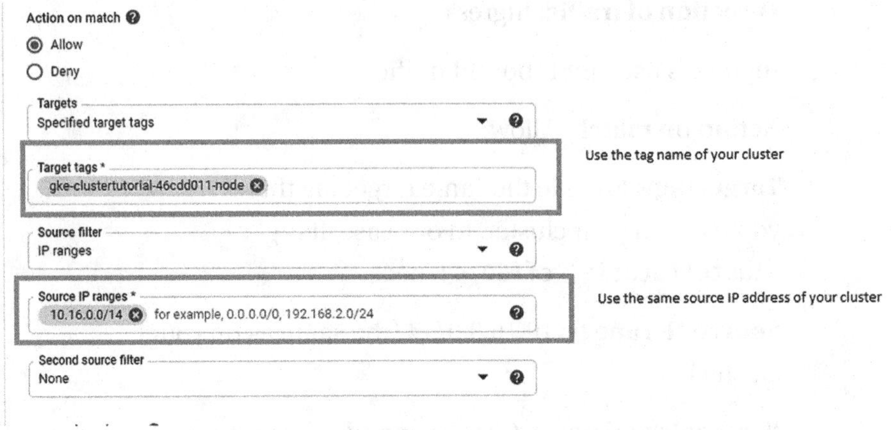

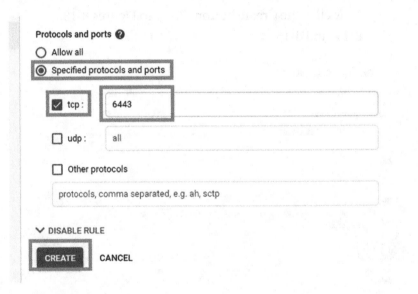

Figure 8-14. *Inbound firewall rule creation—continued*

Figure 8-15. *Inbound firewall rule creation—continued*

Step 4: Verify the created inbound firewall rule
search rule with the name you have given, e.g.,
sysdig-agent-inbound, as shown in Figure 8-16.

☐	k8s-f14e5ea21eb04f69-node-http-hc	Ingress	gke-clustertutc	IP ranges: 130.21	tcp:10256	Allow	1000	default
☐	k8s-fw-a3c600ff8530011ea9ae542010a80014	Ingress	gke-clustertutc	IP ranges: 0.0.0.0	tcp:80	Allow	1000	default
☐	k8s-fw-afc265d10523f11ea9ae542010a80014	Ingress	gke-clustertutc	IP ranges: 0.0.0.0	tcp:80,443	Allow	1000	default
☐	sysdig-agent-inbound	Ingress	gke-clustertutc	IP ranges: 10.16.I	tcp:6443	Allow	1000	default
☐	default-allow-icmp	Ingress	Apply to all	IP ranges: 0.0.0.0	icmp	Allow	65534	default
☐	default-allow-internal	Ingress	Apply to all	IP ranges: 10.128	tcp:0-65535 udp:0-65535 icmp	Allow	65534	default

Figure 8-16. *Inbound Firewall rule creation—continued*

Step 5: Fill in the Create firewall rule form for outbound rules, as per the following:

Name: Give an appropriate name

Logs: Choose the Off option

Network: default

Priority: 1000

Direction of traffic: Egress

Egress use for outbound traffic

Action on match: Allow

Target tags: Provide the same tag that you used on your cluster. In our case, it is gke-clustertutorial-cff607d3-node.

Destination IP ranges: 10.16.0.0/14

Protocols and ports: Check tcp and select port 6443.

Now click the Create button. Refer to Figures 8-17, 8-18, and 8-19.

←   Create a firewall rule

Firewall rules control incoming or outgoing traffic to an instance. By default, incoming traffic from outside your network is blocked.Learn more

Name *
sysdig-agent-outbound   ❓

Lowercase letters, numbers, hyphens allowed

Description

Logs
Turning on firewall logs can generate a large number of logs which can increase costs in Stackdriver.Learn more
○ On
◉ Off

Network *
default   ▼   ❓

Priority *
1000   ❓

Priority can be 0–65535Check priority of other firewall rules

Figure 8-17. *Outbound firewall rule creation*

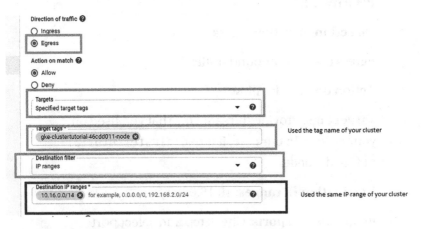

Figure 8-18. *Outbound firewall rule creation—continued*

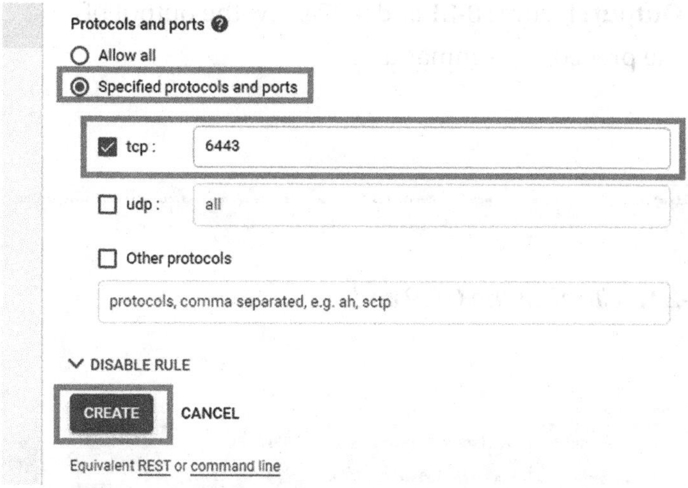

Figure 8-19. *Outbound firewall rule creation—continued*

Step 6: Verify the created outbound firewall rule search rule with name you have given, e.g., sysdig-agent-outbound, as shown in Figure 8-20.

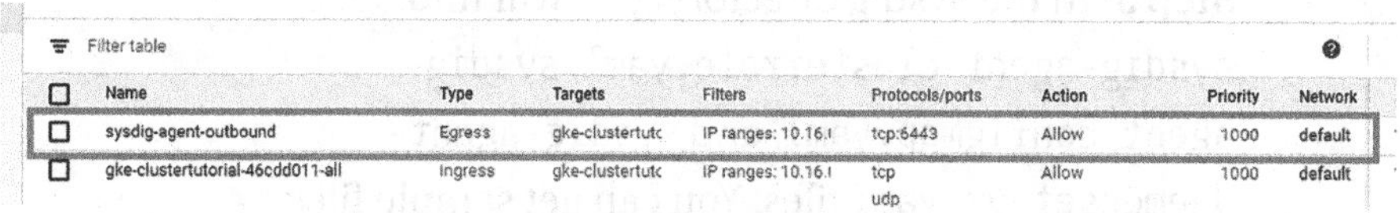

Figure 8-20. *Outbound firewall rule creation—continued*

Installing Sysdig Agent on GKE

Step 1: Connect to GKE and open Cloud Shell.

Step 2: Execute the following command under Prometheus, to clone GCP, which contains `sysdig-agent-clusterrole.yaml`, `sysdig-agent-configmap.yaml`, and `sysdig-agent-daemonset-v2.yaml` files:.$ git clone https://github.com/dryice-devops/GCP.git

Output: Figures 8-21 and 8-22 show the output of the preceding command.

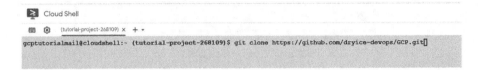

Figure 8-21. *Cloning the GCP code*

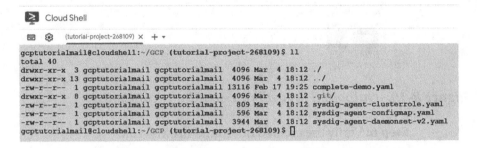

Figure 8-22. *Clone the GCP code—continued*

Step 3: In the Sysdig directory, you will find `sysdig-agent-clusterrole.yaml`, `sysdig-agent-configmap.yaml`, and `sysdig-agent-daemonset-v2.yaml` files. You can get sample files from the following GitHub link: `https://github.com/draios/sysdig-cloud-scripts/tree/master/agent_deploy/kubernetes`

In the `sysdig-agent-configmap.yaml` file, you will find the following section: `k8s_cluster_name`. Pass the value of the GCP EKS cluster (Prometheus, in our case), as shown in Figure 8-23.

```
########################################
new_k8s: true
k8s_cluster_name: "clustertutorial"
prometheus:
  enabled: true
```

Figure 8-23. *Passing the value of the GCP EKS cluster*

Next, open the `sysdig-agent-daemonset-v2.yaml` file. You don't have to modify anything in this file.

Step 4: Create a namespace for the Sysdig agent, by executing following command from the GCP directory.

Command: $ `kubectl create ns sysdig-agent`

Output: Figure 8-24 shows the output of the preceding command.

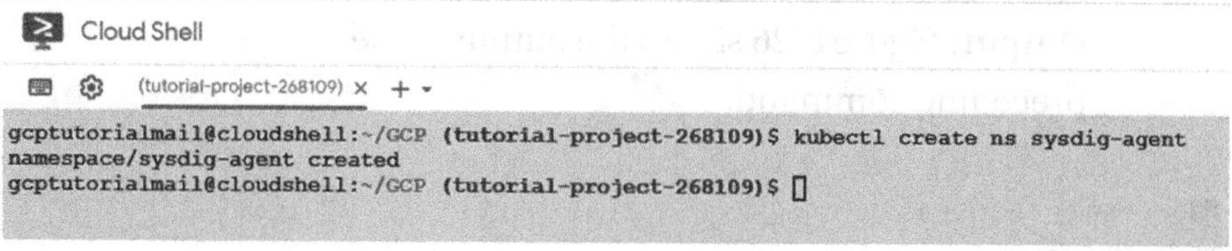

```
Cloud Shell
(tutorial-project-268109) ×  + ▾
gcptutorialmail@cloudshell:~/GCP (tutorial-project-268109)$ kubectl create ns sysdig-agent
namespace/sysdig-agent created
gcptutorialmail@cloudshell:~/GCP (tutorial-project-268109)$ []
```

Figure 8-24. *Sysdig agent namespace creation*

Step 5: Create secrets for the Sysdig agent, by executing the following command. This will use the key (highlighted) we got when we created the evaluation account for Sysdig (while selecting Kubernetes from the welcome screen).

Command: $ `kubectl create secret generic sysdig-agent --from-literal=access-`

key=9b63d2de-4e52-49a9-b287-ef3c3dd39934 -n
sysdig-agent

Output: Figure 8-25 shows the output of the
preceding command.

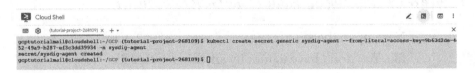

Figure 8-25. *Sysdig agent secret creation*

Step 6: Execute the following command, to deploy
the Sysdig agent cluster role. The clusterrole file is
the same one we created in previous steps.

Command: $ kubectl apply -f sysdig-agent-
clusterrole.yaml -n sysdig-agent

Output: Figure 8-26 shows the output of the
preceding command.

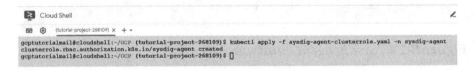

Figure 8-26. *Sysdig agent cluster role deployment*

Step 7: Execute the following command, to create a
service account in the Sysdig agent namespace.

Command: $ kubectl create serviceaccount
sysdig-agent -n sysdig-agent

Output: Figure 8-27 shows the output of the
preceding command.

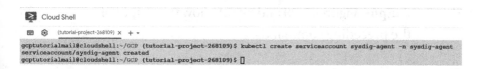

Figure 8-27. *Sysdig agent service account for sysdig namespace*

Step 8: Execute the following command, to create cluster role binding in the Sysdig namespace.

Command: $ kubectl create clusterrolebinding sysdig-agent --clusterrole=sysdig-agent --serviceaccount=sysdig-agent:sysdig-agent

Output: Figure 8-28 shows the output of the preceding command.

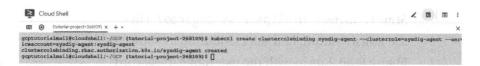

Figure 8-28. *Sysdig agent cluster role binding creation*

Step 9: Execute the following commands, to complete installation of the Sysdig agent.

Command: $ kubectl apply -f sysdig-agent-configmap.yaml -n sysdig-agent

Command: $kubectl apply -f sysdig-agent-daemonset-v2.yaml -n sysdig-agent

Output: Figures 8-29 and 8-29.1 show the output of the preceding commands.

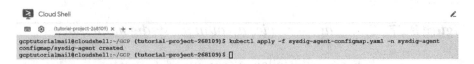

Figure 8-29. *Sysdig agent configmap creation*

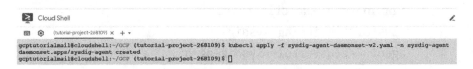

Figure 8-29.1. *Sysdig agent daemonset installation*

Now we will navigate to the Sysdig console, to review the monitoring metrics.

Step 1: Navigate to `https://sysdig.com/`, click the Log in button, and select Monitor, as shown in Figure 8-30. Log in with the username/password used at the registration stage.

Figure 8-30. *Sysdig login*

Step 2: After logging in, you will see the welcome to Sysdig page. You will also see a "You have 3 agents connected!" notification. Click Go to Next Step! to navigate to the next screen, as shown in Figure 8-31.

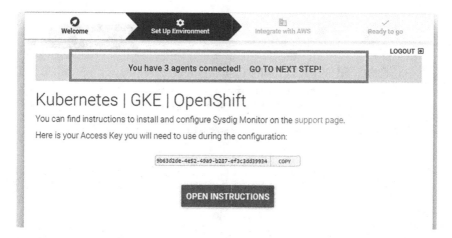

Figure 8-31. *Sysdig welcome page*

Step 3: Leave the Integrate with AWS section blank and click the Skip button, as shown in Figure 8-32, thus completing the Sysdig setup (Figures 8-33 and 8-34).

Figure 8-32. *Skipping the AWS account*

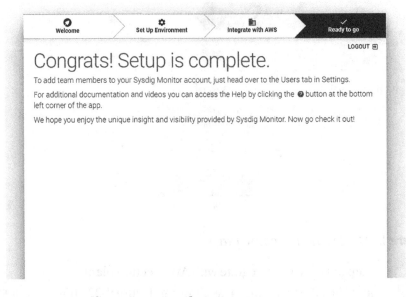

Figure 8-33. *Sysdig setup completion*

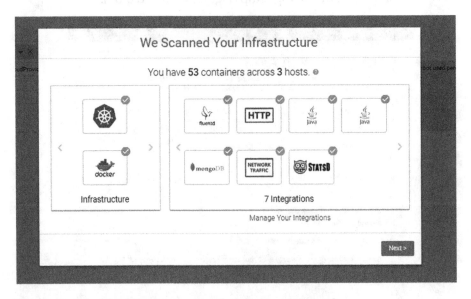

Figure 8-34. *Sysdig setup completion—continued*

Now let's navigate across various reports on the Sysdig console for container monitoring. By clicking the Next button, you will see new a window with the following message: "Your Environment Is Ready To Go." Click the Complete Onboarding button, as shown in Figure 8-35.

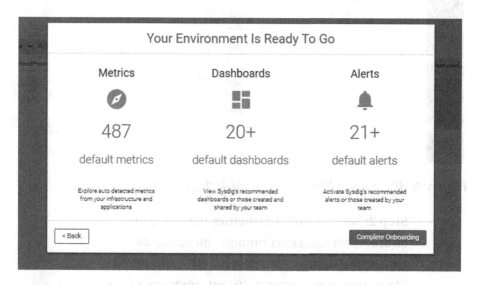

Figure 8-35. *Sysdig home dashboard screen*

Navigating GKE Monitoring Reports

To navigate GKE monitoring reports, execute the following steps:

> **Step 1:** To view the deployed Pods in Sysdig, click Explore. Now and select Host & Containers from the drop-down option. On the other node, select Kubernetes Health Overview under the Kubernetes category (a subcategory of Default Dashboards), as shown in Figure 8-36.

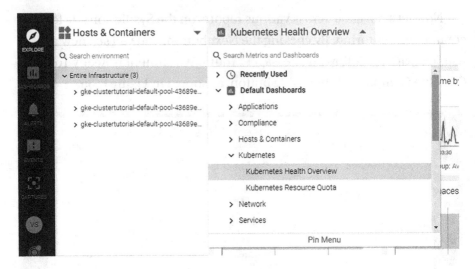

Figure 8-36. *Sysdig Kubernetes health dashboard*

> **Step 2:** You will find rich metrics regarding the entire Kubernetes environment, including by top namespace (by container), CPU/memory/ file system usage, network in/out, as shown in Figures 8-37 and 8-38.

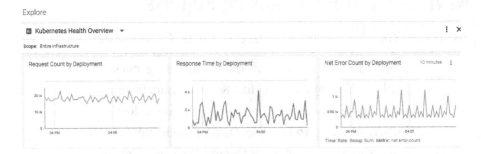

Figure 8-37. *Sysdig Kubernetes health dashboard*

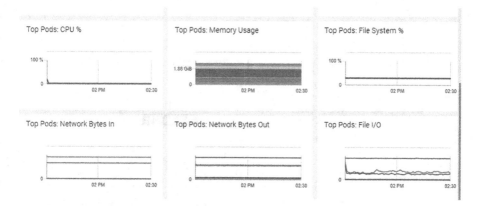

Figure 8-38. *Sysdig Kubernetes health dashboard—continued*

Step 3: Select Container Limits from the drop-down
menu at the far right of the page, to view CPU/
memory share and quotas, as shown in Figures 8-39
and 8-40.

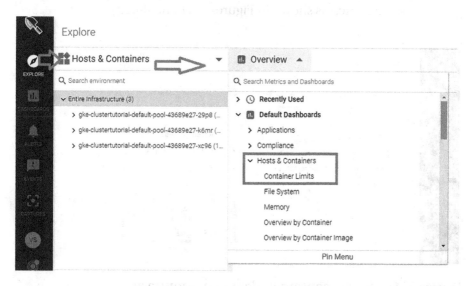

Figure 8-39. *Sysdig Container limit monitoring*

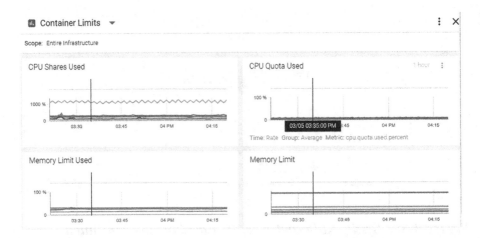

Figure 8-40. *Sysdig Container limit monitoring—continued*

> **Step 4:** Select File System from the drop-down
> menu at the right side of the page, to view number
> of bytes free/bytes used/number of inodes in the file
> system, etc., as shown in Figures 8-41 and 8-42.

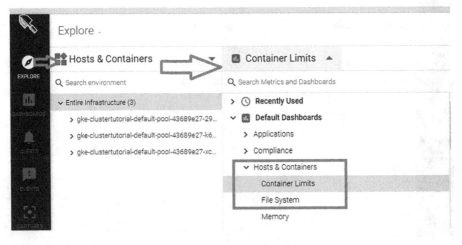

Figure 8-41. *Sysdig container file system monitoring*

File System ▼

Scope: Entire Infrastructure

File System

fs.mountDir	fs.device	fs.type	fs.bytes.total GiB	fs.bytes.used GiB	fs.bytes.free GiB	fs.used.percent %
/home/kubernetes/containerized_mounter/...	/dev/sda1	ext4	94.3	5.7	88.6	6.1
/home/kubernetes/containerized_mounter/...	/dev/sda1	ext4	94.3	5.5	88.8	5.8
/home/kubernetes/containerized_mounter	/dev/sda1	ext4	94.3	5.5	88.8	5.8
/var/lib/kubelet	/dev/sda1	ext4	94.3	5.5	88.8	5.8
/home/kubernetes/bin	/dev/sda1	ext4	94.3	5.5	88.8	5.8
/home/kubernetes/flexvolume	/dev/sda1	ext4	94.3	5.5	88.8	5.8
/var/lib/docker	/dev/sda1	ext4	94.3	5.5	88.8	5.8
/var/lib/google	/dev/sda1	ext4	94.3	5.5	88.8	5.8
/var/lib/toolbox	/dev/sda1	ext4	94.3	5.5	88.8	5.8

Figure 8-42. *Sysdig container file system monitoring—continued*

Step 5: Select the Overview option under Network, from the right side of the drop-down menu, to view such metrics as inbound network bytes, outbound network bytes, and total network bytes, as shown in Figures 8-43, 8-44, and 8-45.

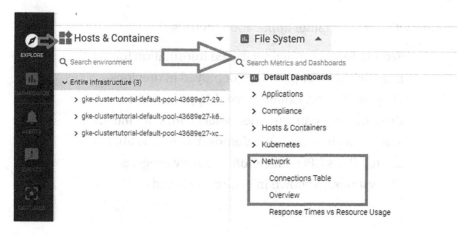

Figure 8-43. *Sysdig Container network monitoring*

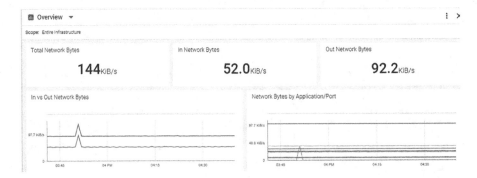

Figure 8-44. Sysdig Container network monitoring—continued

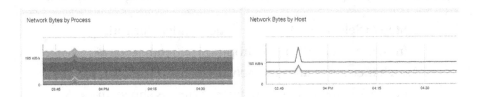

Figure 8-45. Sysdig Container network monitoring—continued

Now let's view container application metrics.

> **Step 1:** To view container-based information for
> our Sock Shop application (deployed in previous
> chapters), select Containerized Apps from the
> drop-down menu, and then select container names,
> starting with weaveworksdemos. You will be able to
> see top Pods CPU utilization, memory usage, and
> file systems, as shown in Figures 8-46 and 8-47.

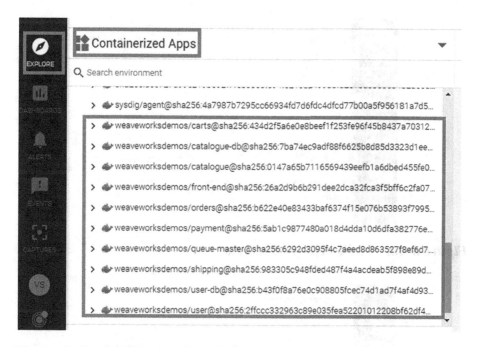

Figure 8-46. *Sysdig containerized application view*

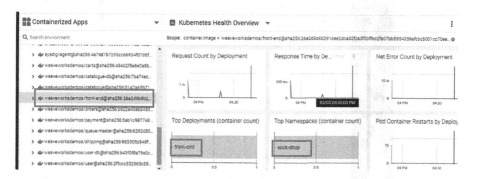

Figure 8-47. *Sysdig containerized application view—continued*

Step 2: To view deployments, select Deployments
from the drop-down menu and select sock-shop, as
in Figures 8-48, 8-49, and 8-50.

Figure 8-48.   Sysdig deployment view

Figure 8-49.   Sysdig deployment view—continued

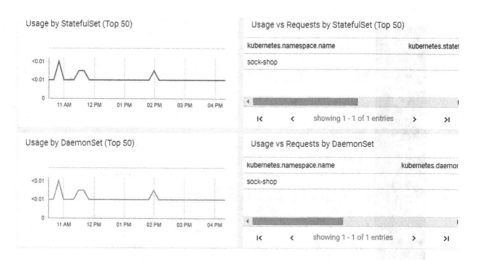

Figure 8-50. *Sysdig deployment view—continued*

Select Kubernetes CPU Allocation Optimization
under the Kubernetes category.

Now let's explore other metrics provided by Sysdig specific to the
application layer.

Step 1: Click Explore, at the left-hand side panel
and choose the Hosts & Containers option from the
drop-down menu. Select HTTP from the second
drop-down menu on the right. You will see metrics
such as top HTTP request, average/maximum
request time, slowest URLs, etc., as shown in
Figures 8-51, 8-52, 8-53, and 8-54.

Figure 8-51. *Sysdig HTTP monitor*

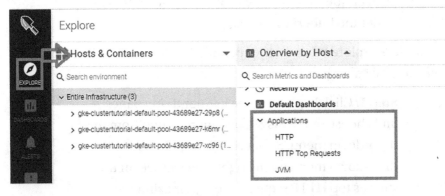

Figure 8-52. *Sysdig HTTP monitor Default Dashboards*

Figure 8-53. *Sysdig HTTP monitor metrics*

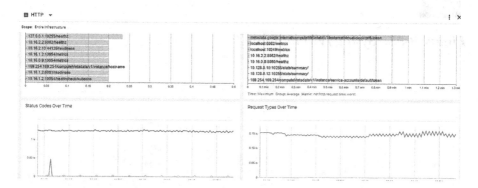

Figure 8-54. *Sysdig HTTP monitor metrics—continued*

Step 2: Select JVM, instead of HTTP, to view JVM-related metrics. This will show such metrics as allocated heap memory usage by process over time and garbage collector collection time, as shown in Figures 8-55 and 8-56.

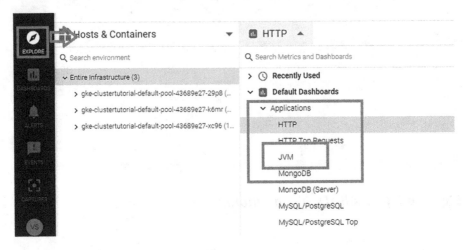

Figure 8-55. *Sysdig JVM monitor*

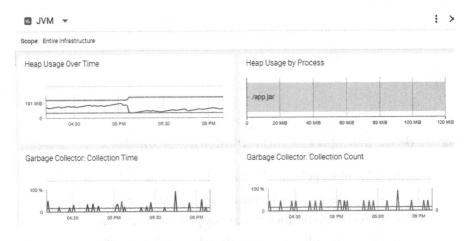

Figure 8-56. *Sysdig JVM monitor metrics*

Step 3: Select MongoDB (Server), instead of JVM, from the drop-down menu at the right of the page, to view MongoDB-related metrics, such as total number of connections created, amount of virtual memory used by the MongoDB process, etc., as shown in Figures 8-57 and 8-58.

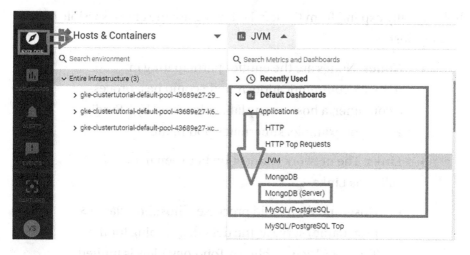

Figure 8-57. *Sysdig MongoDB monitor*

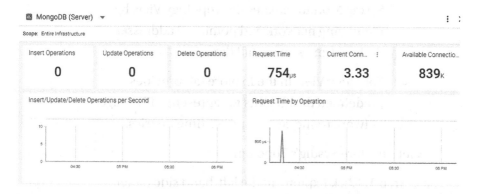

Figure 8-58. *Sysdig MongoDB monitor metrics*

Sysdig Topology View provides interface to visualize how different components in your application system interact with one another in real time. By default, the interface shows a selected host's top processes and their interaction with processes on remote hosts or host groups. The interaction is depicted as nodes and links. Links connect nodes. Nodes and links radially expand from the left. Following are the entities visible on the Sysdig console:

- **Nodes**: Nodes are the entities participating in network communication. A node could be a process, a container, a host, or any label identified by a Sysdig agent, for example, kubernetes.pod.name.

- **Links**: The network connection between nodes is called as Links.

  - Hosts and their child processes (host.hostName > proc.name) serve as the default grouping for the Topology View. Scaling a Topology View is limited by the number of processes and connections. Sysdig Monitor creates the Topology View by identifying network end points (IP addresses) derived from system call data.

  - Topology View in the Explore tab provides predefined dashboards to represent CPU usage, network traffic, and response time metrics.

Now let's explore Sysdig's Topology View.

Step 1: Click Explore, in the left-hand side panel, and choose the Hosts & Containers option from the drop-down menu. Select Topology, then CPU Usage. Click each icon, to drill down on CPU usage by application node and container, with topology mapping, as shown in Figures 8-59 and 8-60.

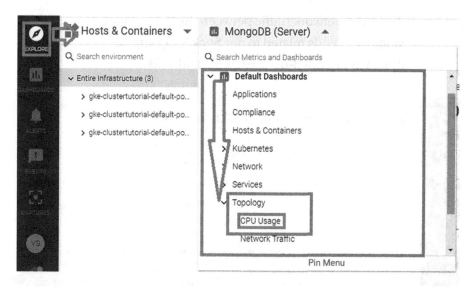

Figure 8-59. *Sysdig Topology View CPU Usage option*

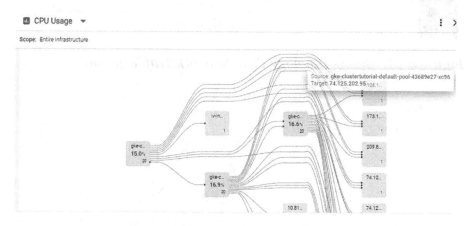

Figure 8-60. *Sysdig Topology View CPU usage metrics*

Step 2: Select the Network Traffic option from the second drop-down menu, instead of CPU usage. You can drill down to view the specific flow. For example, we selected the Python-based box that

293

shows the network traffic between the Python and Mongo DB Pods related to our Sock Shop app, as shown in Figures 8-61, 8-62, 8-63, and 8-64.

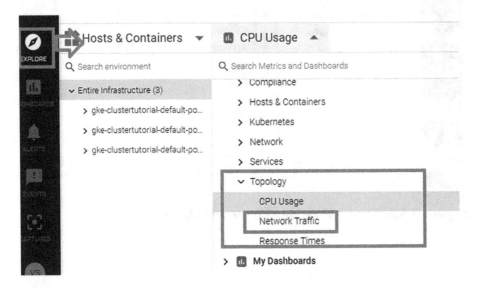

Figure 8-61. *Sysdig Topology View Network Traffic option*

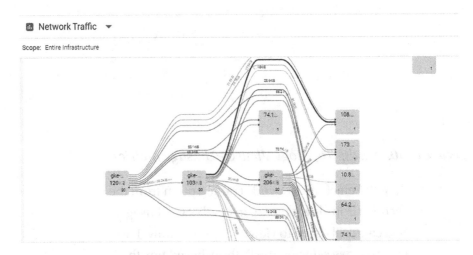

Figure 8-62. *Sysdig Topology View Network Traffic metrics*

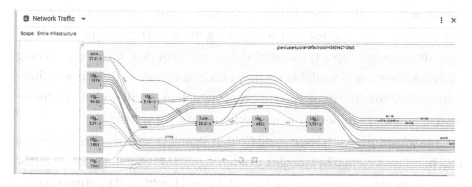

Figure 8-63. Additional Sysdig Topology View Network Traffic metrics

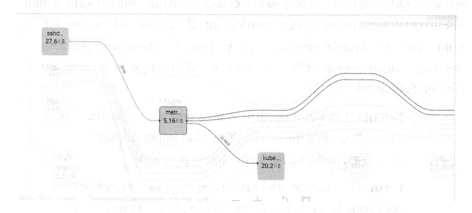

Figure 8-64. Sysdig Topology View network traffic between Pods

Classic monitoring tools are usually based on static configuration files and were designed to monitor machines, not microservices or containers. In the container world, things work very differently on the account that containers may scale up or down, based on the scaling policy and incoming traffic on the application. Additionally containers are created and destroyed at an incredible pace, and it is impossible to keep track of such dynamic entities from monitoring perspective.

Most of the modern platform systems provide huge variety of metrics each of which may provide an insight to how platform is behaving. It is quite difficult for human brain to analyze so much data and gain insights into how application is performing. Imagine a application on container platform that is being heavily used and is generating loads of metrics regarding various aspects like availability, performance, errors etc. As long as the application is available we may perceive that everything is working however we may overlook certain events which over a period of time may lead to an outage or performance bottleneck in the system.

Google resolved this issue using Golden Signals (a term used in the Google SRE handbook coined by Google). Golden Signals are essentially four metrics that will provide you a very good idea of the real health and performance of your application, as seen by the systems interacting with that application service. Golden Signals can help to detect issues of a microservices application. These signals are a reduced set of metrics that offer a wide view of a service from a user or consumer perspective, so you can detect potential problems that might be directly affecting the behavior of the application. The four Golden Signals are

> **Latency**: Latency is the time your system takes to serve a request against the service. This is an important sign to detect a performance degradation problem.

> **Errors**: The rate of errors returned by your service is a very good indicator of deeper issues. It is very important to detect not only explicit errors but implicit errors too.

> **Traffic/Connections**: This is an indicator of the amount of use of your service per time unit. It can be many different values, depending on the nature of the system, such as the number of requests to an API or the bandwidth consumed by a streaming app.

> **Saturation**: Usually, saturation is expressed as a percentage of the maximum capacity, but each system will have different ways to measure saturation. The percentage could mean the number of users or requests obtained directly from the application or based on estimations.

Now let's see how we can view Golden Signal metrics using Sysdig.

Step 1: Click Explore at the left-hand side panel and choose the Services option from the drop-down menu.

Step 2: Select Kubernetes Service Golden Signals from the second drop-down menu on right, as shown Figures 8-65, 8-66, and 8-67.

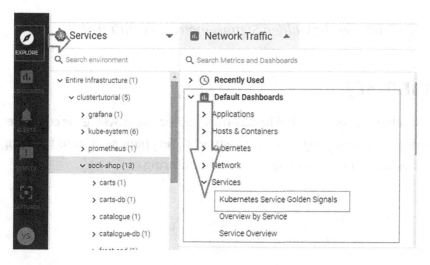

***Figure 8-65.** Sysdig Golden Signals option*

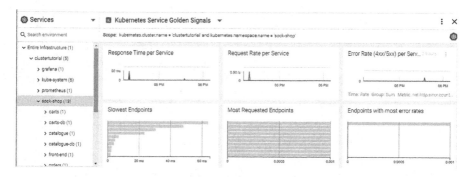

***Figure 8-66.** Sysdig Golden Signals metrics*

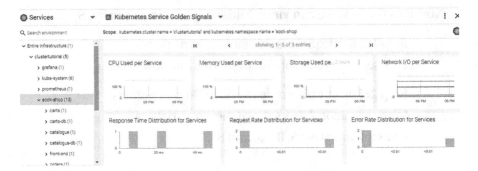

Figure 8-67. *Sysdig Golden Signals metrics—continued*

Summary

In this chapter, we provided hands-on steps for using Sysdig for container application monitoring. The next chapter covers hands-on steps for using Prometheus for container application monitoring.

CHAPTER 9

GKE Monitoring Using Prometheus

This chapter provides hands-on steps to guide you through the use of Prometheus for GKE monitoring. In addition, it covers the following:

- Overview of Prometheus

- Prometheus Architecture

- Prometheus on Google Kubernetes Engine

- Setting Up Prometheus on a Kubernetes Cluster

- Exporters

Introduction

Prometheus is a monitoring service that provides IT teams with performance data about applications and VMs running on the GCP and AWS public cloud. It includes capabilities that specially focus on Kubernetes operators and other features of Kubernetes, such as CPU and memory utilization. Cluster information can be viewed by infrastructure, workloads, and containers.

© Navin Sabharwal, Piyush Pandey 2020
N. Sabharwal and P. Pandey, *Pro Google Kubernetes Engine*,
https://doi.org/10.1007/978-1-4842-6243-6_9

In this chapter, you will learn how to install Prometheus. We will use the Sock Shop application that we deployed on a GKE cluster in Chapter 8 and configure Prometheus to monitor the GKE cluster and extract the various matrices related to CPU utilization, etc.

Overview of Prometheus

Container-based technologies are affecting elements of infrastructure management services, such as backup, patching, security, high availability, disaster recovery, etc. Monitoring is one such element that has evolved leaps and bounds with the rise of container technology. Prometheus is one of the container monitoring tools that comes up most frequently as an open source monitoring and alerting solution. Prometheus was initially conceived at SoundCloud, and slowly, it became one of the favorite tools for container monitoring. It's predominantly written in Go language and is one of the first Cloud Native Computing Foundation graduated projects.

Prometheus supports a multidimensional data model based on key-value pairs, which helps in collecting container monitoring as time series data. It also provides a powerful query language called Prometheus Query Language (PromQL). PromQL allows selection and aggregation of time series data in real time. The data can either be viewed as a graph, as tabular data, or used by external systems via API calls. Prometheus also supports various integrations with third-party systems for reporting, alerting, dashboarding, and exporters, for fetching data from various sources.

Prometheus Architecture

Now let's look at the core components of the Prometheus architecture. Figure 9-1 illustrates the architecture of Prometheus and its main components.

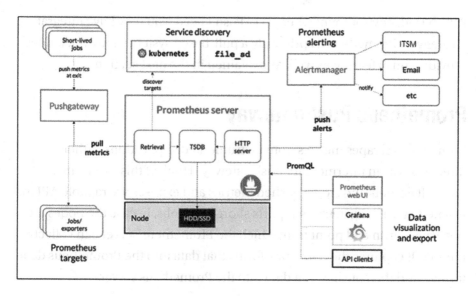

Figure 9-1. *Prometheus architecture*

Prometheus Server

This is a main central component server that collects the metrics from multiple nodes and stores them locally. The Prometheus server works on the principle of scraping, i.e., invoking the metrics end points of the various nodes that it is configured to monitor. It collects these metrics at regular intervals and stores them locally.

The Prometheus server scrapes and stores metrics. This means that your application must expose an end point for which metrics are available and instruct the Prometheus server on how to scrape it.

Note that the Prometheus server uses a persistence layer, which is part of the server and not expressly mentioned in the documentation. Each node of the server is autonomous and does not rely on distributed storage. The time at which Prometheus performs that scrape is not guaranteed. Therefore, if you have a use case that requires accurate second-by-second scrapes, Prometheus may not be a good choice. Also, Prometheus is unreservedly HTTP-focused. If you operate in a monolithic SOAP-based, or

301

RPC-based, environment where HTTP isn't used, you may have integration challenges. Prometheus is primarily a pull-based system; however, it does provide a push feature as well, as explained in the next section.

Prometheus Pushgateway

Prometheus scrapes metrics from instrumented applications, either directly or via an intermediary push gateway. Think of this as a form of buffer. It accepts and stores pushed metrics and exposes a scrapable API for Prometheus. Pushgateway supports short-lived jobs, in case the nodes are not exposing an end point from which the Prometheus server can collect metrics. It captures the data, transforms that data into the Prometheus data format, and then pushes that data into the Prometheus server.

Exporters

Exporters run on a monitored host that gets existing metrics from a third-party system (such as a Linux server, MySQL daemon, etc.) and exports them to the metric in Prometheus and pushes the data to the Prometheus server.

Alertmanager

Prometheus has an alerting module, called Alertmanager, to send alerts and route them to the correct receiver integration, such as email, Slack, etc.

Web-UI

The web UI allows users to access, visualize, and chart stored data. Prometheus provides its own UI, but you can also configure other visualization tools, such as Grafana, to access the Prometheus server, using PromQL.

Key Container Monitoring Features

Following are the key features provided by Prometheus for container monitoring.

Multidimensional Data Model

The model is based on key-value pairs, similar to how Kubernetes itself organizes infrastructure metadata with labels. It allows for flexible and accurate time series data, powering its PromQL.

Accessible Format and Protocols

Exposing Prometheus metrics is a pretty straightforward task. Metrics are human-readable, in a self-explanatory format, and published using a standard HTTP transport. You can check that the metrics are correctly exposed just by using your web browser.

Service Discovery

The Prometheus server is in charge of periodically scraping targets, so that applications and services don't have to worry about emitting data (metrics are pulled, not pushed). Prometheus servers have several methods to auto-discover scrape targets. Some servers can be configured to filter and match container metadata, making them an excellent fit for ephemeral Kubernetes workloads.

Modular and Highly Available Components

Metric collection, alerting, graphical visualization, etc., are performed by different composable services. All these services are designed to support redundancy and sharding.

Native Query Language Support

As mentioned in the overview, Prometheus provides a functional query language, PromQL, that allows users to select and aggregate time series data in real time. The result of an expression can either be represented as graphical or tabular data in Prometheus's expression browser, or it can be consumed by external systems, via the HTTP API.

Support for Dashboarding and Reporting

Prometheus supports integration with various reporting solutions, such as Grafana and Splunk, for getting Kubernetes metrics view for operational usage. This simplifies operations management tasks for container ecosystem for inventory management, performance management, and incident management.

Prometheus on Google Kubernetes Engine

In Chapter 8, while deploying our Sock Shop application, we used a YAML configuration file to provide details required for deploying applications on the target/worker node. Before installing Prometheus and Alertmanager, we want to give you an overview of the basics of the YAML file structure. YAML is a human-readable data-serialization language. It is commonly used for configuration files and in applications in which data is being stored or transmitted. YAML was created specifically for common-use cases, such as the following:

- Configuration files

- Log files

- Cross-language data sharing

- Complex data structures

At a high-level, the following are the building blocks of a YAML file, exemplified in Figure 9-2.

Key-value pair: The basic type of entry in a YAML file is of a key-value pair. After the key and colon, there is a space and then the value.

Arrays/Lists: Lists have a number of items under their name. The elements of a list begin with a "-."

Dictionary/Map: A more complex type of YAML file is a dictionary or a map.

Key-Value Pair	Array/Lists	Dictionary/Map
Fruit: Apple Vegetable: Radish Liquid: Water Meat: Goat	Fruits: - Orange - Banana - Mango Vegetables: - Potato - Tomato - Carrot	Banana: Calories: 200 Fat: 0.5g Carbs: 30g Grapes: Calories: 100 Fat: 0.4g Carbs: 20g

Figure 9-2. YAML file building blocks

These days, Kubernetes resources, such as Pods, services, and deployments, are created by using YAML files. In the upcoming sections, we will cover the creation of the deployment resource, by using a YAML file and will provide you with an overview of key fields used in the same.

Now let's start with setting up Prometheus and Alertmanager. We will use the same container environment set up in Chapter 8 for this exercise.

Setting Up Prometheus on a Kubernetes Cluster

Let's start setting up Prometheus in a Kubernetes environment. Figure 9-3 provides an overview of the task flows that we will follow to deploy Prometheus.

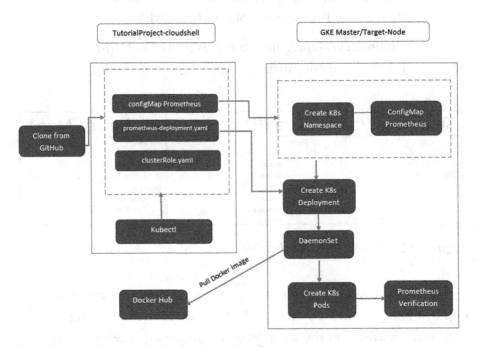

Figure 9-3. *Prometheus deployment flow*

The sequence of steps to be taken for Prometheus deployment is as follows:

1. We will first connect to Cloud Shell in the working project.

2. We will then clone the configuration files from GitHub.

3. We will then use kubectl, which is preconfigured in Google Cloud Shell, to create a namespace on the GKE cluster.

4. We will create a cluster role and cluster role binding on the GKE cluster.

5. We will create config map and then deploy Prometheus, using this config map on the GKE cluster.

6. We will then create a service for Prometheus for end-user access.

7. Finally, we will test the status of Prometheus deployment, using command-line and web browser access.

Installing and Setting Up Prometheus on GKE

Cloning Prometheus Code from GitHub

Before cloning Prometheus from GitHub, first, we will create the gcptutorialmail folder, under the /home directory, and under gcptutorialmail, we will create the prometheus folder. This prometheus folder contains all the configuration files required to install Prometheus on GKE.

> **Step 1:** Execute the following command, to create the gcptutorialmail and prometheus folders.
>
> **Command:**
>
> cd /home
>
> mkdir gcptutorialmail

Output: Figure 9-4 shows the output of the preceding command.

```
gcptutorialmail@cloudshell:/home (tutorial-project-268109)$ mkdir gcptutorialmail
```

Figure 9-4. *Creating the* `gcptutorialmail` *directory*

Navigate to the `gcptutorialmail` folder by executing the following command.

Command:

```
cd /gcptutorialmail
```

Output: Figure 9-4.1 shows the output of the preceding command.

```
gcptutorialmail@cloudshell:/home (tutorial-project-268109)$ cd gcptutorialmail/
gcptutorialmail@cloudshell:~ (tutorial-project-268109)$ pwd
/home/gcptutorialmail
gcptutorialmail@cloudshell:~ (tutorial-project-268109)$
```

Figure 9-4.1. *Moving to the* `gcptutorialmail` *directory*

Now create the `prometheus` folder under gcptutorialmail, by executing the following command.

Command: `mkdir prometheus`

Output: Figure 9-4.2 shows the output of the preceding command.

```
gcptutorialmail@cloudshell:~ (tutorial-project-268109)$ mkdir prometheus
```

Figure 9-4.2. *Creating the* `prometheus` *directory*

Navigate to the prometheus folder, by executing the following command.

Command: cd /prometheus

Output: Figure 9-4.3 shows the output of the preceding command.

```
gcptutorialmail@cloudshell:~ (tutorial-project-268109)$ cd prometheus/
gcptutorialmail@cloudshell:~/prometheus (tutorial-project-268109)$ pwd
/home/gcptutorialmail/prometheus
gcptutorialmail@cloudshell:~/prometheus (tutorial-project-268109)$
```

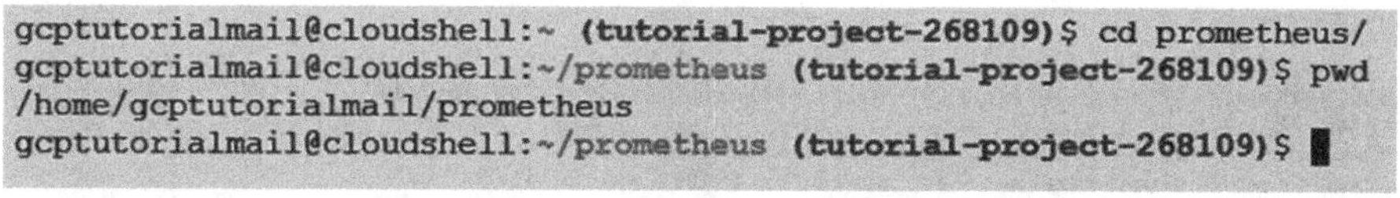

Figure 9-4.3. *Navigationg to the prometheus directory*

Step 2: Clone the code from GitHub (https://github.com/dryice-devops/gcp-prometheus.git), by executing the following command.

Command: git clone https://github.com/dryice-devops/gcp-prometheus.git

Output: Figure 9-4.4 shows the output of the preceding command.

```
gcptutorialmail@cloudshell:~/prometheus (tutorial-project-268109)$ git clone https://github.com/dryice-devops/gcp-prometheus.git
```

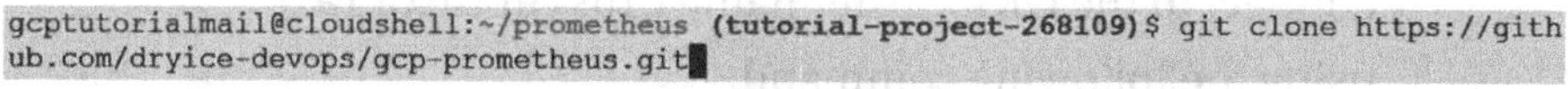

Figure 9-4.4. *Cloning Prometheus code from GitHub*

Verifying the Cloned Files: After cloning the files from GitHub, you will see the following files:

clusterRole.yaml

configMap.yaml

prometheus-deployment.yaml

To verify that the preceding configuration files are successfully cloned to the local prometheus folder, execute the following command.

Command: 11

Output: Figure 9-5 shows the output of the preceding command.

```
gcptutorialmail@cloudshell:~/prometheus (tutorial-project-268109)$ ll
total 24
drwxr-xr-x  2 gcptutorialmail gcptutorialmail 4096 Mar  6 20:49 ./
drwxr-xr-x 17 gcptutorialmail gcptutorialmail 4096 Apr 28 15:47 ../
-rw-r--r--  1 gcptutorialmail gcptutorialmail  630 Mar  2 21:31 clusterRole.yaml
-rw-r--r--  1 gcptutorialmail gcptutorialmail 5543 Mar  6 14:44 configMap.yaml
-rw-r--r--  1 gcptutorialmail gcptutorialmail  887 Mar  2 21:48 prometheus-deployment.yaml
gcptutorialmail@cloudshell:~/prometheus (tutorial-project-268109)$
```

Figure 9-5. *Verifying the cloned files*

Creating the Namespace

To install Prometheus, the first step is to create a separate namespace in the existing cluster for logical segregation. To do this, perform the following steps:

Step 1: Before creating the namespace, be sure to connect to the GKE cluster name clustertutorial, using the following command.

Command: gcloud container clusters get-credentials clustertutorial --zone us-central1-a --project tutorial-project-268109

Output: Figure 9-6 shows the output of the preceding command.

```
gcptutorialmail@cloudshell:~/GCP (tutorial-project-268109)$ gcloud container clusters get-credentials clustertut
orial --zone us-central1-a --project tutorial-project-268109
Fetching cluster endpoint and auth data.
kubeconfig entry generated for clustertutorial.
```

Figure 9-6. *Namespace creation for Prometheus monitoring*

Step 2: Execute the following command on Cloud Shell for the tutorial project, to create a new namespace, called prometheus, from the prometheus directory.

Command: kubectl create namespace prometheus

Output: Figure 9-6.1 shows the output of the preceding command.

```
gcptutorialmail@cloudshell:~ (tutorial-project-268109)$ kubectl create namespace prometheus
namespace/prometheus created
```

Figure 9-6.1. *New namespace creation for Prometheus monitoring*

Cluster Role YAML File

Let's deep-dive into the content of the cluster role YAML file (clusterRole.yaml) in the prometheus folder, to understand the section and its relevance. The file has two sections: ClusterRole and ClusterRoleBinding.

Cluster Role Section

apiVersion

The initial section of the file has the field that defines the apiVersion of Kubernetes with which to interact with the Kubernetes API server. It is typically used for creating the object. apiVersion varies, depending upon the Kubernetes version in your environment. We used the following apiVersion: rbac.authorization.k8s.io/v1beta1 for ClusterRole.

kind

The kind field defines the types of the Kubernetes object, e.g., cluster role, deployment, service, Pods, etc. In our case, we are using ClusterRole.

metadata

This section has name subcomponents defined in the file. The name field specifies the name of the object. In our example, we are using prometheus as the name, as shown in Figure 9-6.2.

```
apiVersion: rbac.authorization.k8s.io/vlbetal
kind: ClusterRole
metadata:
   name: prometheus
```

Figure 9-6.2. *Cluster role YAML file walkthrough*

rules

A rule is a set of operations (verbs) that can be carried out on a group of resources that belong to different API groups (also known as legacy groups). In our example, we are creating the rule that allows a user to execute several operations on nodes, proxies, service, end points, and Pods that belong to the core (expressed by " " in the YAML file), apps, and extensions. The API groups rule has several subcomponent elements.

resources: This field defines various Kubernetes resources.

verbs: This field defines the action to be performed on the resources.

nonResourceURLs: This is a set of partial URLs that a user should have access to. Non-resource URLs are not namespaced. This field is only applicable for cluster roles referenced from a cluster role binding. Rules can either apply to API resources (such as "pods" or "secrets") or non-resource URL paths (such as "/api"), but not both, as shown in Figure 9-6.3.

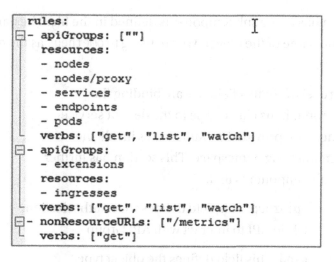

```
rules:
- apiGroups: [""]
  resources:
  - nodes
  - nodes/proxy
  - services
  - endpoints
  - pods
  verbs: ["get", "list", "watch"]
- apiGroups:
  - extensions
  resources:
  - ingresses
  verbs: ["get", "list", "watch"]
- nonResourceURLs: ["/metrics"]
  verbs: ["get"]
```

Figure 9-6.3. *Cluster Role YAML file components*

Cluster Role Binding Section

apiVersion

The initial section of the file has the field that defines the apiVersion of Kubernetes with which to interact with the Kubernetes API server. It is typically used to create the object. apiVersions vary, depending on the Kubernetes version in your environment. For cluster role binding, we use the following API: rbac.authorization.k8s.io/v1beta1.

kind

Kind field defines the types of the Kubernetes object, e.g., ClusterRole, Deployment, Service, Pods, etc. In our case, we are using ClusterRoleBinding.

metadata

This section has name subcomponents defined in the file. The name field specifies the name of the object. We are using prometheus as the name in our example.

roleRef: In this field, we are binding the Prometheus cluster role to the default service account provided by Kubernetes inside the monitoring namespace. This section has further subcomponents in it.

apiGroup: This field defines rbac.authorization. k8s.io API to interact with API Group

kind: This field defines the object type.

name: The name of the cluster role, e.g., prometheus.

Subjects: This section defines the set of users and processes that must access the Kubernetes API. This section has further subcomponents in it.

kind: This field defines the object type service account.

name: As every Kubernetes installation has a service account called default that is associated with every running Pod, we used the same: default.

namespace: This field defines the namespace
name for the cluster role binding, e.g., monitoring
(which we created in the "Creating the
Namespace" section), as shown in Figure 9-6.4.

```
apiVersion: rbac.authorization.k8s.io/v1beta1
kind: ClusterRoleBinding
metadata:
  name: prometheus
roleRef:
  apiGroup: rbac.authorization.k8s.io
  kind: ClusterRole
  name: prometheus
subjects:
- kind: ServiceAccount
  name: default
  namespace: prometheus
```

Figure 9-6.4. *Cluster role YAML file components and subcomponents*

Now we will create for Prometheus the cluster role and cluster role
binding that was just created.

Step 1: Create the role, using the following
command on Cloud Shell for tutorial project, under
the prometheus folder.

Command:

kubectl create -f clusterRole.yaml

Output: Figure 9-7 shows the output of the
preceding command.

```
gcptutorialmail@cloudshell:~/prometheus (tutorial-project-268109)$ kubectl create -f clusterRole.yaml
clusterrole.rbac.authorization.k8s.io/prometheus created
clusterrolebinding.rbac.authorization.k8s.io/prometheus created
```

Figure 9-7. *Cluster role and cluster role binding creation for
Prometheus*

Creating a ConfigMap

ConfigMap will be used to decouple any configuration artifacts from image content and alerting rules, which will be mounted to the Prometheus container in /etc/prometheus as prometheus.yaml and prometheus.rules files.

> **Step 1:** We will use a Config-Map YAML file in the prometheus folder to create ConfigMap. Now let's review the content of this YAML file. ConfigMap incorporates the prometheus.rules and prometheus.yaml files under the data section.
>
> apiVersion: The initial section of the file defines the field with which the apiVersion of Kubernetes is to interact with the Kubernetes API server. It is typically used for creating the object. apiVersion varies, depending on the Kubernetes version in your environment.
>
> kind: The kind field defines the types of the Kubernetes objects, e.g., cluster role, deployment, service, Pods, etc. We are using ConfigMap as the object.
>
> metadata: This section has name subcomponents defined in the file that contains the ConfigMap data.
>
>> name: This field has the name of the ConfigMap. In our example, we are using prometheus-server-conf.
>>
>> labels: This field defines the label for ConfigMap, e.g., prometheus-server-conf.
>>
>> namespace: This field defines the namespace in which ConfigMap will be created, e.g., monitoring, as shown in Figure 9-8.

```
apiVersion: v1
kind: ConfigMap
metadata:
  name: prometheus-server-conf
  labels:
      name: prometheus-server-conf
  namespace: prometheus
```

Figure 9-8. *Config Map YAML file components and subcomponents*

data: This field defines the prometheus.rules and prometheus.yml content and passes their information at runtime to ConfigMap.

prometheus.rules: This section contains the alerting rules used to generate the Alert, on the basis of various conditions, e.g., out of memory, out of disk space, etc. We chose High Pod Memory usage.

prometheus.yml: Prometheus is configured through a configuration file, which is prometheus.yml. The configuration file defines everything related to scraping jobs and their instances, as well as which rule files to load. prometheus.yml contains all the configuration that helps to dynamically discover Pods and services running in the Kubernetes cluster. Following are scrape jobs in our Prometheus scrape configuration:

kubernetes-apiservers: This gets all the metrics from the API servers.

kubernetes-nodes: All Kubernetes node metrics will be collected with this job.

kubernetes-pods: All the Pod metrics will be discovered, if the Pod metadata is annotated with prometheus.io/scrape and prometheus.io/port annotations.

kubernetes-cadvisor: Collects all cAdvisor metrics.

kubernetes-service-endpoints: All the service end points will be scrapped if the service metadata is annotated with prometheus.io/scrape and prometheus.io/port annotations. It will use blackbox monitoring.

prometheus.rules: This contains all the alert rules for sending alerts to Alertmanager.

global: The global configuration specifies parameters that are valid in all other configuration contexts. global has various subcomponents, as follows:

scrape_interval: How frequently to scrape targets by default. We chose 20s for our example.

evaluation_interval: The length of time until a scrape request times out. We chose 20s for our example.

rule_files: This specifies a list of globs. Rules and alerts are read from all matching files that we defend under prometheus.rules and the path defined as /etc/prometheus/prometheus.rules, as shown in Figure 9-9.

```
data:
  prometheus.rules: |-
    groups:
    - name: devopscube demo alert
      rules:
      - alert: High Pod Meory
        expr: sum(container_memory_usage_bytes) > 1
        for: 1m
        labels:
          severity: slack
        annotations:
          summary: High Memory Usage
  prometheus.yml: |-
    global:
      scrape_interval: 20s
      evaluation_interval: 20s
    rule_files:
    - /etc/prometheus/prometheus.rules
    alerting:
      alertmanagers:
      - scheme: http
        static_configs:
        - targets:
          - "alertmanager.monitoring.svc:9093"
```

Figure 9-9. *ConfigMap YAML file fields and subfields*

Step 2: Execute the following command to create the ConfigMap from the prometheus folder.

Command: kubectl create -f config-map.yaml -n prometheus

Output: Figure 9-10 shows the output of the preceding command.

```
gcptutorialmail@cloudshell:~/prometheus (tutorial-project-268109)$ kubectl create -f configMap.yaml -n promethe
s
configmap/prometheus-server-conf created
```

Figure 9-10. *ConfigMap creation for Prometheus*

Prometheus Deployment

After setting up the roles and configuration and environment for Prometheus deployment, perform the following steps to install Prometheus on the Kubernetes cluster created on GKE.

To deploy Prometheus on the Kubernetes cluster, we will use the `prometheus-deployment.yaml` file in `prometheus` folder.

We will use the official Prometheus Docker image v2.12.0 from the Docker hub. In this configuration, the Prometheus ConfigMap mounting is as a file inside `/etc/Prometheus`.

Following are details of the Prometheus deployment file:

> `apiVersion:` The beginning section of this file defines the field with which the apiVersion of Kubernetes is to interact with the Kubernetes API server. It is typically used for creating the object. apiVersion varies depending upon the Kubernetes version in your environment.

> `kind:` The `kind` field defines the types of the Kubernetes object, e.g., cluster role, deployment, service, Pods, etc. We are using the object as deployment.

> `metadata:` This section has name subcomponents defined in the file.

>> `name:` This field specifies the name of service object, e.g., prometheus-deployment.

>> `namespace:` This field specifies the namespace of the service object, e.g., monitoring, as shown in Figure 9-11.

```
apiVersion: extensions/v1beta1
kind: Deployment
metadata:
    name: prometheus-deployment
    namespace: prometheus
```

Figure 9-11. *Prometheus deployment YAML file walkthrough*

spec: This field specifies the service.

> replicas: This field provides data about the number of Pods to be available at a particular instance.

> selector: This section provides details about the service selector.

>> matchLabels: This is the name that will be used to match and identify the service, as shown in Figure 9-12.

```
spec:
    replicas: 1
    selector:
      matchLabels:
        app: prometheus-server
```

Figure 9-12. *Prometheus deployment YAML file walkthrough*

template: The type of port used by the service

> metadata: name will be used to match and identify the service.

>> labels: A key-value pair that is attached to the object intended to be used to specify identifying attributes

>>> app = key

>>> prometheus-server = value

The preceding is illustrated in Figure 9-13.

```
template:
  metadata:
    labels:
      app: prometheus-server
```

Figure 9-13. *Prometheus deployment YAML file walkthrough—*
continued

Spec:

    containers: detail of container object

    name: name of the container

    image: image with version

    args: argument used at the time of container creation

        "--config.file=/etc/prometheus/ prometheus.yml" file name to be used at the time of deployment

        "-storage.tsdb.path=/prometheus/" this determines where Prometheus writes its database

    ports:

        containerport - application listening port as shown in Figure 9-14.

```
spec:
  containers:
  - name: prometheus
    image: prom/prometheus:v2.6.1
    args:
      - "--config.file=/etc/prometheus/prometheus.yml"
      - "--storage.tsdb.path=/prometheus/"
    ports:
      - containerPort: 9090
```

Figure 9-14. *Prometheus deployment YAML file walkthrough—*
continued

volumeMounts: A storage volume allows an
existing StorageOS volume to be mounted into your
Pod. Two volumeMounts are created: prometheus-
config-volume and prometheus-storage-volume.
prometheus-config-volume will be using our
ConfigMap to manage prometheus.yml. With
prometheus-storage-volume, we are creating an
emptyDir to store the Prometheus data.

Name: This is the name of the volume.

mouthPath: This defines the mounted path, as
shown in Figure 9-15.

```
volumeMounts:
  - name: prometheus-config-volume
    mountPath: /etc/prometheus/
  - name: prometheus-storage-volume
    mountPath: /prometheus/
```

Figure 9-15. *Prometheus deployment YAML file walkthrough—*
continued

volume: This is a directory with data that is accessible to all containers running in a Pod and gets mounted onto each container's filesystem. Its lifetime is identical to the lifetime of the Pod. Decoupling the volume lifetime from the container lifetime allows the volume to persist across container crashes and restarts. Further, volumes can be backed by a host's filesystem or by persistent block storage volumes, such as AWS EBS, or a distributed filesystem.

name: Name of the volume

configMap: Volume using ConfigMap

defaultMode

name Defined name of the ConfigMap that has to be used.

name:

emptyDir: The emptyDir volume is first created when a Pod is assigned to a node and exists as long as that Pod is running on that node we used to store the Prometheus data, as shown in Figure 9-16.

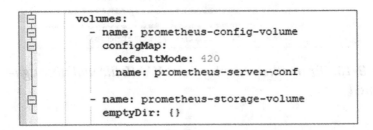

```
volumes:
  - name: prometheus-config-volume
    configMap:
      defaultMode: 420
      name: prometheus-server-conf

  - name: prometheus-storage-volume
    emptyDir: {}
```

Figure 9-16. *Prometheus deployment YAML file walkthrough—continued*

Follow the next steps, to install Prometheus on the Kubernetes cluster.

Step 1: Execute the following command from the prometheus directory.

Command: `kubectl apply -f prometheus-deployment.yaml -n prometheus`

Output: Figure 9-17 shows the output of the preceding command.

```
gcptutorialmail@cloudshell:~/prometheus (tutorial-project-268109)$ kubectl create -f prometheus-deployment.yaml
-n prometheus
deployment.extensions/prometheus-deployment created
```

Figure 9-17. *Prometheus deployment*

To verify the deployment, list the Pod, using the following command.

Command: `kubectl get pods -n prometheus`

Output: Figure 9-18 shows the output of the preceding command.

```
gcptutorialmail@cloudshell:~/prometheus (tutorial-project-268109)$ kubectl get pods -n prometheus
NAME                                      READY   STATUS    RESTARTS   AGE
prometheus-deployment-78fb5694b4-m46rq    1/1     Running   0          7h23m
```

Figure 9-18. *Prometheus deployment—continued*

Step 2: To enable the service to access the Prometheus UI, use the port forwarding command with the Prometheus Pod name we received previously.

Command: `kubectl port-forward prometheus-deployment-78fb5694b4-m46rq 8080:9090 -n prometheus`

Output: Figure 9-19 is the output of the port forwarding. It will set Grafana to run on port 9090.

```
gcptutorialmail@cloudshell:~/prometheus (tutorial-project-268109)$ kubectl port-forward prometheus-deployment-7
fb5694b4-jncrn 8080:9090 -n prometheus
Forwarding from 127.0.0.1:8080 -> 9090
```

***Figure 9-19.** Port forwarding to run Prometheus*

Step 3. To test the status of Prometheus deployment, go to the web preview in Cloud Shell, to access the UI, after changing the port to 8080. Go to web preview ➤ Change port ➤ 8080, as shown in Figures 9-20 and 9-21.

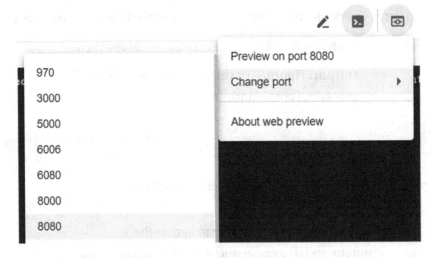

***Figure 9-20.** Forwarding to port 8080*

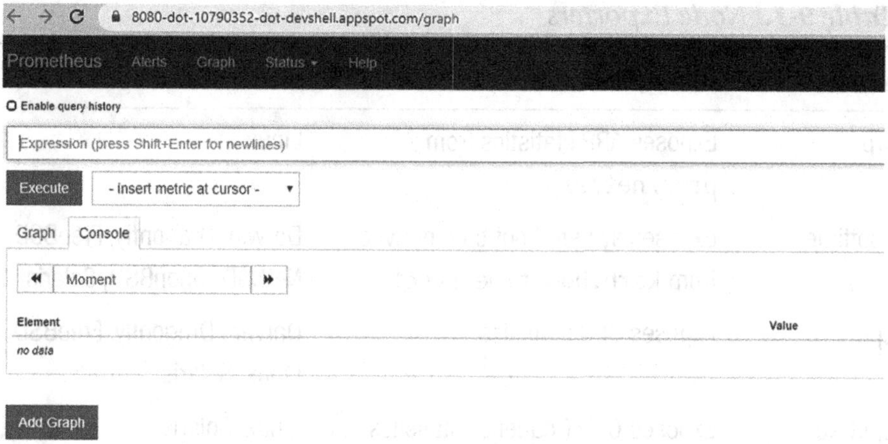

Figure 9-21. *Prometheus screen*

Exporters

Exporters help to fetch state/logs/metrics from the application/
Kubernetes service and provide data to Prometheus. They are similar
to adapters or plug-ins in other monitoring tools available on the
market. Prometheus provides a list of official and externally contributed
exporters. Let's explore some that are useful for container infrastructure
monitoring, by accessing the following: `https://prometheus.io/docs/`
`instrumenting/exporters/`.

Node Exporter

Node Exporter is a Prometheus exporter for fetching metrics for hardware
and OS metrics exposed by Unix/Linux kernels. It is written in the Go
language, with pluggable metric collectors. Collectors differ according to
OS type usage. Table 9-1 provides a few examples.

Table 9-1. *Node Exporters*

Name	Description	OS
arp	Exposes ARP statistics from /proc/net/arp	Linux
boottime	Exposes system boot time derived from `kern.boottime sysctl`	Darwin, Dragonfly, FreeBSD, NetBSD, OpenBSD, Solaris
cpu	Exposes CPU statistics	Darwin, Dragonfly, FreeBSD, Linux, Solaris
cpufreq	Exposes CPU frequency statistics	Linux, Solaris
diskstats	Exposes disk I/O statistics	Darwin, Linux, OpenBSD
filesystem	Exposes filesystem statistics, such as disk space used	Darwin, Dragonfly, FreeBSD, Linux, OpenBSD
hwmon	Exposes hardware monitoring and sensor data from `/sys/class/hwmon/`	Linux
meminfo	Exposes memory statistics	Darwin, Dragonfly, FreeBSD, Linux, OpenBSD
netclass	Exposes network interface info from `/sys/class/net/`	Linux
netdev	Exposes network interface statistic, such as bytes transferred	Darwin, Dragonfly, FreeBSD, Linux, OpenBSD
netstat	Exposes network statistics from `/proc/net/netstat`. This is the same information as `netstat -s`.	Linux
nfs	Exposes NFS client statistics from `/proc/net/rpc/nfs`. This is the same information as `nfsstat -c`.	Linux

(*continued*)

Table 9-1. *(continued)*

Name	Description	OS
nfsd	Exposes NFS kernel server statistics from `/proc/net/rpc/nfsd`. This is the same information as `nfsstat -s`.	Linux
uname	Exposes system information as provided by the uname system call	Darwin, FreeBSD, Linux, OpenBSD

Installation of Node Exporter in Prometheus Using a Helm Chart

To install Node Exporter, Helm and Tiller are required. Helm and Tiller are preconfigured with the Cloud Shell explained in the "Deploying Grafana" section of Chapter 7.

Step 1: Execute the following command to update Tiller and assign a service account role.

Command: `helm init --service-account tiller --history-max 200 –upgrade`

Now run the following command, to verify that Helm and Tiller are running smoothly. You should now see both the client and server version information.

Command: `helm version`

Output: Figure 9-22 shows the output of the preceding command.

```
gcptutorialmail@cloudshell:~/prometheus (tutorial-project-268109)$ helm version
Client: &version.Version{SemVer:"v2.14.1", GitCommit:"5270352a09c7e8b6e8c9593002a73535276507c0", GitTreeState:"
lean"}
Server: &version.Version{SemVer:"v2.14.1", GitCommit:"5270352a09c7e8b6e8c9593002a73535276507c0", GitTreeState:"
lean"}
```

Figure 9-22. *Prometheus screen*

Step 2: Execute the following command. It will download the exporter from the following GitHub URL and install the Node Exporter on the GKE cluster.

https://github.com/helm/charts/tree/master/ stable/prometheus-node-exporter

Command: helm install --name node-exporter stable/prometheus-node-exporter

Output: Figures 9-23 and 9-24 show the output of the preceding command.

```
gcptutorialmail@cloudshell:~$ helm install --name node-exporter stable/prometheus-node-exporter[]
```

Figure 9-23. *Node Exporter installation*

```
==> v1/Pod(related)
NAME                                          READY  STATUS            RESTARTS  AGE
node-exporter-prometheus-node-exporter-8v5rf  0/1    ContainerCreating  0        1s
node-exporter-prometheus-node-exporter-dnrqf  0/1    ContainerCreating  0        1s
node-exporter-prometheus-node-exporter-lv8gq  0/1    ContainerCreating  0        1s

==> v1/Service
NAME                                    TYPE       CLUSTER-IP    EXTERNAL-IP  PORT(S)   AGE
node-exporter-prometheus-node-exporter  ClusterIP  10.81.13.221  <none>       9100/TCP  1s

==> v1/ServiceAccount
NAME                                    SECRETS  AGE
node-exporter-prometheus-node-exporter  1        1s

==> v1beta1/PodSecurityPolicy
NAME                                    PRIV   CAPS     SELINUX   RUNASUSER  FSGROUP    SUPGROUP   READONLYROOTFS  VOLUMES
node-exporter-prometheus-node-exporter  false  RunAsAny RunAsAny  MustRunAs  MustRunAs  false      configMap,emptyDir,projected,secret,down
ardAPI,persistentVolumeClaim,hostPath

NOTES:
1. Get the application URL by running these commands:
     export POD_NAME=$(kubectl get pods --namespace default -l "app=prometheus-node-exporter,release=node-exporter" -o jsonpath="{.items[0].me
adata.name}")
     echo "Visit http://127.0.0.1:9100 to use your application"
     kubectl port-forward --namespace default $POD_NAME 9100
```

Figure 9-24. *Node Exporter installation—continued*

Step 3: Now let's verify that the Node Exporter service is running, using the following command.

Command: kubectl get svc

Output: Figure 9-25 shows the output of the preceding command.

```
▶  Cloud Shell

☷  ⚙   cloudshell ✕  + ▾

gcptutorialmail@cloudshell:~$ kubectl get svc
NAME                                        TYPE        CLUSTER-IP      EXTERNAL-IP   PORT(S)     AGE
gke-postgresql                              ClusterIP   10.81.9.139     <none>        5432/TCP    6m26s
gke-postgresql-headless                     ClusterIP   None            <none>        5432/TCP    6m26s
gke-postgresql-metrics                      ClusterIP   10.81.9.38      <none>        9187/TCP    6m26s
kubernetes                                  ClusterIP   10.81.0.1       <none>        443/TCP     8h
node-exporter-prometheus-node-exporter      ClusterIP   10.81.13.221    <none>        9100/TCP    82s
gcptutorialmail@cloudshell:~$ []
```

***Figure 9-25.** Service list*

The node-exporter-prometheus-node-exporter service should be visible and in a running state, as highlighted in Figure 9-25. Note, too, the cluster IP for the service, as it will be used in the next step.

Step 4: Next is to configure the installed Node Exporter from the previous step.

Navigate to the prometheus folder and open the config-map.yaml file. Under the scarpe_config section, find the job_name: node_exporter section and details for job name and static_configs, as shown in Figure 9-26.

```
      - job_name: node-exporter
        static_configs:
          - targets: ['10.81.13.221:9100']
```

***Figure 9-26.** Node Exporter setting*

job_name: This field represents the job name for Node Exporter. We are using the value node-exporter as job_name.

static_configs: This section has a subsection named targets. "Targets" refers to the job target, 10.81.13.221 (cluster IP), and 9100, the service port on which Node Export is running. You can use the following command to verify your cluster IP and port information.

Command: kubectl get svc

Output: Figure 9-27 shows the output of the preceding command.

```
Cloud Shell

cloudshell ×  + ▾

gcptutorialmail@cloudshell:~$ kubectl get svc
NAME                                         TYPE        CLUSTER-IP     EXTERNAL-IP   PORT(S)      AGE
gke-postgresql                               ClusterIP   10.81.9.139    <none>        5432/TCP     6m26s
gke-postgresql-headless                      ClusterIP   None           <none>        5432/TCP     6m26s
gke-postgresql-metrics                       ClusterIP   10.81.9.38     <none>        9187/TCP     6m26s
kubernetes                                   ClusterIP   10.81.0.1      <none>        443/TCP      8h
node-exporter-prometheus-node-exporter       ClusterIP   10.81.13.221   <none>        9100/TCP     82s
gcptutorialmail@cloudshell:~$ []
```

Figure 9-27. *Service list*

Step 5: Execute the following commands to reflect the Prometheus ConfigMap changes made in the previous steps.

Commands:

- kubectl delete configmaps prometheus-server-conf -n=prometheus

- kubectl create -f config-map.yaml

- `kubectl delete deployment prometheus-deployment -n prometheus`

- `kubectl apply -f prometheus-deployment.yaml -n prometheus`

  Step 6: Verify Node Exporter from the Prometheus UI, by logging in and navigating to Status and then Targets on Prometheus. Then execute the following command.

  `$ kubectl port-forward prometheus-deployment-78fb5694b4-7z6dd 8080:9090 -n prometheus`

  The code highlighted in yellow is a Pod name of Prometheus that you can get by executing the following command.

  Command: `kubectl get pod -n prometheus`

  Output: The output of the preceding command is shown in Figure 9-28.

```
NAME                                         READY    STATUS     RESTARTS   AGE
prometheus-deployment-78fb5694b4-7z6dd        1/1      Running    0          19m
gcptutorialmail@cloudshell:~/prometheus (tutorial-project-268109)$ []
```

Figure 9-28. Getting the Prometheus Pod name

  The output of port forwarding is shown in Figure 9-29.

```
gcptutorialmail@cloudshell:~/prometheus (tutorial-project-268109)$ kubectl port-forward prometheus-deployment-7
fb5694b4-jncrn 8080:9090 -n prometheus
Forwarding from 127.0.0.1:8080 -> 9090
```

Figure 9-29. Port forwarding

Open Prometheus in the browser and go to Targets, under the Status drop-down menu, as shown in Figure 9-30.

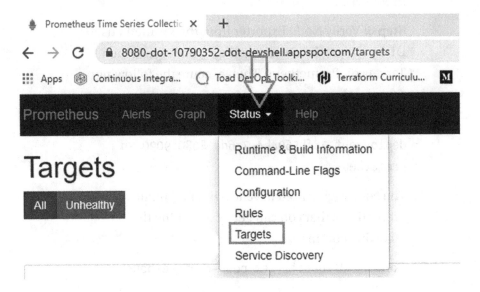

Figure 9-30. Prometheus screen

Search node-exporter and verify that its state is UP, as shown in Figure 9-31.

Figure 9-31. Exporter list

Step 7: Now let's execute a query, to start collecting
and displaying the node metrics. Click the Graph
tab. Under the expression section (text box), type
"node_load15" and click the Execute button, as
shown in Figure 9-32.

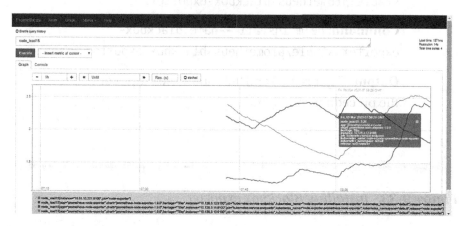

Figure 9-32. *Node metric*

Node Exporter is principally used to monitor infra elements of
container infrastructure and not processes/services.

Blackbox Exporter

Blackbox exporter is used to monitor network end points leveraging HTTP,
HTTPS (via HTTP prober), DNS, TCP, and ICMP. It is used for blackbox
monitoring scenarios in which monitoring for targets is performed from
external sources, and master the monitoring solution does not have
knowledge of the target systems internal mechanics details. Following are
the steps to configure Blackbox exporter.

Step 1: Navigate to the `prometheus` folder and execute the following Helm command, to install the Blackbox exporter. Blackbox exporter content will be downloaded from the following GitHub URL: `https://github.com/helm/charts/tree/master/stable/prometheus-blackbox-exporter`.

Command: `helm install --name blackbox-exporter stable/prometheus-blackbox-exporter`

Output: Figures 9-33 and 9-34 show the output of the preceding command.

Cloud Shell
(tutorial-project-268109)
gcptutorialmail@cloudshell:~/prometheus (tutorial-project-268109)$ helm install --name blackbox-exporter stable/prometheus-blackbox-exporter

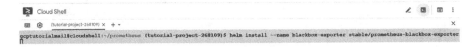

***Figure 9-33.** Installing Blackbox exporter*

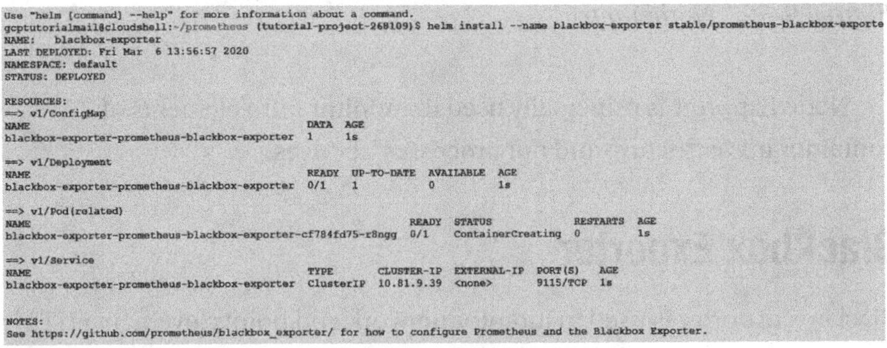
Use "helm [command] --help" for more information about a command.
gcptutorialmail@cloudshell:~/prometheus (tutorial-project-268109)$ helm install --name blackbox-exporter stable/prometheus-blackbox-exporte
NAME: blackbox-exporter
LAST DEPLOYED: Fri Mar 6 13:56:57 2020
NAMESPACE: default
STATUS: DEPLOYED
RESOURCES:
==> v1/ConfigMap
NAME DATA AGE
blackbox-exporter-prometheus-blackbox-exporter 1 1s
==> v1/Deployment
NAME READY UP-TO-DATE AVAILABLE AGE
blackbox-exporter-prometheus-blackbox-exporter 0/1 1 0 1s
==> v1/Pod(related)
NAME READY STATUS RESTARTS AGE
blackbox-exporter-prometheus-blackbox-exporter-cf784fd75-r8ngg 0/1 ContainerCreating 0 1s
==> v1/Service
NAME TYPE CLUSTER-IP EXTERNAL-IP PORT(S) AGE
blackbox-exporter-prometheus-blackbox-exporter ClusterIP 10.81.9.39 <none> 9115/TCP 1s
NOTES:
See https://github.com/prometheus/blackbox_exporter/ for how to configure Prometheus and the Blackbox Exporter.

***Figure 9-34.** Installing Blackbox exporter—continued*

Step 2: Execute the following command from the `prometheus` folder, to get the Blackbox service details, e.g., clusterip (10.81.9.39) and port (9115/TCP), required to configure the Blackbox exporter in the Prometheus ConfigMap file.

Command: kubectl get svc

Output: Figure 9-35 shows the output of the preceding command.

Figure 9-35.   Getting Blackbox exporter service details

Step 3: Now let's configure HTTP Probe through Blackbox exporter in Prometheus. Navigate to prometheus folder and open the configMap.yaml. Find the section named "job_name: 'blackbox' and modify the following entries:

job_name: This field represents the name of the job, which is blackbox in our example.

metrics_path: This field represents the HTTP resource path used for fetching metrics from the target application.

params: This section has a subsection named modules under it. We are using the module for HTTP 200 response monitoring.

static_configs: This section has a subsection named targets. The URL mentioned under targets refers to the URL of the application you want to monitor. You can replace this with the sock Shop application URL we deployed in Chapter 8.

relabel_configs: In this section, modify the URL entry under replacement with the Blackbox service IP:port value we fetched previously, e.g., 10.81.9.39:9115, as shown in Figure 9-36.

```
1    - job_name: 'blackbox'
2      metrics_path: /probe
3      params:
4        module: [http_2xx]  # Look for a HTTP 200 response.
5      static_configs:
6        - targets:
7          - http://34.70.226.32:80/   # Target to probe (webpress application url) with http.
8      relabel_configs:
9        - source_labels: [__address__]
10         target_label: __param_target
11       - source_labels: [__param_target]
12         target_label: instance
13       - target_label: __address__
14         replacement: 10.81.9.39:9115  # The blackbox exporter's real hostname:port.
```

Figure 9-36. *Port update*

Step 4: Execute the following commands, to apply
the changes in the Prometheus ConfigMap and
deployment from the prometheus folder.

- `$kubectl delete configmaps prometheus-server-conf -n=prometheus`

- `$kubectl create -f configMap.yaml`

- `$kubectl delete deployment prometheus-deployment -n prometheus`

- `$kubectl apply -f prometheus-deployment.yaml -n prometheus`

Step 5: Execute the following command, to verify
that the Prometheus ConfigMap and deployment
are running smoothly, from the prometheus folder.

Command: `kubectl get all -n= prometheus`

Step 6: Log in to the Prometheus GUI via
`https://8080-dot-10790352-dot-devshell.appspot.com/targets` to view the `blackbox_http`
end points, as shown in Figure 9-37.

Figure 9-37. *Exporter list*

Step 7: Click Graph in the Prometheus GUI
and execute the following query to get the
duration of the HTTP request, by connecting
the phase for the Sock Shop application URL,
http://34.70.226.32:80, and job, "blackbox" (the
Sock Shop application URL shown in Figure 9-38
could be different in your case).

Query:

```
probe_http_duration_seconds{instance=
"http://34.70.226.32/",job="blackbox",
phase="connect"}
```

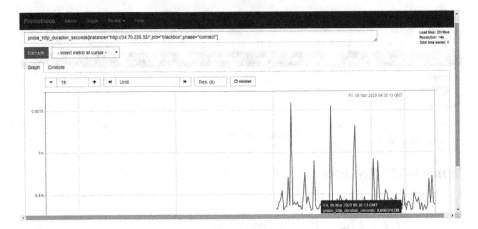

Figure 9-38. *Blackbox metric*

Summary

In this chapter, you learned to use Prometheus for monitoring GKE. In the next chapter, you will see, through hands-on exercises, how to enabled container monitoring, using CI/CD-based automated pipelines.

CHAPTER 10

Automation of GKE Cluster, Application, and Monitoring Deployments

This chapter provides hands-on steps for using infrastructure as code (IaC) and a CI/CD pipeline to automate deployment of container ecosystem infrastructure, applications, and monitoring and covers the following:

- Cleaning Up the GKE Environment Namespace

- Installing Jenkins

- Creating a Service for the Jenkins Slave

- GKE Provisioning, Application Deployment, and Sysdig Agent, Using a Jenkins Pipeline

- Deleting the GKE Cluster from the Jenkins Pipeline.

© Navin Sabharwal, Piyush Pandey 2020
N. Sabharwal and P. Pandey, *Pro Google Kubernetes Engine*,
https://doi.org/10.1007/978-1-4842-6243-6_10

Introduction

With the rise of new platforms and ever changing technologies setting up of infrastructure and then deploying applications over it is becoming complex and time consuming task. Additionally using manual approach of setting up of application and infrastructure increases the probability of human errors and security risks. Also once provisioning of infrastructure and application deployment is completed one has to also manage other aspects like maintainability, scalability, fault-tolerance performance etc.

The rise of IaC or Infrastructure as Code has enabled the reconstruction of application services from nothing but a source code repository, an application data backup, and underline hybrid cloud IaaS or PaaS resources. We leverage codified definition of Infrastructure and application components to provisions and manages our infrastructure in a predictable way. That means that an application, regardless of its environment or where it is hosted, can be spun up with a predefined list of requirements entirely from scratch. That same code can run in production, in staging, and on your local dev environment.

Another key benefit is the consistency of build. If you must manage several environments, such as Dev, QA, Staging, Prod, etc., spinning those up from the same code base ensures they all behave the exact same way and adhere to same set of policies/standards.

Following is a high-level view of how IaC tools operate (Figure 10-1):

1. You describe the desired infrastructure resources in a file (e.g., a virtual network with three public subnets, a compute instance on one of them with a block volume attached to it). We don't need to describe how to create the resources because IaC solutions manage that complexity and provide an abstract view to Developers or Infrastructure operations team to focus on service definition part.

2. The IaC tool typically scan through code in which you have described your service definition and validates whether resource is already present or not before creating new one.

3. If the resources are not present, they are created.

4. If the resources are already present with the same attributes, no action is taken (as what you expect is already present).

5. If matching resources are found with differences, the IaC tool assumes you want them changed and makes the change happen.

6. The tool does not throw errors/fail/create unintended duplicate resources in any of these cases, because these operations are idempotent.

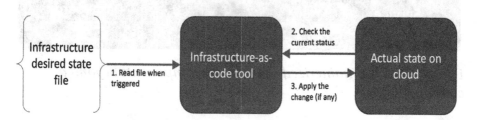

Figure 10-1. *How IaC works*

As DevOps continue to evolve, developers find ways to strengthen the integration of IaC and containers, as they complement each other. Containers incorporate IaC into development cycles as a core component.

We might have to configure a container orchestrator, such as Kubernetes, to keep a certain number of copies of the image running, and we might require other infrastructure and resources, such as a load balancer, DNS entries, TLS certificates, dashboards, alarms, and logging.

A containerized application in the cloud might look something like the following diagram (Figure 10-2), where a container image is only part of the full application.

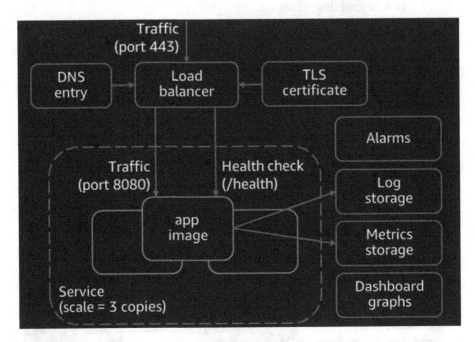

Figure 10-2. *Containerized application components beyond a container image*

The complete application is typically a combination of the container image and an IaC template containing all this configuration. The image bundles all of the application's dependencies, such as system libraries, so ideally it should run exactly the same in Dev and Prod environments. However in case the environments are manually deployed then due to the difference in the configurations same image might not work across multiple environments. It's now also important to have the exact same infrastructure configuration across those environments as well, in order for the application to behave the same.

With the use of IaC solution with in the CI/CD pipeline, we can now manage provisioning and modification of infrastructure and application components easily without any worry about configuration mismatch, security risk, human error etc. A simplified example of our release process is shown in Figure 10-3.

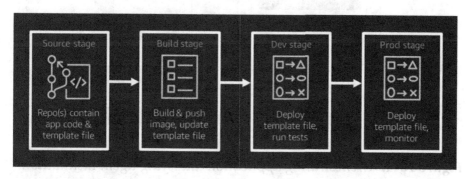

Figure 10-3. *CI/CD pipeline leveraging IaC to automate container monitoring*

The IaC template contains both the container-related configuration and the underlying infrastructure (for example, a load balancer). In the "build" stage of the pipeline, the container image is built and pushed, and the unique ID for the new container image is inserted into the infrastructure as code template. Each stage of the pipeline, like "Dev" and "Prod," then deploys the same infrastructure as code template. This ensures each environment is deployed in predictable, standardized and accelerated manner with all the required controls and best practices as per requirement. Same concept now can be extended to also include enabling of operational controls like monitoring, security, backup etc. to ensure application service has all the necessary operations component integration available the moment it is deployed in any environment.

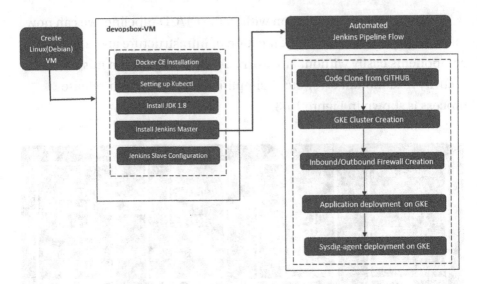

Figure 10-4. *Orchestrating application and sydig-agent installation*

In the upcoming section, we will take you through a hands-on exercise to enable use of the `gcloud` command-line interface tool and Jenkins. We will also cover application deployment scenario using Jenkins as well later in this chapter.

Cleaning Up the GKE Environment Namespace

Before we begin, let's clean up the GKE environment created in Chapter 9. After cleaning, we will set up the automated process in Jenkins to create a cluster, firewall, application deployment, Sysdig agent installation, and cluster deletion. First we will delete the existing GKE cluster name `clustertutorial` in GCP, the Sock Shop application that we covered in previous chapters, and Sysdig agent, which was configured manually in previous chapters.

Log in to the GCP console and navigate to Kubernetes Engine and click Clusters. Next, select the check box of the cluster name: start with clustertutorial, then click the Delete button, which is on the extreme right at the top of that page, to delete the cluster, as shown in Figure 10-5.

Figure 10-5. *GKE cluster clustertutorial deletion*

Environment Setup

In this section, we will use `gcloud` to create/delete GKE cluster and firewall rules. Sysdig will be used to monitor the container ecosystem. To orchestrate all these steps, we will use Jenkins.

Before installing Jenkins (version V2.2.4.5), we will first create a VM in GCP, and then install Java, kubectl, and Docker on the VM.

> **Step 1:** Log in to the GCP console and navigate to Compute Engine, then select VM instances, as shown in Figure 10-6.

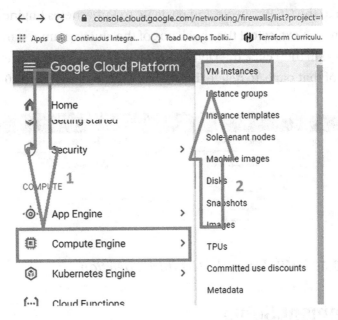

Figure 10-6. GCP Compute Engine

Step 2: Once the VM instances page opens, click on the Create Instance button, to create a new VM (Figure 10-7).

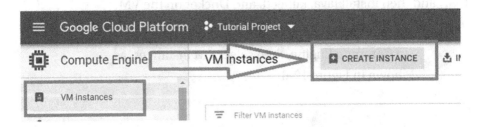

Figure 10-7. GCP VM instances for creating VM

Step 3: Choose any appropriate name (e.g., we named our VM devopsbox) and select as Region us-central1 (Iowa) and as Zone us-central1-a (Figure 10-8).

Name ⓘ
Name is permanent

devopsbox

Labels ⓘ (Optional)

+ Add label

Region ⓘ
Region is permanent

us-central1 (Iowa) ▼

Zone ⓘ
Zone is permanent

us-central1-a ▼

Figure 10-8. *GCP VM instance Creation*

Step 4: Create a VM with the Machine type n1-standard-2 (Figures 10-8.1 and 10-8.2).

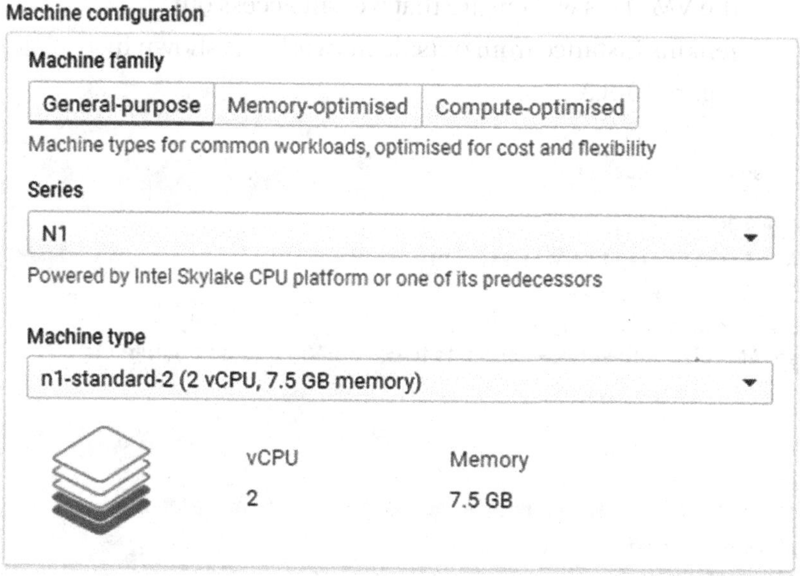

Machine configuration

Machine family

| General-purpose | Memory-optimised | Compute-optimised |

Machine types for common workloads, optimised for cost and flexibility

Series

N1 ▼

Powered by Intel Skylake CPU platform or one of its predecessors

Machine type

n1-standard-2 (2 vCPU, 7.5 GB memory) ▼

	vCPU	Memory
	2	7.5 GB

Figure 10-8.1. *Creating a VM in GCP*

349

Boot disk

Select an image or snapshot to create a boot disk; or attach an existing disk. Can't find what you're looking for? Explore hundreds of VM solutions in Marketplace.

| Public images | Custom images | Snapshots | Existing disks |

☐ Show images with Shielded VM features ⊘

Operating system
Debian ▾

Version
Debian GNU/Linux 9 (stretch) ▾

amd64 built on 20200309

Boot disk type ⊘   Size (GB) ⊘
Standard persistent disk   ▾   10

Figure 10-8.2. *Creating a VM in GCP—continued*

> **Step 5:** Select App Engine default for the Service
> account and check Allow HTTP traffic in the Firewall
> section. Click on the create button, to provision
> the VM. This will ensure that we can access our
> Jenkins instance from outside networks, as shown in
> Figure 10-8.3.

Identity and API access ⊘

Service account ⊘
App Engine default service account ▾

Access scopes ⊘
Use IAM roles with service accounts to control VM access Learn more

Firewall ⊘
Add tags and firewall rules to allow specific network traffic from the Internet.

☑ Allow HTTP traffic
☐ Allow HTTPS traffic

Figure 10-8.3. *Creating VM in GCP—continued*

Step 6: Once a new VM is created, you will see the same on the VM instances page, as shown in Figure 10-8.4.

Figure 10-8.4. *Creating VM in GCP—continued*

Step 7: To connect with the newly created VM, click start and then select Open in browser window, as shown in Figure 10-8.5.

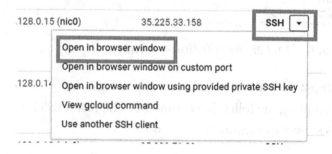

Figure 10-8.5. *Connecting the VM*

Setting Up the Docker CE

Now we will set up the Docker-based container ecosystem, using the 19.03.8 edition of Docker CE on GCP VM.

Step 1: Update the packages by executing the following command. The result will be as shown in Figures 10-9 and 10-9.1.

```
$ sudo apt update
```

```
gcptutorialmail@devopsbox:~$ sudo apt update
Ign:1 http://deb.debian.org/debian stretch InRelease
Get:2 http://security.debian.org stretch/updates InRelease [94.3 kB]
Get:3 http://deb.debian.org/debian stretch-updates InRelease [91.0 kB]
Get:4 http://packages.cloud.google.com/apt cloud-sdk-stretch InRelease [6,377 B]
Get:5 http://deb.debian.org/debian stretch-backports InRelease [91.8 kB]
Get:6 http://packages.cloud.google.com/apt google-compute-engine-stretch-stable InRelease [3,843 B]
Hit:7 http://deb.debian.org/debian stretch Release
Hit:8 http://packages.cloud.google.com/apt google-cloud-packages-archive-keyring-stretch InRelease
Get:9 http://security.debian.org stretch/updates/main Sources [209 kB]
Get:10 http://security.debian.org stretch/updates/main amd64 Packages [520 kB]
Get:11 http://security.debian.org stretch/updates/main Translation-en [230 kB]
```

Figure 10-9. *Docker installation*

```
Get:24 http://deb.debian.org/debian stretch-backports/main Translation-en 2020-03-20-2036.50.pdiff [4,658 B]
Get:24 http://deb.debian.org/debian stretch-backports/main Translation-en 2020-03-20-2036.50.pdiff [4,658 B]
Fetched 1,459 kB in 1s (1,457 kB/s)
Reading package lists... Done
Building dependency tree
Reading state information... Done
1 package can be upgraded. Run 'apt list --upgradable' to see it.
```

Figure 10-9.1. *Docker installation—continued*

Step 2: Install other prerequisite packages, by executing the following command. The result will be as shown in Figures 10-9.2 and 10-9.3.

```
$ sudo apt install apt-transport-https ca-certificates
curl gnupg2 software-properties-common
```

```
gcptutorialmail@devopsbox:~$ sudo apt install apt-transport-https ca-certificates curl gnupg2 software-properties-common
Reading package lists... Done
Building dependency tree
Reading state information... Done
ca-certificates is already the newest version (20161130+nmu1+deb9u1).
curl is already the newest version (7.52.1-5+deb9u10).
```

Figure 10-9.2. *Docker installation*

```
Setting up packagekit (1.1.5-2+deb9u1) ...
Setting up software-properties-common (0.96.20.2-1) ...
Setting up packagekit-tools (1.1.5-2+deb9u1) ...
Processing triggers for sgml-base (1.29) ...
Processing triggers for libc-bin (2.24-11+deb9u4) ...
Processing triggers for systemd (232-25+deb9u12) ...
Processing triggers for dbus (1.10.28-0+deb9u1) ...
```

Figure 10-9.3. *Docker installation—continued*

Step 3: Add a GPG key for the Docker repository, by executing the following command. The output is shown in Figure 10-9.4.

```
$ curl -fsSL https://download.docker.com/linux/debian/
gpg | sudo apt-key add -
```

```
 ssh.cloud.google.com/projects/tutorial-project-268109/zones/us-central1-a/instances/devopsbox?authuser=0&hl=en_GB&projectNumber=353345307101
goptutorialmail@devopsbox:~$ curl -fsSL https://download.docker.com/linux/debian/gpg | sudo apt-key add -
OK
goptutorialmail@devopsbox:~$ ▌
```

Figure 10-9.4. *Docker installation—continued*

Step 4: Add the Docker repository to APT sources, by executing the following command. The output for this command is shown in Figure 10-9.5.

```
$ sudo add-apt-repository "deb [arch=amd64]
https://download.docker.com/linux/debian
$(lsb_release -cs) stable"
```

```
goptutorialmail@devopsbox:~$ sudo add-apt-repository "deb [arch=amd64] https://download.docker.com/linux/debian $(lsb_release -cs) stable"▌
```

Figure 10-9.5. *Docker installation*

Step 5: Update the package database with the Docker packages from the newly added repo, by executing the following command. The result is shown in Figure 10-9.6.

```
$ sudo apt update
```

```
gcptutorialmail@devopsbox:~$ sudo apt update
Hit:1 http://security.debian.org stretch/updates InRelease
Ign:2 http://deb.debian.org/debian stretch InRelease
Hit:3 http://deb.debian.org/debian stretch-updates InRelease
Hit:4 http://deb.debian.org/debian stretch-backports InRelease
Hit:5 http://packages.cloud.google.com/apt cloud-sdk-stretch InRelease
Hit:6 http://deb.debian.org/debian stretch Release
Hit:7 http://packages.cloud.google.com/apt google-compute-engine-stretch-stable InRelease
Hit:8 http://packages.cloud.google.com/apt google-cloud-packages-archive-keyring-stretch InRelease
Get:9 https://download.docker.com/linux/debian stretch InRelease [44.8 kB]
Get:11 https://download.docker.com/linux/debian stretch/stable amd64 Packages [13.1 kB]
Fetched 57.9 kB in 0s (71.2 kB/s)
Reading package lists... Done
Building dependency tree
Reading state information... Done
1 package can be upgraded. Run 'apt list --upgradable' to see it.
gcptutorialmail@devopsbox:~$
```

Figure 10-9.6. *Docker installation—continued*

Step 6: Execute the following command, make sure to install from the Docker repo instead of the default Debian repo. The results of the command are shown in Figures 10-9.7 and 10-9.8.

```
$ apt-cache policy docker-ce
```

```
gcptutorialmail@devopsbox:~$ apt-cache policy docker-ce
```

Figure 10-9.7. *Docker installation—continued*

```
18.03.0~ce-0-debian 500
    500 https://download.docker.com/linux/debian stretch/stable amd64 Packages
17.12.1~ce-0-debian 500
    500 https://download.docker.com/linux/debian stretch/stable amd64 Packages
17.12.0~ce-0-debian 500
    500 https://download.docker.com/linux/debian stretch/stable amd64 Packages
17.09.1~ce-0-debian 500
    500 https://download.docker.com/linux/debian stretch/stable amd64 Packages
17.09.0~ce-0-debian 500
    500 https://download.docker.com/linux/debian stretch/stable amd64 Packages
17.06.2~ce-0-debian 500
    500 https://download.docker.com/linux/debian stretch/stable amd64 Packages
17.06.1~ce-0-debian 500
    500 https://download.docker.com/linux/debian stretch/stable amd64 Packages
17.06.0~ce-0-debian 500
    500 https://download.docker.com/linux/debian stretch/stable amd64 Packages
17.03.3~ce-0-debian-stretch 500
    500 https://download.docker.com/linux/debian stretch/stable amd64 Packages
17.03.2~ce-0-debian-stretch 500
    500 https://download.docker.com/linux/debian stretch/stable amd64 Packages
17.03.1~ce-0-debian-stretch 500
    500 https://download.docker.com/linux/debian stretch/stable amd64 Packages
17.03.0~ce-0-debian-stretch 500
    500 https://download.docker.com/linux/debian stretch/stable amd64 Packages
```

Figure 10-9.8. *Docker installation—continued*

Step 7: Run the following command to install
Docker Community Edition 19.03.8. The results are
shown in Figures 10-9.9 and 10-9.10.

```
$ sudo apt install docker-ce
```

```
gcptutorialmail@devopsbox:~$ sudo apt install docker-ce
Reading package lists... Done
Building dependency tree
Reading state information... Done
The following additional packages will be installed:
    aufs-dkms aufs-tools binutils cgroupfs-mount containerd.io cpp cpp-6 dkms docker-ce-cli fakero
    libatomic1 libc-dev-bin libc6-dev libcc1-0 libcilkrts5 liberror-perl libfakeroot libgcc-6-dev
    libmpc3 libmpfr4 libmpx2 libperl5.24 libquadmath0 libtsan0 libubsan0 linux-compiler-gcc-6-x86
    linux-headers-4.9.0-12-common linux-headers-amd64 linux-kbuild-4.9 linux-libc-dev make manpage
    pigz rename rsync
Suggested packages:
    aufs-dev binutils-doc cpp-doc gcc-6-locales python3-apport menu gcc-multilib autoconf automake
    gcc-6-multilib gcc-6-doc libgcc1-dbg libgomp1-dbg libitm1-dbg libatomic1-dbg libasan3-dbg libl
    libcilkrts5-dbg libmpx2-dbg libquadmath0-dbg git-daemon-run | git-daemon-sysvinit git-doc git-
    git-cvs git-mediawiki git-svn glibc-doc make-doc ed diffutils-doc perl-doc libterm-readline-gn
The following NEW packages will be installed:
    aufs-dkms aufs-tools binutils cgroupfs-mount containerd.io cpp cpp-6 dkms docker-ce docker-ce-
    libasan3 libatomic1 libc-dev-bin libc6-dev libcc1-0 libcilkrts5 liberror-perl libfakeroot libg
    libltdl7 libmpc3 libmpfr4 libmpx2 libperl5.24 libquadmath0 libtsan0 libubsan0 linux-compiler-g
    linux-headers-4.9.0-12-common linux-headers-amd64 linux-kbuild-4.9 linux-libc-dev make manpage
    pigz rename rsync
0 upgraded, 52 newly installed, 0 to remove and 1 not upgraded.
Need to get 139 MB of archives.
After this operation, 632 MB of additional disk space will be used.
Do you want to continue? [Y/n] y
```

Figure 10-9.9. *Docker Community Edition installation*

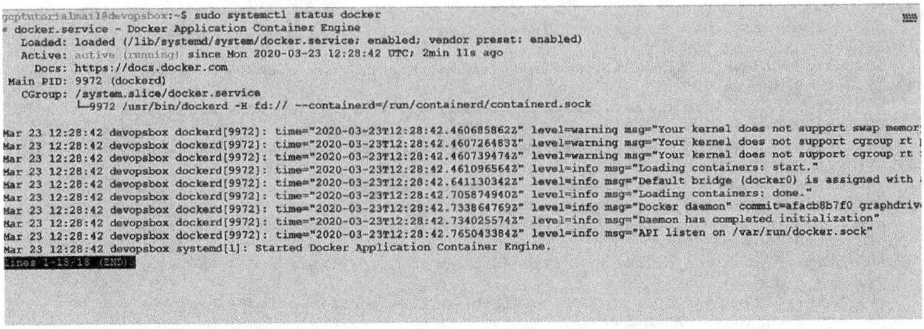

Figure 10-9.10. Docker Community Edition installation—continued

Step 8: Check the status of the Docker service by executing the following command. The result of the command is shown in Figure 10-9.11.

```
$ sudo systemctl status docker
```

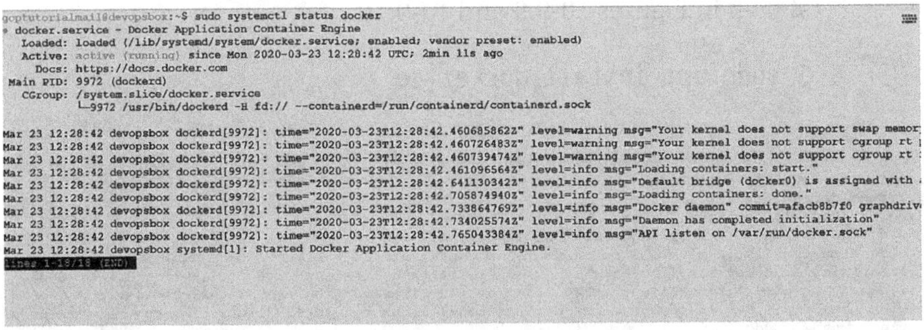

Figure 10-9.11. Checking the status of the Docker installation

Step 9: To avoid typing sudo whenever you run the Docker command, add username to the Docker group, by executing the following command. The result is shown in Figure 10-9.12.

```
$ sudo usermod -aG docker ${USER}
```

```
gcptutorialmail@devopsbox:~$ sudo usermod -aG docker ${USER}
```

Figure 10-9.12. Docker installation—username added

> **Step 10**: To verify the change, exit from the VM and connect again.
>
> **Step 11**: Verify the Docker version by executing the following command. The result is shown in Figure 10-9.13.
>
> ```
> $ docker version
> ```

```
gcptutorialmail@devopsbox:~$ docker version
Client: Docker Engine - Community
 Version:           19.03.8
 API version:       1.40
 Go version:        go1.12.17
 Git commit:        afacb8b7f0
 Built:             Wed Mar 11 01:26:02 2020
 OS/Arch:           linux/amd64
 Experimental:      false

Server: Docker Engine - Community
 Engine:
  Version:          19.03.8
  API version:      1.40 (minimum version 1.12)
  Go version:       go1.12.17
  Git commit:       afacb8b7f0
  Built:            Wed Mar 11 01:24:36 2020
  OS/Arch:          linux/amd64
  Experimental:     false
 containerd:
  Version:          1.2.13
  GitCommit:        7ad184331fa3e55e52b890ea95e65ba581ae3429
 runc:
  Version:          1.0.0-rc10
  GitCommit:        dc9208a3303feef5b3839f4323d9beb36df0a9dd
 docker-init:
  Version:          0.18.0
  GitCommit:        fec3683
gcptutorialmail@devopsbox:~$
```

Figure 10-9.13. Verifying the Docker version

Setting Up kubectl

In order to connect and deploy the application and Sysdig agent on GKE, kubectl must be installed on the VM.

Step 1: Execute the following command to install kubectl.

```
$ curl -LO https://storage.googleapis.com/kubernetes-
release/release/`curl -s https://storage.googleapis.
com/kubernetes-release/release/stable.txt`/bin/linux/
amd64/kubectl
```

The output of the preceding code is shown in Figure 10-10.

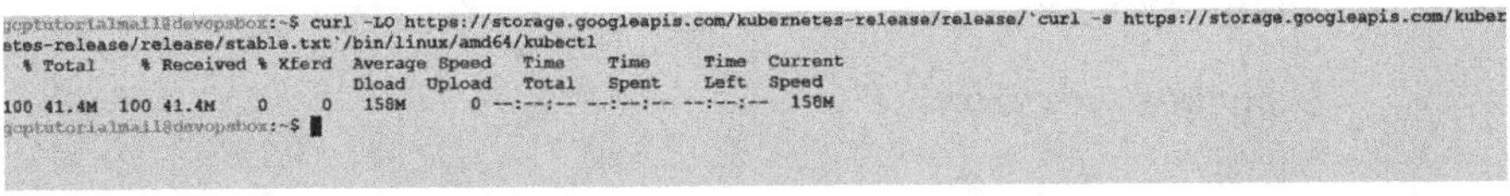

Figure 10-10. Installing kubectl

Step 2: Make kubectl executable with the following command. The result is shown in Figure 10-10.1.

```
$ chmod +x ./kubectl
```

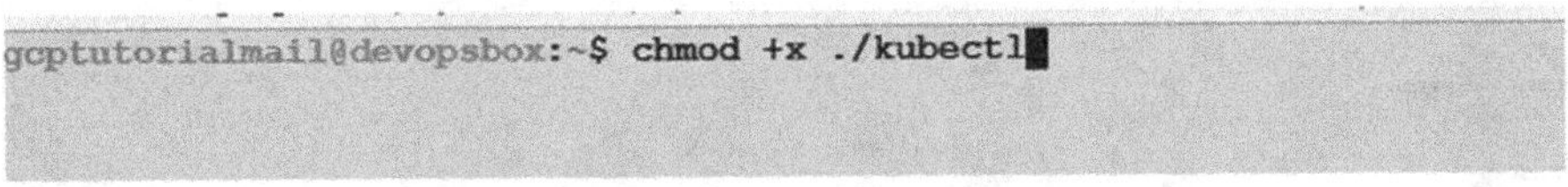

Figure 10-10.1. Making kubectl executable

Step 3: Move kubectl to usr/local/bin with the following command.

```
$ sudo mv ./kubectl /usr/local/bin/kubectl
```

Step 4: Verify the kubectl installation by executing the following command. The result is shown in Figure 10-10.2.

```
$ kubectl version -client
```

```
gcptutorialmail@devopsbox:~$ kubectl version --client
Client Version: version.Info{Major:"1", Minor:"17", GitVersion:"v1.17.4", GitCommit:"8d8aa39598534325ad77120c120a22b3a990b5ea", GitTreeState:
clean", BuildDate:"2020-03-12T21:03:42Z", GoVersion:"go1.13.8", Compiler:"gc", Platform:"linux/amd64"}
gcptutorialmail@devopsbox:~$
```

Figure 10-10.2.   kubectl installation verification

Installing the Java Development Kit (JDK)

In order to configure the Jenkins slave JDK is required to be installed on VM. Execute the following steps to install Java version 1.8.0_242.

Step 1: Update the package by executing the following command. The result is shown in Figure 10-11.

```
$ sudo apt-get update
```

```
gcptutorialmail@devopsbox:~$ sudo apt-get update
Hit:1 http://security.debian.org stretch/updates InRelease
Ign:2 http://deb.debian.org/debian stretch InRelease
Hit:3 http://packages.cloud.google.com/apt cloud-sdk-stretch InRelease
Hit:4 http://deb.debian.org/debian stretch-updates InRelease
Hit:5 http://deb.debian.org/debian stretch-backports InRelease
Hit:6 http://deb.debian.org/debian stretch Release
Hit:7 http://packages.cloud.google.com/apt google-compute-engine-stretch-stable InRelease
Hit:8 http://packages.cloud.google.com/apt google-cloud-packages-archive-keyring-stretch InRelease
Hit:9 https://download.docker.com/linux/debian stretch InRelease
Reading package lists... Done
```

Figure 10-11.   JDK installation

Step 2: Execute the following command, to install JDK. The result is shown in Figure 10-11.1.

```
$ sudo apt-get install default-jdk
```

```
gcptutorialmail@devopsbox:~$ sudo apt-get install default-jdk
Reading package lists... Done
Building dependency tree
Reading state information... Done
The following additional packages will be installed:
```

Figure 10-11.1. JDK installation

Step 3: Press Y to continue the Java setup, as shown
in Figure 10-11.2.

```
  openjdk-8-jre-headless x11-common x11-utils x11proto-core-dev x11proto-ir
0 upgraded, 160 newly installed, 0 to remove and 1 not upgraded.
Need to get 112 MB of archives.
After this operation, 495 MB of additional disk space will be used.
Do you want to continue? [Y/n] y
```

Figure 10-11.2. JDK installation—continued

Step 4: Verify the Java installation by executing
the following command. The result is shown in
Figure 10-11.3.

```
$ java -version
```

```
gcptutorialmail@devopsbox:~$ java -version
openjdk version "1.8.0_242"
OpenJDK Runtime Environment (build 1.8.0_242-8u242-b08-1~deb9u1-b08)
OpenJDK 64-Bit Server VM (build 25.242-b08, mixed mode)
```

Figure 10-11.3. JDK installation verification

Installing Jenkins

In order to orchestrate the GKE provisioning and application deployment,
we will use Jenkins version 2.204.1. Execute the following steps to install
and configure Jenkins.

Step 1: Execute the below command to create Jenkins_home directory. This is where Jenkins will keep all its configuration and jobs, under the home directory of the user (e.g., /home/gcptutorial). The result of the command is shown in Figure 10-12.

```
$ mkdir Jenkins_home
```

```
gcptutorialmail@devopsbox ~ $ pwd
/home/gcptutorialmail
gcptutorialmail@devopsbox ~ $ mkdir jenkins_home
gcptutorialmail@devopsbox ~ $ ls
jenkins_home
gcptutorialmail@devopsbox ~ $ ▮
```

Figure 10-12. *Jenkins home directory installation*

Step 2: Execute the following command to install Jenkins. The results are shown in Figures 10-12.1 and 10-12.2.

```
$ docker run -d --name jenkins -p 8080:8080 -p
50000:50000 -v /home/gcptutorialmail/jenkins_
home:/var/jenkins_home jenkins/jenkins:lts
```

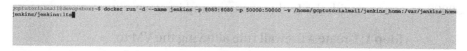

Figure 10-12.1. *Jenkins installation*

```
Mar 20, 2020 1:28:49 PM jenkins.InitReactorRunner$1 onAttained
INFO: Listed all plugins
Mar 20, 2020 1:28:51 PM jenkins.InitReactorRunner$1 onAttained
INFO: Prepared all plugins
Mar 20, 2020 1:28:51 PM jenkins.InitReactorRunner$1 onAttained
INFO: Started all plugins
Mar 20, 2020 1:28:51 PM jenkins.InitReactorRunner$1 onAttained
INFO: Augmented all extensions
Mar 20, 2020 1:28:53 PM jenkins.InitReactorRunner$1 onAttained
INFO: Loaded all jobs
Mar 20, 2020 1:28:53 PM hudson.model.AsyncPeriodicWork$1 run
INFO: Started Download metadata
Mar 20, 2020 1:28:54 PM jenkins.util.groovy.GroovyHookScript execute
INFO: Executing /var/jenkins_home/init.groovy.d/tcp-slave-agent-port.groovy
Mar 20, 2020 1:28:54 PM jenkins.InitReactorRunner$1 onAttained
INFO: Completed initialization
Mar 20, 2020 1:28:55 PM org.springframework.context.support.AbstractApplicationContext prepareRefresh
INFO: Refreshing org.springframework.web.context.support.StaticWebApplicationContext@5955b1f6: display name [Root WebApplication
ontext]; startup date [Fri Mar 20 13:28:55 UTC 2020]; root of context hierarchy
Mar 20, 2020 1:28:55 PM org.springframework.context.support.AbstractApplicationContext obtainFreshBeanFactory
INFO: Bean factory for application context [org.springframework.web.context.support.StaticWebApplicationContext@5955b1f6]: org.s
ringframework.beans.factory.support.DefaultListableBeanFactory@4aa571f2
Mar 20, 2020 1:28:55 PM org.springframework.beans.factory.support.DefaultListableBeanFactory preInstantiateSingletons
INFO: Pre-instantiating singletons in org.springframework.beans.factory.support.DefaultListableBeanFactory@4aa571f2: defining be
s [authenticationManager]; root of factory hierarchy
Mar 20, 2020 1:28:55 PM org.springframework.context.support.AbstractApplicationContext prepareRefresh
```

Figure 10-12.2. *Jenkins installation—continued*

> **Step 3**: Execute the following command to fetch the
> Jenkins secrets password. The result is shown in
> Figure 10-12.3.

```
$ sudo cat jenkins-data/secrets/initialAdminPassword
```

🔒 ssh.cloud.google.com/projects/tutorial-project-268109/zones/us-central1-a/instances/devopsbox?authuser=0&hl=en_GB&

```
gcptutorialmail@devopsbox ~/jenkins_home/secrets $ sudo cat initialAdminPassword
0c████████████████████████
gcptutorialmail@devopsbox ~/jenkins_home/secrets $ █
```

Figure 10-12.3. *Fetching the Jenkins initial admin password*

We have to set up the firewall rule to allow access on ports 8080 and
50000, to connect with the Jenkins master and its slave.

> **Step 1**: Create a firewall rule allowing the VM to
> get inbound connection for ports 8080 and 50000
> for Jenkins. Go to VPC network, then click Firewall
> rules, as shown in Figure 10-13.

Figure 10-13. *Firewall rules page*

> **Step 2**: Click on Create Firewall Rule on the Firewall
> page, as shown in Figure 10-13.1.

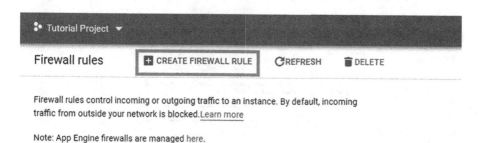

Figure 10-13.1. *Creating the firewall rule for Jenkins*

> **Step 3**: Fill in the firewall options, as follows:
>
> **Name**: As mentioned, choose a meaningful name,
> e.g., firewall-rule-devopsbox.
>
> **Logs option**: Choose Off.
>
> **Network**: Choose default.
>
> **Priority**: 1000
>
> **Direction of traffic**: Ingress
>
> **Action on match**: Allow

Targets: Select Specified target tags and give devopsbox as the name of the **Target tag** on which this firewall rule will apply.

Source IP range: The aforementioned 0.0.0.0/0

Protocols and Ports: Choose Specified protocols.

Ports: Select tcp as the protocol and the aforementioned ports 8080 and 50000.

Click the Create button, as shown in Figures 10-14, 10-14.1, and 10-14.2.

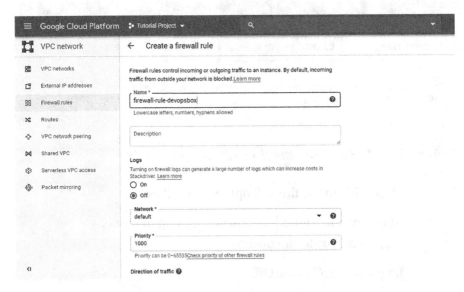

Figure 10-14. *Creating the firewall rule for Jenkins—continued*

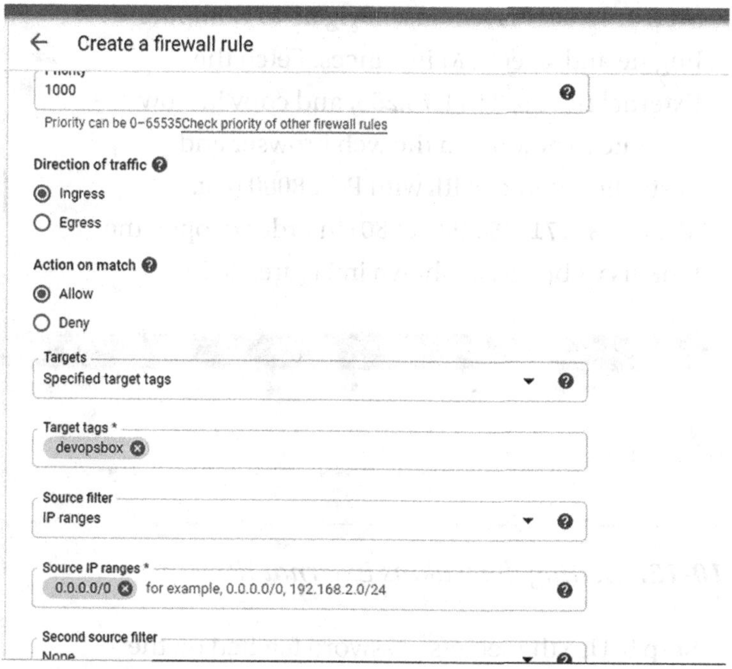

Figure 10-14.1. *Creating the firewall rule for Jenkins—continued*

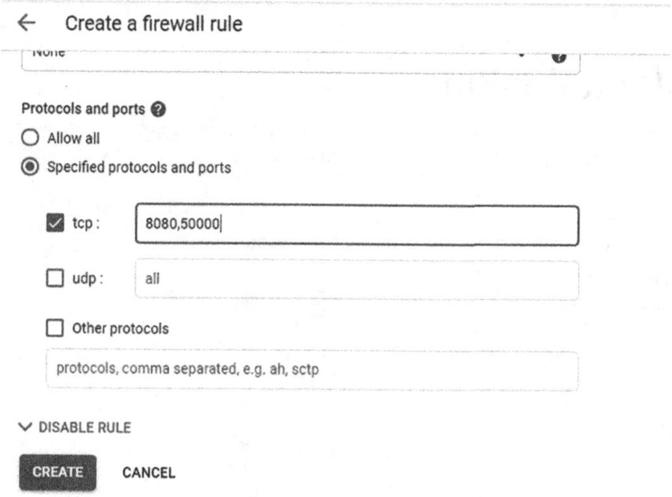

Figure 10-14.2. *Creating the firewall rule for Jenkins—continued*

Step 4: To access Jenkins, navigate to Compute Engine and select VM instances. Fetch the External IP, e.g., 34.71.75.255, and copy it. Now navigate to new tab in the web browser and paste the external URL with Port 8080 (e.g. http://34.71.75.255:8080) in order to open the Jenkins webpage, as shown in Figure 10-15.

Figure 10-15. *Getting the Jenkins External IP*

Step 5: Use the secrets password fetched on the Unlock Jenkins page from Step 3 of the "Installing Jenkins" section and click the Continue button, as shown in Figure 10-16.

Unlock Jenkins

To ensure Jenkins is securely set up by the administrator, a password has been written to the log (not sure where to find it?) and this file on the server:

```
/var/jenkins_home/secrets/initialAdminPassword
```

Please copy the password from either location and paste it below.

Administrator password

```
································|
```

Continue

Figure 10-16. *Accessing the Jenkins console for the first time*

Step 6: Click on the Install suggested plugins
option to install various plug-ins required to create
pipelines, as shown in Figure 10-17.

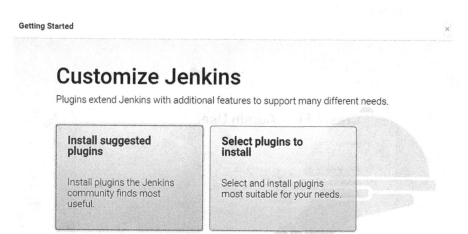

Figure 10-17. *Selection of additional Jenkins features*

Step 7: Click Continue to proceed, as shown in
Figure 10-18.

✔ GitHub Branch Source Plugin	✔ Pipeline: GitHub Groovy Libraries	✔ Pipeline: Stage View
✔ Subversion	✔ SSH Slaves	✔ Matrix Authorization Strategy Plugin
✔ LDAP	✔ Email Extension	✔ Mailer Plugin

Continue   Retry

Figure 10-18. *Selection of suggested Jenkins plug-ins options*

Step 8: Fill in details for Username, Password, Full name, and Email address on the form that comes up and click Save and Continue, as shown in Figure 10-19.

Figure 10-19. *Jenkins First Admin User setup*

Step 9: Click Save and Finish to proceed, as shown in Figure 10-20.

Getting Started

Instance Configuration

Jenkins URL: `http://34.71.75.225:8080/`

The Jenkins URL is used to provide the root URL for absolute links to various Jenkins resources. That means this value is required for proper operation of many Jenkins features including email notifications, PR status updates, and the BUILD_URL environment variable provided to build steps.

The proposed default value shown is **not saved** yet and is generated from the current request, if possible. The best practice is to set this value to the URL that users are expected to use. This will avoid confusion when sharing or viewing links.

Jenkins 2.204.5   Not now   Save and Finish

Figure 10-20. Jenkins Instance Configuration page

> **Step 10**: Click on the Start using Jenkins button to complete the installation, as shown in Figure 10-21.

Getting Started

Jenkins is ready!

Your Jenkins setup is complete.

Start using Jenkins

Figure 10-21. Jenkins is ready!

> You will see the following screen for the Jenkins console (Figure 10-22).

Figure 10-22. *First-time Jenkins console*

Jenkins Slave Setup

Perform the following steps to set up the Jenkins slave executable.

Step 1: Navigate to /home `directory of user`
`and create sub directory jenkins_slave` and
give 700 permission, by executing the following
commands by root user. `Jenkins_node directory`
will be used by the Jenkins node to connect and
execute the command.

```
$ cd ~
$ mkdir jenkins_slave
$ chmod 700 jenkins_slave
```

Step 2: Navigate to the Jenkins URL which was used
in previous steps to access Jenkins. Use your admin
password set up in the previous steps. Navigate to
Manage Jenkins ➤ Manage Nodes ➤ New Node, as
shown in Figures 10-22.1 and 10-22.2.

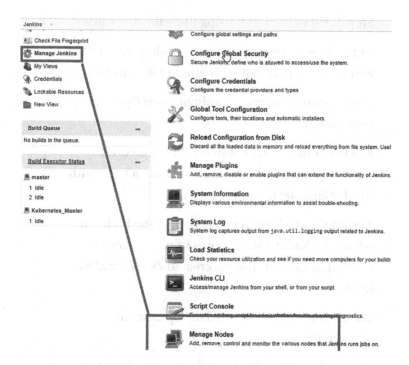

Figure 10-22.1. *Setting up the Jenkins node*

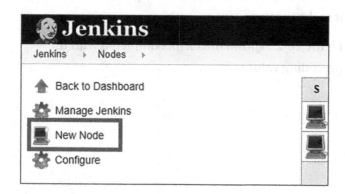

Figure 10-22.2. *Setting up the Jenkins node—continued*

Step 3: Fill in the form, using the following values:

Name: Use any name of your choosing. In our case, we chose the previously mentioned devopsbox.

Description: Use any meaningful description, e.g., devopsbox.

# of executors: As mentioned, we entered 1, to represent the number of executors associated with this Jenkins slave.

Remote root directory: The path of the folder in which the Jenkins slave stores its workspace and configuration. For this, we created /var/Jenkins_ home.

Label: The aforementioned devopsbox label was used.

Usage: Select Use this node as much as possible.

Launch method: Select Launch agent by connecting it to the master.

Figure 10-23 shows the form, completed with the preceding values.

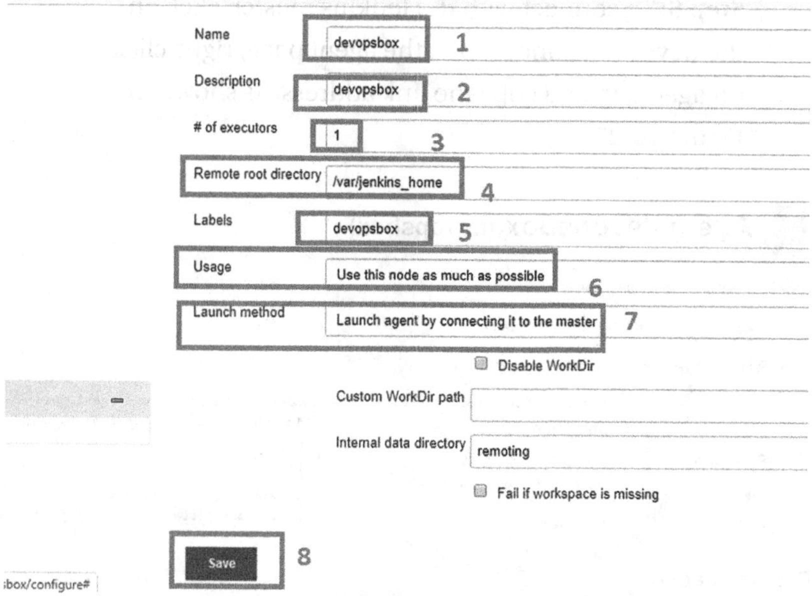

Figure 10-23. Setting up the Jenkins node

Step 4: Click the Save button, to save the configuration.

Step 5: Verify that the agent is configured successfully, by reviewing the Jenkins console status.

The agent is configured but not yet connected with the Jenkins master, as shown in Figure 10-24.

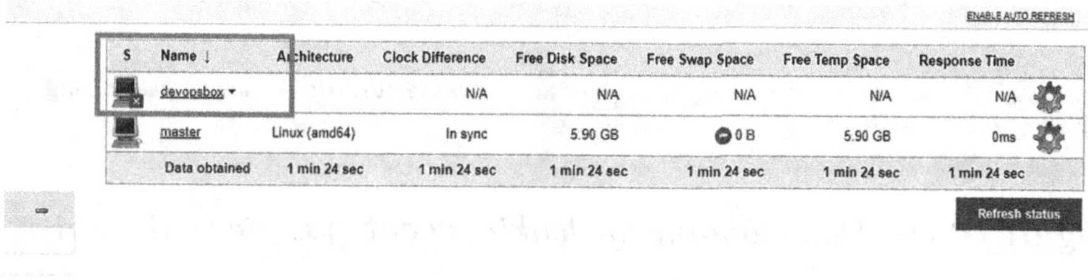

Figure 10-24. Verifying the Jenkins node

373

Step 6: To connect with the Jenkins master, click on the devopsbox once, open the agent page, right-click on agent.jar, and copy the link address, as shown in Figure 10-25.

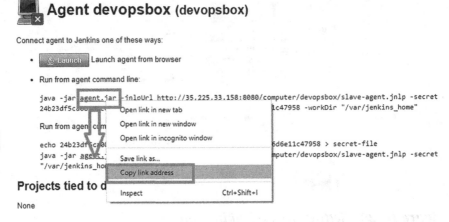

Figure 10-25. *Copying the* agent.jar *link URL of the Jenkins node*

Step 7: Now log into the VM and navigate to the jenkins_slave directory, and execute the following command in order to download the Jenkins slave jar. The result of the command is shown in Figures 10-26 and 10-27.

```
$ cd Jenkins_slave
$ wget http://35.192.203.53:8080/jnlpJars/agent.jar
```

gcptutorialmail@devopsbox:~/jenkins_slave$ **wget http://35.192.203.53:8080/jnlpJars/agent.jar**

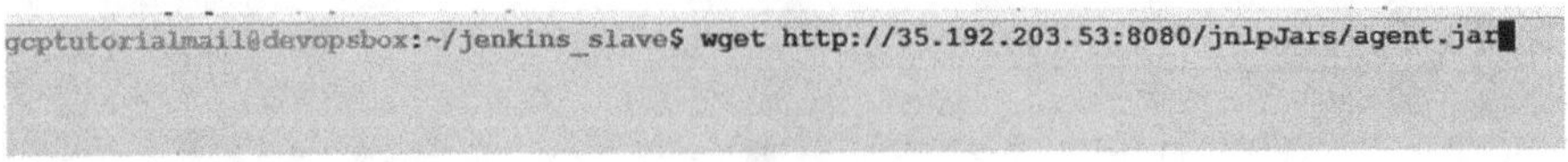

Figure 10-26. *Downloading the Jenkins* agent.jar *file on the VM*

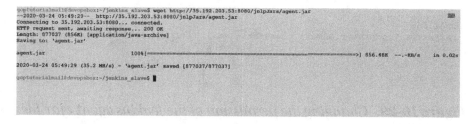

Figure 10-27. *Completed download of the Jenkins* agent.jar *file on the VM*

Step 8: Verify that *agent.jar* downloaded, by executing the following command. The result is shown in Figure 10-28.

```
$ ls -ltr
```

```
gcptutorialmail@devopsbox:~/jenkins_slave$ ls -ltr
total 860
-rw-r--r-- 1 gcptutorialmail gcptutorialmail 877037 Mar 23 12:50 agent.jar
gcptutorialmail@devopsbox:~/jenkins_slave$
```

Figure 10-28. *Verifying the Jenkins* agent.jar *file on the VM*

Step 9: Change permission to 700 and verify the permission of *agent.jar*, by executing the following command. The result is shown in Figure 10-29.

```
$ chmod 700 agent.jar
$ ls -ltr
```

```
gcptutorialmail@devopsbox:~/jenkins_slave$ ls -ltr
total 860
-rwxrwxrwx 1 gcptutorialmail gcptutorialmail 877037 Mar 23 12:50 agent.jar
gcptutorialmail@devopsbox:~/jenkins_slave$ █
```

Figure 10-29. *Changing the permission of the Jenkins* agent.jar *file on the VM*

Creating a Service for the Jenkins Slave

Now we will create the Linux-based service to connect the Jenkins slave from the Jenkins master machine.

> **Step 1**: Navigate to the /etc/systemd/system
> directory and create a jenkinsslave.service file.
> Copy the following content and save the file, as
> shown in Figures 10-30 and 10-31.
>
> [Unit]
> Description=jenkinsslave
> Wants=network-online.target
> After=network-online.target
> [Service]
> Type=simple
> ExecStart=/usr/bin/java -jar /home/
> gcptutorialmail/jenkins_slave/agent.jar -jnlpUrl
> http://35.225.33.158:8080/computer/devopsbox/slave-
> agent.jnlp \
> -secret 24b23df5ca08cc4ece2f3a511e41ffc
> 1c96729fc81ea8cdfb1786d6e11c47958 -workDir
> "/var/jenkins_home"

```
Restart=always
RestartSec=1
[Install]
WantedBy=multi-user.target
```

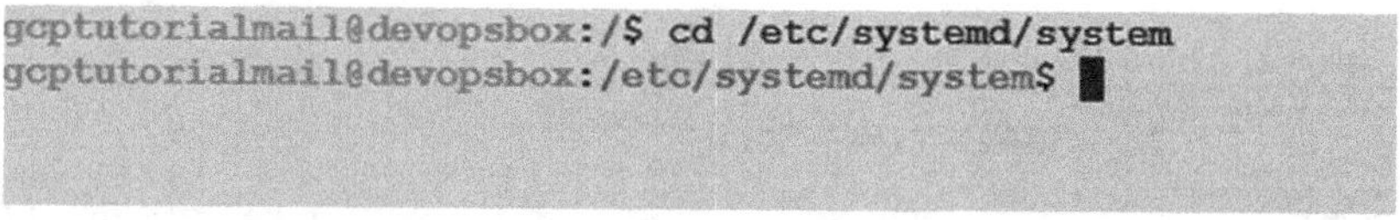

```
gcptutorialmail@devopsbox:/$ cd /etc/systemd/system
gcptutorialmail@devopsbox:/etc/systemd/system$
```

Figure 10-30. *Creating the Jenkins slave service on the VM*

```
gcptutorialmail@devopsbox:/etc/systemd/system$ vi jenkinsslave.service
```

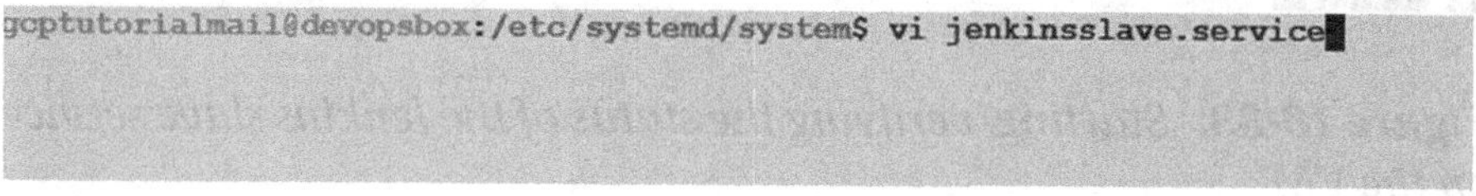

Figure 10-31. *Creating the Jenkins Slave service on the VM—continued*

Step 2: To start the service, switch to root user, by executing the following command. The result of the preceding command is shown in Figure 10-32.

```
$ sudo su -
```

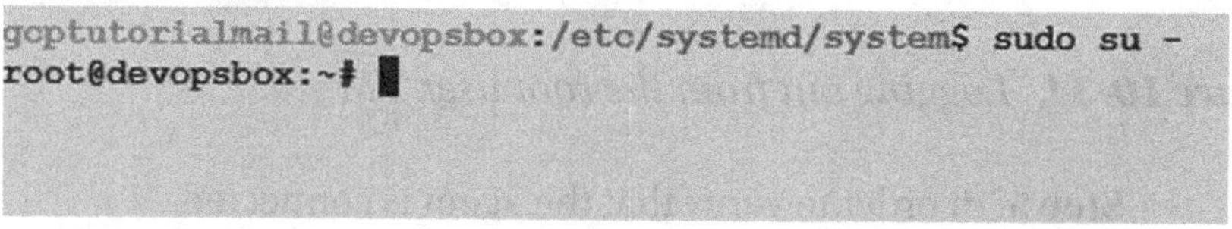

```
gcptutorialmail@devopsbox:/etc/systemd/system$ sudo su -
root@devopsbox:~#
```

Figure 10-32. *Creating the Jenkins slave service on the VM—continued*

377

Step 3: Execute below commands to start and then verify the service. The result is shown in Figure 10-33.

```
$ systemctl start jenkinsslave
$ systemctl status jenkinsslave
```

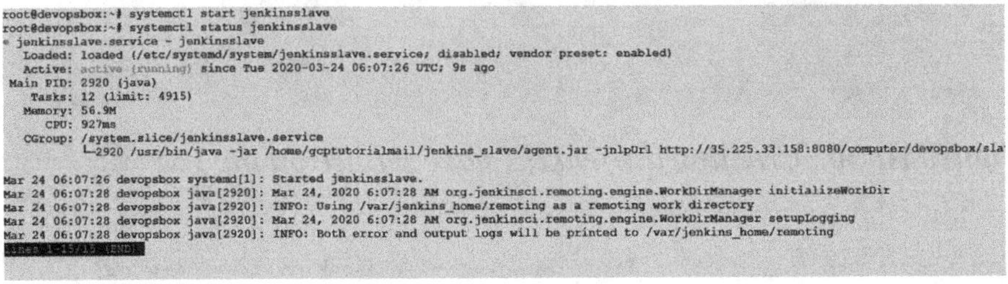

Figure 10-33. *Starting/verifying the status of the Jenkins slave service on the VM*

Step 4: Execute the following command to exit the root user session. The result is shown in Figure 10-34.

```
$ exit
```

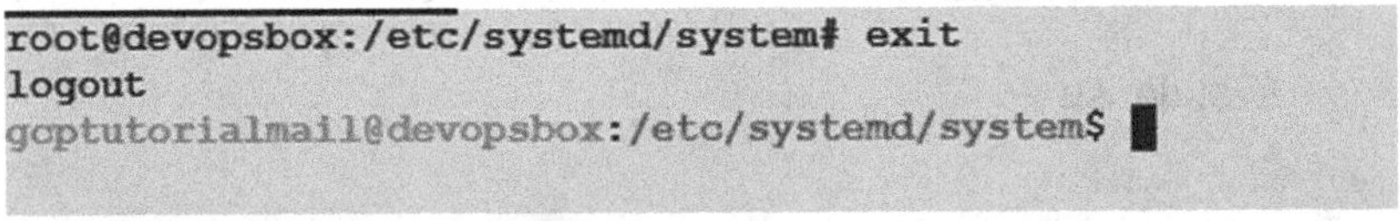

Figure 10-34. *Logging out from the root user VM*

Step 5: In order to verify that the agent is connected and running navigate to Jenkins ➤ Nodes, then click devopsbox.

You will see that the agent is connected, as shown in Figure 10-35.

Agent devopsbox (devopsbox)

Agent is connected.

Projects tied to devopsbox

None

Figure 10-35. *Verifying that the Jenkins agent is connected on the Jenkins node page*

GKE Provisioning, Application Deployment, and Sysdig Agent, Using a Jenkins Pipeline

Now we will create the Jenkins Pipeline CICD-GKEProv-Sysdig to automate the following processes.

> **Code clone**: Clone the Sock Shop and Sysdig agent deployment code from the following GitHub repository: https://github.com/dryice-devops/GCP.git.

> **Create cluster**: Create a Kubernetes cluster clustertutorial on GKE with gcloud.

> **Create firewall rule**: Create an ingress/egress firewall rule for port 6443 of the Sysdig agent.

> **Deploy application**: Deploy the Sock Shop application on EKS, through kubectl.

> **Deploy Sysdig Agent**: Deploy the Sysdig agent on EKS through kubectl.

Step 1: Navigate to the following URL, to access Jenkins. Use the admin password set up in the previous steps. Click New item, as shown in Figure 10-36.

URL: `http://EXTERNAL_IP:8080`

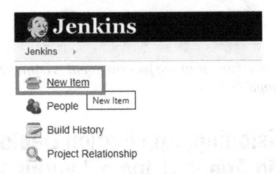

Figure 10-36. *Creating the Jenkins Pipeline*

Step 2: Fill in the form. Enter "CICD-GKEProv-Sysdig" as the Item name and choose Pipeline since we are using Pipeline as a code in Jenkins to automate the previously defined processes. Click on OK, as shown in Figure 10-36.1 to continue.

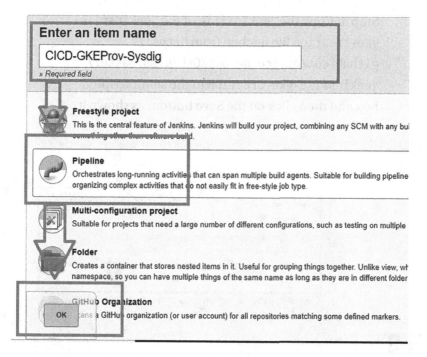

Figure 10-36.1. *Creating the Jenkins Pipeline*

Step 3: Click on Pipeline and it will display a script box in which we will compose our Jenkins script as shown in Figure 10-37.

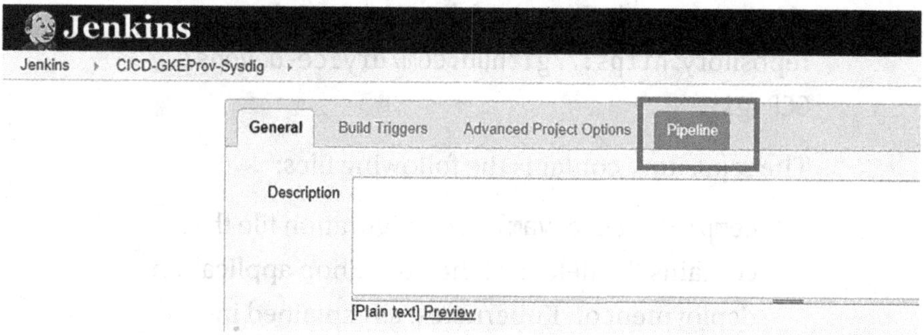

Figure 10-37. *Composing the Jenkins script*

Step 4: Copy the jenkinsfile of the jenkinsfile-gke-creation file fetched from https://github.com/dryice-devops/GKE/blob/master/jenkinsfile-gke-creation to the same script box and then click on the Save button, as shown in

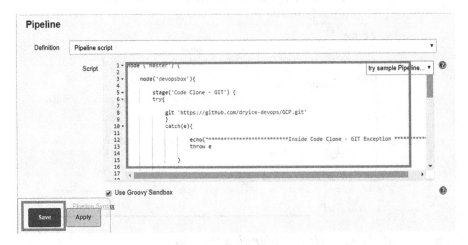

Figure 10-37.1. *Saving the Jenkins script*

Figure 10-37.1.

The Jenkinsfile creation consists of the following five stages:

1. **Code Clone from GitHub**: In this stage, we are cloning the code from the following GitHub repository: https://github.com/dryice-devops/GCP.git.

   The repository contains the following files:

   1.1 complete-demo.yaml: A configuration file that contains the details of the Sock Shop application deployment on Kubernetes, as explained in Chapter 4.

1.2 `sysdig-agent-clusterrole.yaml`: A configuration file for creating the cluster role for the Sysdig agent. This was covered in Chapter 7.

1.3 `sysdig-agent-configmap.yaml`: A configuration file for creating ConfigMap for the Sysdig agent. This was explained in Chapter 7.

1.4 `sysdig-agent-daemonset-v2.yaml`: A configuration file for creating a daemonset for the Sysdig agent, which was explained in in Chapter 7.

2. **Creating the cluster clustertutorial in GKE**: In this stage, we are creating three node-based Kubernetes clusters named `clustertutorial` in GKE, through `gcloud` in the us-central1-a zone by using the following command.

```
sh "gcloud container clusters create
clustertutorial --num-nodes=3 --zone=us-
central1-a"
```

3. **Creating an inbound/outbound firewall in GKE**: In the third stage of the Jenkinsfile configuration we are creating a stateful firewall rule for both inbound and outbound connections on port 6443, for the Sysdig agent by using the `gcloud` command as shown in Figures 10-37.2 and 10-37.3.

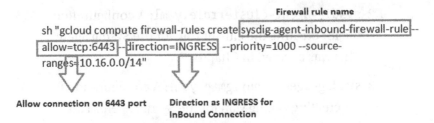

Figure 10-37.2. *Inbound/outbound firewall rule in the Jenkins script*

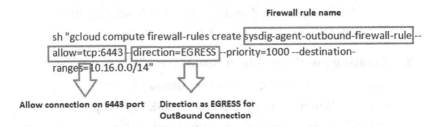

Figure 10-37.3. *Inbound/outbound firewall rule in the Jenkins script—continued*

4. **Deploying the application on the GKE cluster**: In this stage, we are creating the sock-shop namespace and deploying the Sock Shop application on the GKE cluster, by using the following kubectl commands.

```
sh " export KUBECONFIG=~/.kube/config &&
kubectl create namespace sock-shop "

sh " export KUBECONFIG=~/.kube/config && kubectl
apply -f '${WORKSPACE}/complete-demo.yaml'  "
```

5. **Sysdig deployment on GKE**: In this stage, we are deploying the Sysdig agent on GKE, through kubectl.

5.1 The ns namespace is created by executing the
following command:

```
sh " export KUBECONFIG=~/.kube/config &&
kubectl create ns sysdig-agent"
```

5.2 In the following command, you must change the
access-key as per your Sysdig setup access-key,
highlighted in yellow.

```
sh " export KUBECONFIG=~/.kube/config
&& kubectl create secret generic
sysdig-agent --from-literal=access-
key=effdab9c-9554-4274-9042-9e8331e1d78b
-n sysdig-agent "
```

5.3 Create a cluster role for the Sysdig agent, by
executing the following command:

```
sh " export KUBECONFIG=~/.kube/config &&
kubectl apply -f '${WORKSPACE}/sysdig-
agent-clusterrole.yaml' -n sysdig-agent "
```

5.4 Create a service account for the Sysdig agent in the
GKE cluster, by following this command:

```
sh " export KUBECONFIG=~/.kube/config &&
kubectl create serviceaccount sysdig-
agent -n sysdig-agent "
```

5.5 Define the cluster role binding that grants the
Sysdig agent roles in the cluster role.

```
sh " export KUBECONFIG=~/.kube/config
&& kubectl create clusterrolebinding
sysdig-agent --clusterrole=sysdig-agent
--serviceaccount=sysdig-agent:sysdig-
agent "
```

5.6 Apply `sysdig-agent-configmap.yaml` file, using
the following command. You do not have to change
anything in this file.

```
sh " export KUBECONFIG=~/.kube/config &&
kubectl apply -f '${WORKSPACE}/sysdig-
agent-configmap.yaml' -n sysdig-agent"
```

5.7 Apply the `daemonset-v2.yaml` file, using the
following command. You do not have to change
anything in this file.

```
sh "export KUBECONFIG=~/.kube/config &&
kubectl apply -f '${WORKSPACE}/sysdig-
agent-daemonset-v2.yaml' -n sysdig-
agent"
```

Step 5: Execute the Jenkins job by clicking Build
Now, as indicated in Figure 10-38.

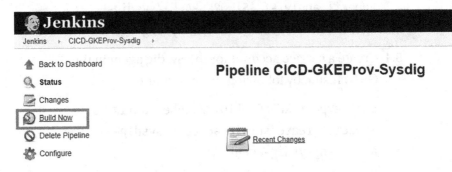

Figure 10-38. *Executing the Jenkins script*

Step 6: Once the job has been executed successfully, the following build history will indicate the build number in blue. If there is an error, it will be red. It also shows the stages, under Stage view. To view logs, click the build number (#). Next, Click Console Output. Figures 10-39, 10-39.1, and 10-39.2 illustrate the preceding.

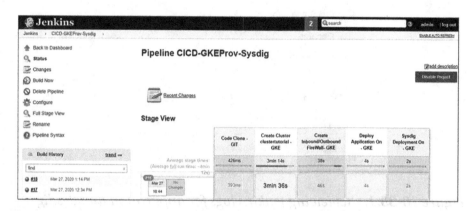

Figure 10-39. *Reviewing Jenkins logs for application and Sysdig agent deployment*

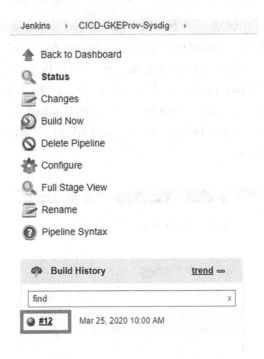

Figure 10-39.1. *Reviewing Jenkins logs for application and Sysdig agent deployment—continued*

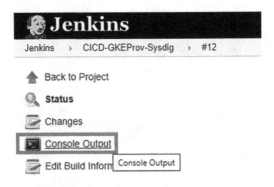

Figure 10-39.2. *Reviewing Jenkins logs for application and Sysdig agent deployment—continued*

In the log console, scroll down three-quarters of the screen to get the newly created EKS node details, as shown in Figures 10-39.3, 10-39.4, 10-39.5, and 10-39.6.

⬤ **Custom Console Output**

```
Started by user admin
Running in Durability level: MAX_SURVIVABILITY
[Pipeline] Start of Pipeline
[Pipeline] node
Running on Jenkins in /var/jenkins_home/workspace/CICD-GKEProv-Sysdig
[Pipeline] {
[Pipeline] node
Running on devopsbox in /var/jenkins_home/workspace/CICD-GKEProv-Sysdig
[Pipeline] {
[Pipeline] stage
[Pipeline] { (Code Clone - GIT)
[Pipeline] git
No credentials specified
Fetching changes from the remote Git repository
Checking out Revision 91048de54a0d86594c3a1a729e9709da4eda3bc7 (refs/remotes/origin/master)
Commit message: "update sysdig-agent-daemonset-v2.yaml"
 > git rev-parse --is-inside-work-tree # timeout=10
 > git config remote.origin.url https://github.com/dryice-devops/GCP.git # timeout=10
Fetching upstream changes from https://github.com/dryice-devops/GCP.git
 > git --version # timeout=10
 > git fetch --tags --progress -- https://github.com/dryice-devops/GCP.git +refs/heads/*:refs/remotes/origin/* # timeout=10
 > git rev-parse refs/remotes/origin/master^{commit} # timeout=10
 > git rev-parse refs/remotes/origin/origin/master^{commit} # timeout=10
 > git config core.sparsecheckout # timeout=10
```

Figure 10-39.3. *Reviewing Jenkins logs for application and Sysdig agent deployment—continued*

```
.........................................................................................
...........................................................................done.
Created [https://container.googleapis.com/v1/projects/tutorial-project-268109/zones/us-central1-a/clusters/clustertutorial].
To inspect the contents of your cluster, go to: https://console.cloud.google.com/kubernetes/workload /gcloud/us-central1-
a/clustertutorial?project=tutorial-project-268109
WARNING: environment variable HOME or KUBECONFIG must be set to store credentials for kubectl
NAME            LOCATION       MASTER_VERSION  MASTER_IP      MACHINE_TYPE   NODE_VERSION   NUM_NODES  STATUS
clustertutorial us-central1-a  1.14.10-gke.24  34.70.204.58   n1-standard-1  1.14.10-gke.24  3          RUNNING
[Pipeline] sleep
Sleeping for 20 sec
```

Figure 10-39.4. *Reviewing Jenkins logs for application and Sysdig agent deployment—continued*

```
: kubectl apply -f /var/jenkins_home/workspace/CICD-GKEDemo-Sysdig/complete-demo.yaml
deployment.apps/carts-db created
service/carts-db created
deployment.apps/carts created
service/carts created
deployment.apps/catalogue-db created
service/catalogue-db created
deployment.apps/catalogue created
service/catalogue created
deployment.apps/front-end created
service/front-end created
deployment.apps/orders-db created
service/orders-db created
deployment.apps/orders created
service/orders created
deployment.apps/payment created
service/payment created
deployment.apps/queue-master created
service/queue-master created
deployment.apps/rabbitmq created
service/rabbitmq created
deployment.apps/shipping created
service/shipping created
deployment.apps/user-db created
service/user-db created
deployment.apps/user created
```

Figure 10-39.5. *Reviewing Jenkins logs for application and Sysdig
agent deployment—continued*

```
clustertutorial  us-central1-a  1.14.10-gke.24  35.226.198.183  n1-standard-1  1.14.10-gke.24  3       RUNNING
[Pipeline] sleep
Sleeping for 20 sec
[Pipeline] sh
+ export KUBECONFIG=~/.kube/config
+ gcloud container clusters get-credentials clustertutorial --zone=us-central1-a --project=tutorial-project-268109
Fetching cluster endpoint and auth data.
kubeconfig entry generated for clustertutorial.
[Pipeline] echo
**************CLUSTER CREATED ***************
[Pipeline] }
[Pipeline] // stage
[Pipeline] stage
[Pipeline] { (Create Inbound/Outbound FireWall- GKE)
[Pipeline] echo
************************** Create Inbound/Outbound FireWall- Start***************************
[Pipeline] sh
+ gcloud compute firewall-rules create sysdig-agent-inbound-firewall-rule --allow=tcp:6443 --direction=INGRESS --priority=1000 --
source-ranges=10.16.0.0/14
Creating firewall...
.....Created [https://www.googleapis.com/compute/v1/projects/tutorial-project-268109/global/firewalls/sysdig-agent-inbound-firewall-
rule].
done.
NAME                                NETWORK DIRECTION PRIORITY ALLOW     DENY DISABLED
sysdig-agent-inbound-firewall-rule  default INGRESS   1000     tcp:6443       False
[Pipeline] sleep
Sleeping for 30 sec
[Pipeline] sh
+ gcloud compute firewall-rules create sysdig-agent-outbound-firewall-rule --allow=tcp:6443 --direction=EGRESS --priority=1000 --
destination-ranges=10.16.0.0/14
```

Figure 10-39.6. *Reviewing Jenkins logs for application and Sysdig
agent deployment—continued*

Step 7: Navigate to your GCP account console and click Compute. Next, select Kubernetes Engine and then Clusters, as in Figure 10-40.

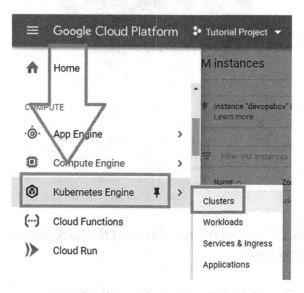

Figure 10-40. *Reviewing the GCP console*

You will see the GKE clustertutorial cluster in active state. This is the same cluster that we created through Jenkins and gcloud (see Figure 10-40.1).

Figure 10-40.1. *Reviewing the GCP Console—continued*

Now click on Services & Ingress, to fetch the URL of
the Sock Shop application, as shown in Figure 10-40.2.

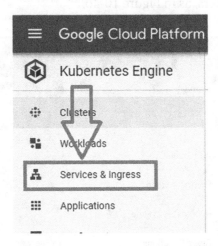

Figure 10-40.2. *Getting the IP address of the Sock Shop application
from the GCP console*

Navigate to the front-end service and copy the
end point which is of type Load balancer in order
to open the Sock Shop application, as shown in
Figures 10-40.3 and 10-40.4.

	Name ↑	Status	Type	Endpoints	Pods	Namespace	Cluster
☐	carts	✓ OK	Cluster IP	10.19.245.199	1/1	sock-shop	clustertutorial
☐	carts-db	✓ OK	Cluster IP	10.19.250.244	1/1	sock-shop	clustertutorial
☐	catalogue	✓ OK	Cluster IP	10.19.249.41	1/1	sock-shop	clustertutorial
☐	catalogue-db	✓ OK	Cluster IP	10.19.248.209	1/1	sock-shop	clustertutorial
☐	front-end	✓ OK	Load balancer	34.71.55.37:80 ☑	1/1	sock-shop	clustertutorial
☐	orders	✓ OK	Cluster IP	10.19.252.146	1/1	sock-shop	clustertutorial
☐	orders-db	✓ OK	Cluster IP	10.19.240.193	1/1	sock-shop	clustertutorial

Figure 10-40.3. *Getting the IP address of the Sock Shop application
from the GCP Console—continued*

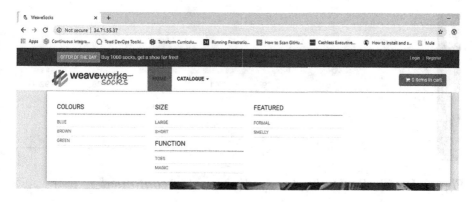

Figure 10-40.4. *Opening the Sock Shop application*

> **Step 8**: Now let's navigate to the Sysdig console and
> confirm that our GKE cluster has been added under
> Monitor. Navigate to the Sysdig URL (`https://`
> `sysdig.com/`) and log in with your credentials, as
> shown in Figure 10-41.

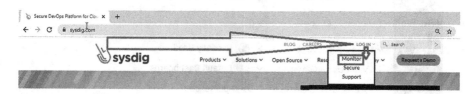

Figure 10-41. *Reviewing the Sysdig console*

> Navigate to Explore ➤ Hosts & Containers and
> then select the overview by container, as shown in
> Figure 10-42.

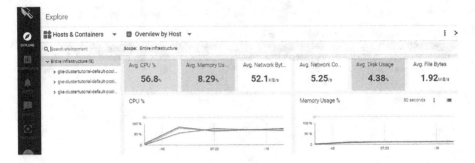

Figure 10-42. *Reviewing the Sysdig console—continued*

Now, to verify whether the Sock Shop application
deployed, click Explore ➤ Hosts & Container ➤
Containers Limits, as per Figure 10-43.

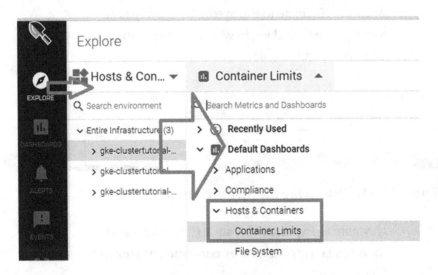

Figure 10-43. *Reviewing Sysdig Console—continued*

Hover the pointer over the Graph of CPU Shares
Used. You will see the Sock Shop containers name
(Figure 10-44).

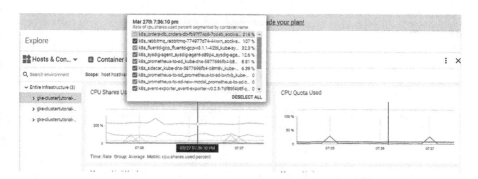

Figure 10-44. *Reviewing the Sysdig console—continued*

Click Hosts & Containers ➤ Network ➤ Overview,
as shown in Figures 10-45 and 10-46.

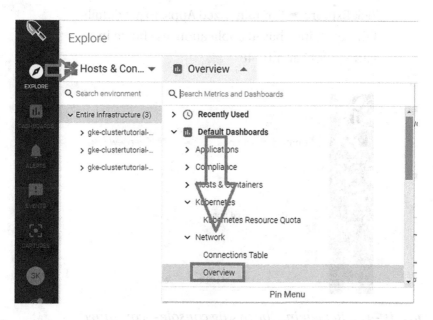

Figure 10-45. *Reviewing the Sysdig console—continued*

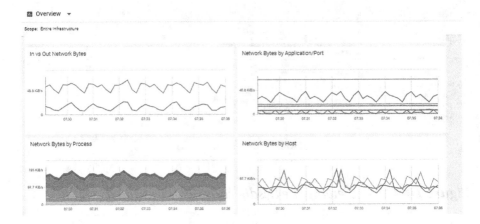

Figure 10-46. *Reviewing the Sysdig console—continued*

Click Explore ➤ Containerized Apps, to get details
of the container-based application, as shown in
Figures 10-47 and 10-48.

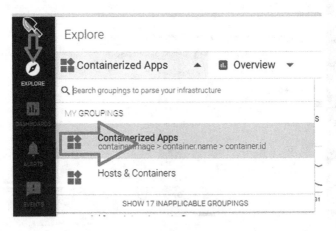

Figure 10-47. *Reviewing the Sysdig console—continued*

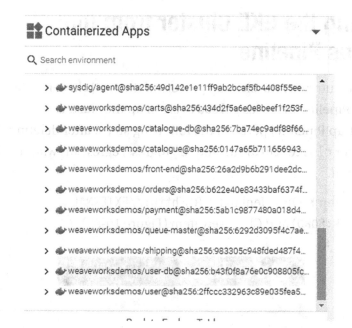

Figure 10-48. *Reviewing the Sysdig console—continued*

Select any container that starts with
weaveworksdemos, to get its details, e.g., In vs Out
Network Bytes, Network Bytes by Application/Port,
etc. (Figure 10-49).

Figure 10-49. *Reviewing the Sysdig Console—continued*

Deleting the GKE Cluster from the Jenkins Pipeline

In order to automate the cleanup process of the GKE cluster, we will create a Jenkins Pipeline that uses `gcloud` to clean up the cluster.

To set up Pipeline, perform the following steps, after deleting the GKE cluster `clustertutorial` and the ingress/egress firewall rule for the Sysdig agent.

> **Step 1**: Open Jenkins (URL: `http://EXTERNAL_IP:8080`) and Click New Item (Figure 10-50).

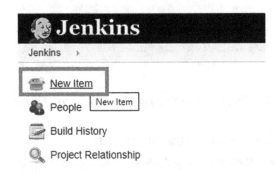

Figure 10-50. *Cleaning up the GKE cluster through Jenkins*

> **Step 2**: Fill in the form by entering "Delete-GKE-Cluster" as the item name and selecting Pipeline, as we are using Pipeline as a code in Jenkins to automate the previously defined cleanup process. Next, click the OK button (Figure 10-51).

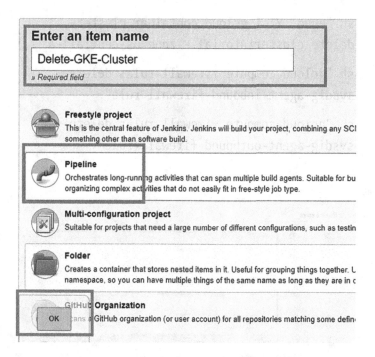

Figure 10-51. *Cleaning up the GKE cluster through Jenkins—
continued*

Step 3: Copy the code from the `jenkinsfile-delete-gke` file from the following GitHub repository: `https://github.com/dryice-devops/GKE`. Paste the file into the Script section and click the Save button.

In this Jenkins file, we use the `gcloud` command to delete the GKE cluster named `clustertutorial` and the created inbound and outbound firewall rules named `sysdig-agent-inbound-firewall-rule` and `sysdig-agent-outbound-firewall-rule`, respectively, by executing the following commands (see also Figure 10-52).

```
sh "echo 'Y' | gcloud container clusters
delete clustertutorial --zone=us-central1-a"
```

```
sh "gcloud compute firewall-rules delete
sysdig-agent-inbound-firewall-rule"
```

```
sh "gcloud compute firewall-rules delete
sysdig-agent-outbound-firewall-rule"
```

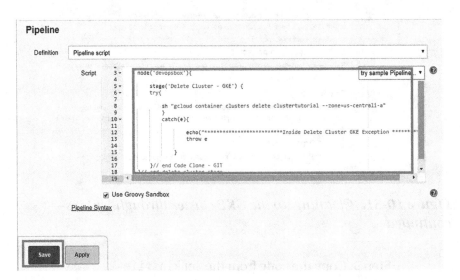

Figure 10-52. *Cleaning up the GKE cluster through Jenkins—deleting* `clustertutorial`

Step 4: Execute the Jenkins job by clicking Build Now, as shown in Figure 10-53.

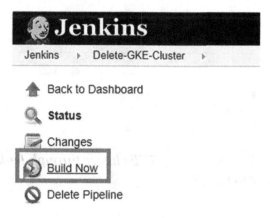

Figure 10-53. *Cleaning up the GKE cluster through Jenkins—Build Now*

Step 5: Once the job is executed successfully, the build history will be shown. Stages are shown under Stage View (Figure 10-54). To view logs, click the build number, as shown in Figure 10-55. Click Console Output (Figure 10-56), and the results of the output are shown in Figure 10-57.

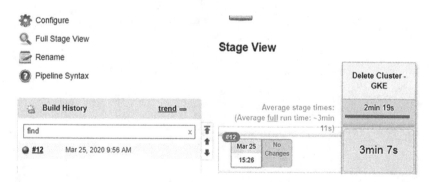

Figure 10-54. *Cleaning up the GKE cluster through Jenkins—Build History*

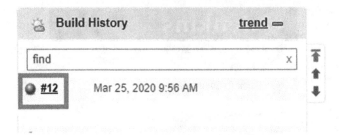

Figure 10-55. *Cleaning up the GKE cluster through Jenkins—clicking the build number to view logs*

Figure 10-56. *Cleaning up the GKE cluster through Jenkins—Console Output*

⬤ Custom Console Output

```
Started by user admin
Running in Durability level: MAX_SURVIVABILITY
[Pipeline] Start of Pipeline
[Pipeline] node
Running on Jenkins in /var/jenkins_home/workspace/Delete-GKE-Cluster
[Pipeline] {
[Pipeline] node
Running on devopsbox in /var/jenkins_home/workspace/Delete-GKE-Cluster
[Pipeline] {
[Pipeline] stage
[Pipeline] { (Delete Cluster - GKE)
[Pipeline] sh
+ gcloud container clusters delete clustertutorial --zone=us-central1-a
+ echo Y
The following clusters will be deleted.
 - [clustertutorial] in [us-central1-a]

Do you want to continue (Y/n)?
Deleting cluster clustertutorial...
...........................................................................
...........................................................................
...........................................................................
...........................................................................
...........................................................................
...........................................................................
...........................................................................
...........................................................................
...........................................................................
...............................done.
WARNING: environment variable HOME or KUBECONFIG must be set to store credentials for kubectl
Deleted [https://container.googleapis.com/v1/projects/tutorial-project-268109/zones/us-central1-a/clusters/clustertutorial].
[Pipeline] sleep
```

Figure 10-57. *Cleaning up the GKE cluster through Jenkins—console output*

In the log console, scroll down the screen to get the
information about the deleted cluster and firewall
rules (Figure 10-58).

```
.........................................................................................................
.........................................................................................................
...............................done.
WARNING: environment variable HOME or KUBECONFIG must be set to store credentials for kubectl
Deleted [https://container.googleapis.com/v1/projects/tutorial-project-268109/zones/us-central1-a/clusters/clustertutorial].
[Pipeline] sleep
Sleeping for 30 sec
[Pipeline] sh
+ gcloud compute firewall-rules delete sysdig-agent-inbound-firewall-rule
The following firewalls will be deleted:
 - [sysdig-agent-inbound-firewall-rule]

Do you want to continue (Y/n)?
Deleted [https://www.googleapis.com/compute/v1/projects/tutorial-project-268109/global/firewalls/sysdig-agent-inbound-firewall-rule].
[Pipeline] sleep
Sleeping for 30 sec
[Pipeline] sh
+ gcloud compute firewall-rules delete sysdig-agent-outbound-firewall-rule
The following firewalls will be deleted:
 - [sysdig-agent-outbound-firewall-rule]

Do you want to continue (Y/n)?
Deleted [https://www.googleapis.com/compute/v1/projects/tutorial-project-268109/global/firewalls/sysdig-agent-outbound-firewall-rule].
[Pipeline] }
[Pipeline] // stage
[Pipeline] }
[Pipeline] // node
[Pipeline] }
[Pipeline] // node
[Pipeline] End of Pipeline
Finished: SUCCESS
```

Figure 10-58. *Cleaning up the GKE cluster through Jenkins—output related to deleted firewall rules*

Step 6: Navigate to your GCP account console and click Compute. Select Kubernetes Engine and then Clusters. You will see the GKE cluster name clustertutorial is being deleted (Figure 10-59).

Figure 10-59. *Cleaning up the GKE cluster in the GCP dashboard*

Wait 5–10 minutes to delete the cluster completely.
Once it has been deleted, you will see the following
screen (Figure 10-60).

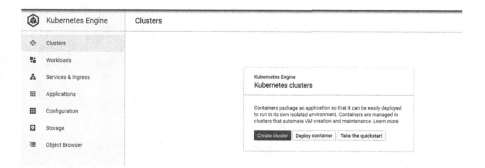

Figure 10-60. *Cleaning up the GKE cluster in the GCP dashboard—continued*

Summary

In this chapter we provided steps for using the cloud-native `gcloud`
command-line tool as an IaC solution and Jenkins as a CI/CD solution, to
automate the deployment of container infrastructure, enable monitoring
through the Sysdig agent, and finally deploying a containerized application
thus bringing us to the conclusion of this book. We have covered various
aspects of GKE lifecycle management in this book and tried to enable
readers with hands on exercises to understand the core concepts
behind GKE management including Networking, Security, Monitoring,
Automation etc.

Index

S, T, U

V, W, X, Y, Z

Printed in the United States
By Bookmasters